Politics in modern Africa

Politics in modern Africa:
The uneven tribal dimension

Kenneth Ingham

London and New York

To Clare

First published 1990
by Routledge
11 New Fetter Lane, London EC4P 4EE

Simultaneously published in the USA and Canada
by Routledge
a division of Routledge, Chapman and Hall, Inc.
29 West 35th Street, New York NY 10001

© 1990 Kenneth Ingham

Typeset by Pat and Anne Murphy,
Highcliffe-on-Sea, Dorset
Printed and bound in Great Britain by
Biddles Ltd, Guildford and King's Lynn

British Library Cataloguing in Publication Data
Ingham, Kenneth
    Politics in modern Africa: the uneven tribal dimension.
    1. Africa. Politics.
    I. Title
    320.96

    ISBN 0-415-02278-9

Library of Congress Cataloging-in-Publication Data
Ingham, Kenneth.
    Politics in modern Africa: the uneven tribal dimension /
by Kenneth Ingham.
        p.   cm.
    Includes bibliographical references.
    ISBN 0-415-02278-9
    1. Africa, Sub-Saharan – Politics and government – 1960–
2. Tribal government –Africa, Sub-Saharan.
3. Ethnicity – Africa, Sub-Saharan.   I. Title.
JQ1879.A15I54   1990   89-77042
320.967′09′045–dc20   –dc20   CIP

Contents

Acknowledgements

My first thanks must go to the Leverhulme Foundation whose generous award of an emeritus fellowship enabled me to return to several African countries which I had not visited for many years. Without that opportunity, it would have been difficult for me to write a number of the chapters in this book. I am also extremely grateful to Mr John Tod, British Council Representative, who did so much to prepare the way for my visits to Senegal and Guinea and who helped me greatly while I was in both those countries. Mr Michael Kelly, Adviser to the English Language Teaching project in Senegal, and Mr David Constable, Head of the English Language Teaching project in Guinea, gave generously of their time to assist me and I am much indebted to them for their kind hospitality.

To the Cheikh Anta Diop University of Dakar, and particularly to M. Aloyse-Raymond Ndiaye, Dean of the Faculty of Letters and Human Sciences, I owe my thanks for permitting me to stay on the university campus where I had such ready access to members of the faculty. M. Boubacar Barry, Head of the History Department, helped me in every way possible as well as devoting considerable time to discussing my project with me. He introduced me to the other members of his department and also allowed me to read the unpublished results of research carried out by students in the department. To all the members of the university, both academic and administrative, who made me so welcome I am deeply indebted.

Dr N. Magassouba, Rector of the University of Conakry, was also extremely helpful, as too, was M. Gouddousy Diallo, Dean of the Faculty of Social Sciences, while M. Nay Dyeng and all the members of the History Department were generous with their comments on my work.

Mr Isaac Tufuoh, Head of the History Department in the University of Legon, shared both his wisdom and experience in discussing the development of his country with me. The students' long essays which he allowed me to read also opened my eyes to a number of issues which had not previously occurred to me. In all these universities I was deeply impressed by the commitment of the faculty members to their subject, sometimes in difficult conditions, and by the patience and readiness with which they shared their expertise with a visitor. I should add that they are in no way accountable for any shortcomings in the book; the responsibility is mine alone.

Finally, my heartfelt thanks are due to my daughter, Clare, and to Dr John Cleave, formerly of the University of Bristol, who with infinite forbearance introduced me to the mysterious workings of a word processor.

Kenneth Ingham

1 The imperial legacy

A high proportion of academics who study Africa would attribute most of the continent's contemporary problems to 'underdevelopment', which is generally deemed to be an imperial or neo-imperial affliction. There are powerful arguments to support that view. The preferred explanation given by even the more discerning sections of the British press, however, is 'tribalism'. Headings such as 'Tribal row threatens Mugabe's party',[1] or 'Tribalism prevents creation of one nation in Nigeria',[2] or 'How Obote fell to tribal strife'[3] are a commonplace of British journalism. Neither 'tribe' nor 'tribalism' is ever defined by the contributors to those publications, though one suspects that the terms are not used with the scrupulous regard for accuracy that an anthropologist might expect. Does this popular view, then, contribute anything to our understanding of Africa?

From the context in which the word appears in the press it would seem that tribalism means loyalty to a socio-political unit smaller than the nation states into which Africa is now divided, and the implication is that such loyalty is detrimental to the successful functioning of those states. It is the element of political allegiance which, I suggest, differentiates tribalism from ethnicity. An ethnic group, though possessing a common culture and a common historical tradition, need not share a common political loyalty. This is a distinction which journalists do not always make and their failure to do so adds confusion to an already complicated issue. The confusion, however, is understandable. It is not easy to anticipate with which socio-political group an African would primarily identify.

Nationalism, meaning allegiance to the contemporary states of Africa, is not yet a universally acknowledged sentiment. Bearing in mind the difficulties encountered by the members of the European Economic Community in trying to reach agreement on joint action, it is not surprising that the inhabitants of African countries, which are

1

equally new creations, do not automatically recognize a national identity. Originally defined to satisfy imperial interests, the boundaries of those countries were sometimes responsible for splitting homogeneous political and social units, and distributing the parts between rival European Powers. More often they lumped together people of differing cultures and traditions, speaking very different languages and owing allegiance to a wide variety of authorities. The diversity of interests among those constituent parts was every bit as great as that among members of the EEC. Nor did the imperial overlords make any serious attempt to foster feelings of loyalty to the countries which they had created, for they had not originally intended that they should have a separate existence. The most that was required of their new subjects was obedience to the representatives of the imperial power, the regular payment of taxes, and co-operation where necessary in the furtherance of imperial economic policies. Reluctant to finance the administration of their new dependencies, the imperial nations were also inclined to rely upon indigenous authorities to do much of their work for them, at least at the level of local government. In many instances this reinforced the people's allegiance to existing authorities rather than directing it towards the new central government.

It would be wrong, however, to assume that imperial overrule merely perpetuated traditional systems of government. African societies rarely responded passively to the imperial situation, though they did not necessarily react violently against it. In many cases they took advantage of new opportunities offered them, particularly for participation in unaccustomed but exciting profitable economic activities. This might involve them in voluntary co-operation with other groups – usually those possessing a common language – in order to create larger units more capable of working for the benefit of their members. Imperial authorities, too, often linked together smaller societies possessing similar characteristics and speaking the same language, to suit their administrative convenience. By both these means, ethnic groups which had previously owned no common political allegiance began, for some of their activities at least, to operate as single, neo-tribal units.

Changes of this sort were not a novelty. Long before the imperial era, African societies were rarely stagnant. New situations had often resulted in new political alignments, sometimes of a temporary, sometimes of a more lasting nature. A common enemy might cause hitherto independent groups to recognize a single military leader to whom they would give their loyalty as long as their position was threatened. Migrant groups, venturing into unknown territory, might discover the value of strong clan affiliations which in a more static situation had seemed unnecessary. By contrast, in more structured societies there were usually means of dismissing an established leader who ignored the rules. Or the rules might be changed where circumstances made such change desirable or when pressure built up in some influential sector. Consequently, there was no inconsistency in changing the system or altering the focus of group loyalty under imperial overlordship. Sometimes the traditional apparatus of government might even be strengthened in the process, while in other instances the foundation of its strength could be shifted from, for example, a spiritual to an economic basis.

Not all the African polities encountered by the European imperialists were small. Some which were described as tribes by the new arrivals might, in a European context, have been recognized as nations or empires, often with a long history of development. Even for them, however, their reaction to the arrival of the Europeans could have revolutionary results. Those which co-operated with the imperialists might find their boundaries enlarged. Those which resisted might have their powers and estates diminished. But, whether rejoicing in the benefits received or rendered resentful by defeat, this type of state usually contrived to retain the loyalty of its people. Thus an alien central authority, striving to operate a uniform administrative system, might be forced to co-exist with widely differing local authorities each of which derived some powers from its imperial masters and some from the traditional loyalty shown by its own people.

Nor were these the only complications. The opportunity offered to enterprising Africans to acquire material wealth by participating in the export economy introduced by the Europeans could also present a serious challenge to traditional authority. The benefits deriving from that source were not shared equally with the people as a whole, and sometimes this led to the formation of a new social group which did not owe its prosperity to traditional communal endeavour but nevertheless wielded considerable power.[4] But one must tread warily. It is easy to overemphasize the revolutionary nature of such a development. Family obligations were never lightly dismissed. In most instances the links between the new entrepreneurial class and the societies from which they had sprung remained strong even if they were modified.

The entrepreneurs were not the only people whose lives were changed by the demands of the new economy. Because of the new direction taken by the economy, labourers were required in agriculture and commerce and increasingly in industry, and there was a growing need for clerical and domestic workers in the towns. The demand for labour did not always coincide with its availability, so a system of migrant labour developed which severed the work-force from the society to which it traditionally belonged – at least for a portion of each year. This did not automatically result in a breakup of those societies, however. The labourers' desire to return with their wages to the families who were dependent upon them remained unchanged. Even where a lengthier residence away from home was required, there was a strong tendency for workers to congregate with others from their home districts, and their attachment to traditional customs was strengthened by their exile – as happens among many migrant communities.

More striking in its impact upon traditional political loyalties was the introduction of European education. Until after the Second World War, imperial governments were often content to leave the education of Africans to missionary societies whose prime concern was to spread the gospel. For the missionaries' purposes it was only necessary for Africans to read and possibly to write. Only those who might be chosen to be teachers or evangelists needed to progress beyond those minimum requirements. This system suited the imperial governments because it also produced a supply of Africans qualified to carry out minor clerical tasks. In parts of West Africa, however, where the earlier progress of evangelization called for an ever-increasing number of qualified Africans, a not inconsiderable number achieved higher levels of education, some of them even travelling to Europe to advance their studies. Only after the Second World War did such a practice become common in other parts of the continent, but when it did occur it meant that students came into contact with European ideas of government and administration very different from anything they had experienced in their own countries. This experience encouraged them to look beyond traditional loyalties and prepared them to contemplate the possibility of becoming the legatees of imperial rule.

Many of those who progressed furthest in the realms of European education were still unwilling to renounce their African heritage completely. They found refuge in the concept of *négritude*, taking pride in traditional African values while simultaneously seeking to gain acceptance from the Europeans by absorbing their culture. Others were sceptical of the prospect of ever sharing power with their European overlords and still more so of any voluntary withdrawal of European control. They believed that their only hope of succeeding to the political kingdom lay in a pan-African movement, a consolidation of dependent entities into an independent whole which would present the imperial powers with a challenge they could not resist and which they could not subsequently undermine by having recourse to their overwhelming economic strength.

The sudden and largely unexpected approach of independence did not destroy the pan-African ideal nor yet expunge the dream of *négritude*, but it pushed both into the background. The total impracticability of creating a structure capable of formulating and administering policies applicable to the whole continent in the time available meant that pan-Africanism must wait. At the same time, *négritude* was really only a cultural statement, not an administrative model. But it was equally inconceivable that the administrative machinery created by the imperial powers should be dismantled in order to introduce a political framework based upon the multiplicity of traditional and neo-traditional identities which had survived, or had been created by, imperial rule. The only possibility was to accept the imperial legacy as it stood and to amend it later.

This was not an unsatisfactory proposition for the new generation of political leaders who aspired to become the heirs to imperial rule. Nor did they find it difficult to carry the majority of the people with them. The idea of freedom from foreign domination was one which could be endowed with pleasant prospects. Because of the employment of indigenous people in the lower ranks of the administration – with which the majority of the population was most frequently in contact – not all Africans had been deeply conscious of the impact of imperial rule. This was increasingly true as the initial impact of imperial conquest became weaker with the passage of time. Many had suffered from oppressive demands for labour, however, and most had been aware of the indifference, even contempt, which some Europeans had shown towards them. The behaviour of many Europeans had had a corrosive effect upon relations between the two races and, singled out for attack in the political rhetoric of the emergent African leaders, probably contributed as much to the surge of popular support for independence as did the hope of greater material prosperity. But there was little evidence that the people as a whole were conscious of having adopted a new national identity to match their newly-won independence. Their ultimate loyalty was still given to traditional or neo-traditional authorities whom they knew and could respect.

For the new elites, who in most cases owed their position to education rather than to tradition, the situation was very different. For them, independence meant opportunities never previously open to them. Even in poor countries, where there was little prospect of widespread benefit, the potential spoils awaiting the fortunate ones were considerable: power, and the wealth that power might engender; patronage, and the strength and status it could provide. In Africa it was political power which brought wealth and commanded patronage, not the reverse; and, the more enterprising Africans believed, where wealth was limited, it was essential to stake an early claim to it. Wealthy African oligarchies capable of dominating the new nations had not yet developed; though in some countries they were beginning to take shape but were still allied with traditional authorities. It was vital, therefore, that the new elites should identify with the successor states which imperialism left behind if they were to be the controllers of the new countries of Africa. At the moment of independence, however, it would be difficult to say whether they had any sincere feelings of national identity with the countries they were destined to govern. Obviously not all the new political leaders were motivated purely by ambition and self-interest. For the moment, however, it was sufficient that they were willing to try to operate the existing machinery of state and that the imperial authorities were gradually accepting that the time had come to hand over control. Some of the retiring governments made last-minute attempts to ensure that their concept of democracy would survive, and that the interests of the minorities would be protected. Otherwise, the fledgling nations were launched with a minimum of preparation.

The transfer of power created a new situation in which, not surprisingly, there was little awareness of unity and nationhood, and in spite of the expectations of the educated elites it was not always easy to agree about who should inherit that power. For a time it was an advantage to have some outstanding figure who could be seen to have led his country to freedom from external rule and upon whom it was possible for the people to focus one aspect of their loyalty. It was still better if he had the support of a popular political party, and it underlined his credentials if, like Jomo Kenyatta in Kenya or Kwame Nkrumah in Ghana, he had suffered for the cause by being sent to prison by the imperial authorities. But such loyalty was precarious. Ultimately its survival depended upon the shared conviction of the mass of the people that participation in the new nation states was preferable to membership of more localized polities. There were many obstacles to be overcome before such a conviction could become universal, not least the fact that the countries had neither been created nor developed with a view to standing on their own.

The inexperience of most of the new rulers placed them at a serious disadvantage when faced with the daunting task of government. They may have been impressive as leaders of protest movements but their knowledge of policy-making and its implementation was slight. They had learnt in schools and universities about European theories of democracy but they had seen little of it in action except for the handful of men from Senegal who had served as deputies in France, and even they had found conditions in their own country were very different. Imperial administrations had been authoritarian in character and bureaucratic in form. Even when elected Africans had been admitted to their country's legislatures their role had been first to voice protest and then to accept the government's decisions. They had never been thought of – until immediately prior to independence – as being potentially capable of forming an alternative government. Once in office, the pressure upon the new leaders to fulfil long-standing obligations to families and supporters by exercising patronage on their behalf could become oppressive, encouraging corruption and dividing societies into envious groups. Having tasted the fruits of power, the temptation to cling to them would also be considerable, with the result that a future of repression and stagnation was not inconceivable whatever opposition it might arouse.

The shortage of qualified and experienced personnel was particularly acute in the intermediate ranges of administration, and perhaps most of all in the economic and commercial field. Even in the more expansive years after the Second World War, education had resembled a slender spire perched upon a squat, lowly building, rather than a regular pyramid. Primary education had become more widespread without reaching the whole population. Universities, too, had made their appearance. But the provision for secondary education, and still more for technical and technological education, had remained totally inadequate to meet the needs of countries striving to create a stable economy. This shortage was exacerbated by the reluctance of many Africans to undertake training in technical subjects. The lessons of European overrule had not been lost upon them. The difference in status between administrators, educated for the most part in the humanities, and the rest of the white community, whether agricultural officers, public-works officials or commercial men, was there for all to see. Only white settlers, with their large landed estates, could challenge the pretensions of the governing elite.

To the shortage of trained personnel was added poverty of natural resources. Few African countries had either the agricultural or industrial potential to satisfy the hopes which had been raised by the prospect of independence. Where the potential did exist, its distribution could be dangerously uneven and local jealousies might easily be aroused. The legacy of dependence upon export crops for foreign exchange in countries where the population was overwhelmingly engaged in farming, left them at the mercy of unsympathetic world markets and distorted the natural patterns of production. As a consequence, some of the people were condemned to the status of hired labourers merely because their land was deemed unsuitable for growing the crops needed for export, while those who were fortunate enough to have suitable land found the prices offered for their produce inexplicably cut because of events taking place at the other side of the world. It was a situation which did not favour contentment and stability, unless the new governments could guarantee new methods of achieving prosperity which might retain the loyalty of the people.

That prospect was seriously threatened by both external and internal forces. The sudden, steep rise in the price of petroleum products placed an appalling burden upon most African countries, which was more than matched by the impact of the sudden, overwhelming growth in the birth-rate. The rise in oil prices completely upset the balance of payments and put a brake on every project which depended for its success on energy derived from petroleum. The latter meant that countries which had formerly produced sufficient food to meet the basic needs of a small population were faced, almost overnight, with the task of feeding many times more people without the trained manpower to instruct the farmers in ways of increasing their output, even where the availability of natural resources made such an increase possible. Within 25 years, populations doubled or nearly trebled (see Table 1.1) – with all that meant, too, by way of a rising demand for employment in countries where opportunities for expansion did not exist. Powers which had readily offered financial assistance at the time of independence, in the hope of sharing in whatever profits might be forthcoming, became more wary. Further help was made dependent upon the fulfilment of onerous conditions which left countries struggling even to pay the interest on loans cheerfully incurred at a time when everyone had had high hopes for the future. Over and above all this, the continent was disturbed by the rivalry of the 'great powers' over their real or imagined strategic interests in the region.

In such a volatile and frequently unpromising situation, the maintenance of security and stability became of increasing importance. In most countries the army was a factor to which little attention was paid at the time of independence. African armies were small and professional. Their officers had been trained by European instructors to stand aside from politics. But their potential importance was

Table 1.1 Growth in population since independence

Country	Date of independence	Estimated population at independence	Estimated population 1987
Uganda	1962	7,016,000	15,514,000
Ghana	1957	4,763,000	13,482,000
Nigeria	1960	35,091,000	100,595,700
Kenya	1963	8,847,000	22,020,000
Senegal	1960	3,110,000	6,793,000
Guinea	1958	2,896,000	6,380,000
Zaire	1960	14,139,000	31,804,000
Angola	1975	6,520,000	9,105,000
Zimbabwe	1980	7,096,000	8,640,000

considerably greater than anyone had anticipated. They were disciplined and they were armed, two significant characteristics which were lacking in the rest of the population. If the new governments proved unable to meet the expectations of the people, the army might well be tempted to intervene politically in the interests of security and stability. In that event, even although it acted with the best of intentions, its efforts could be dangerous. It might restore power quickly to civilian hands, but the possibility that it might intervene again could not be ignored. Also, in many countries the ethnic composition of both the army and the officer corps did not match that of the rest of the country or of the government. In times of stress even professional soldiers might forget that their true allegiance should lie to the state and they might be tempted to protect more local interests.

Perhaps, above all, the absence in many newly independent African countries of a common language provided a serious obstacle to united action. It was a problem that might be partially concealed because the countries' leaders spoke a common European language. But the leaders themselves were often seen by the mass of the people not as national figures but as representatives of local interests, the interests of the people whose language they spoke. Consequently they, too, however wedded they might be to the concept of a new nation, felt the pull of more traditional loyalties.

All these challenges to the prosperity and stability of the new states were challenges to the formation of a new national identity. It was not solely to protect the new nations from outside interference that the Organization of African Unity laid great emphasis in its charter upon the integrity of national boundaries. The political leaders were fully aware of the threat of internal disintegration and of the need to avoid even the appearance of support for breakaway movements. The way in which African countries responded to this threat, as well as to many of the other problems posed by independence, forms the theme of this book. By concentrating on tropical Africa, contrasts and comparisons can be more readily apprehended. The countries selected for examination were all created by European powers, but they differed widely in their composition, their resources, their traditions, and their experience of European administration. Four European countries were involved, each with its own ideas about how to administer African dependencies. Two of the dependencies suffered the presence of white settlers who laid claim to large areas of land which the Africans regarded as traditionally their own. Several came to rely heavily for their revenue upon African-grown export crops. All provided labour, though on a varying scale, for European enterprises. In only isolated cases had Africans been able to acquire notable material wealth before independence. How, then, did Africans respond to their membership of newly-independent nations, and how did their traditional loyalties blend into, or come into conflict with, the new situation in which they found themselves? Is 'tribalism' in the political sense in which we have now defined it the disruptive force which the press would claim it to be?

2 Uganda: the kingdom and the power

If one is seeking for examples of the influence of tribalism on political development one could scarcely do better than to look first at Uganda. Uganda today is a potentially prosperous country striving to recover from the ravages of tyranny and civil war. It is sometimes said to be divided between a predominantly Nilotic north and a Bantu south, the division having had its origins in Britain's decision, during the days of the protectorate, to develop the agricultural resources of the south, for the benefit of British businessmen and British industry, and to leave the north as a reservoir of labour. This decision, the argument goes on, led to the impoverishment of everyone but the handful of southerners who were prepared to act as the economic running dogs of the British.

Uganda is, indeed, desperately impoverished: with inflation rising steeply; with the cost of food to non-producers astronomically high; with exports down; and with the cost of imported goods, when they are available, prohibitive. In addition, there is tension between the north and the south – if the River Nile is deemed to be the dividing line. But these are relatively recent phenomena. The Nile was certainly not the dividing line between the developed south and the 'under-developed' north in the days of the protectorate. Many non-Bantu, both east and north of the river, had benefited considerably from the protectorate authorities' encouragement of export crops, notably cotton and coffee. Nevertheless, after independence they clearly did not align themselves with the other, southern, beneficiaries of protectorate economic policies who wanted to overthrow either of the two governments of the northerner, President Obote. Even today, their acceptance of President Museveni owes more to war weariness than to any feeling of common purpose with the new, 'southern' government. Nor are the Bantu themselves wholeheartedly in favour of the government. Like the rest of the country they simply long for peace and for an opportunity to make up lost ground. In fact, the north/south, Nilotic/Bantu, developed/underdeveloped themes are too simplistic and lack historical depth. Above all, they underestimate the role of the former kingdom of Buganda.

For centuries, since long before Britain became involved in the region until after Uganda became independent, Buganda, a wonderfully fertile land, has insisted upon its unique identity. In so doing it has provided a model which has encouraged hitherto uncoordinated ethnic groups to coalesce into proto-tribal units which have often been at enmity with their archetype and in rivalry with each other. While Buganda was part of a British protectorate this might have been inconvenient but it was not seriously disruptive. Independent Uganda has found the situation more difficult to handle.

At midnight on 31 December 1960, Buganda – at that time a province of the Uganda Protectorate – declared its independence. The British administration dismissed the announcement as preposterous and within a few days the incident was forgotten. But the gesture was profoundly significant. The Ganda leaders had not been primarily concerned with ridding their country of imperial rule. There was already every indication that the British were planning to quit Uganda in the future without prompting from within. What Buganda wished to do was to pre-empt that moment by establishing its independence of the rest of the protectorate. A relationship which was initially tolerable under British overrule had, in the eyes of Buganda's leaders, become rapidly less so since the Second World War. In their estimation it would become wholly intolerable if the kingdom were to become a minority element in a united, independent Uganda, outvoted in parliament over questions of sovereignty and with its economic pre-eminence challenged by envious rivals. Their attitude is understandable if not wholly commendable, but it had a destructive effect upon the rest of Uganda.

Buganda's relationship with Britain began to take shape in the late nineteenth century as a result of the activities of Christian missionaries and it was put on a formal basis by means of an agreement signed in 1900 to which the rest of the protectorate was not a party. Under the terms of that agreement Buganda was, it is true, incorporated into the wider Uganda Protectorate. But there was no apparent reason, it might be argued, why Buganda, as a voluntary signatory of the agreement, should not terminate it if at any time it wished to do so, and in so doing sever its relations with the rest of the country. The kingdom had, after all, existed as an independent political unit for centuries before the British set foot in East Africa. Its people spoke a common language, distinct from that of their neighbours. They had a common culture and a common historical tradition. They were comprehensively governed by a ruler, the *kabaka*, who was supported by an ancient clan system of which he was the head, and by a bureaucracy, the efficiency and loyalty of whose members was ensured by their dependence upon the *kabaka* for preferment. The soil of the country was fertile and could comfortably sustain a large population. Buganda was, by normal criteria, a nation.

The kingdom's relations with its neighbours had sometimes been warlike and had always been conducted warily. Some of those neighbours were monarchies as ancient as Buganda itself. They had their own languages and traditions and their people were as patriotic as the Ganda were, though their administrative hierarchies may not always have been as efficient. To the north and east the situation was different. The region was inhabited by people speaking a number of distinct languages, and the possession of a common language did not usually indicate a common political allegiance. In some instances small groups owed their loyalty to nothing larger than a village community. In others, extensive clan structures had developed and had begun to achieve a measure of permanence. This disparate collection of peoples had been brought together, with Buganda, under the umbrella of the Uganda Protectorate. But the British administration had done nothing to encourage any feelings of national identity. Vernacular languages persisted, dividing one group from another. Those who spoke the languages wanted to retain them and, so far as the administration was concerned, there was no overriding reason why they should not do so. The protectorate authorities did, however, consider it convenient to treat people speaking the same vernacular language as belonging to a single, larger, administrative unit, intermediate between the existing local communities and the alien central government, even when there was no tradition of unity among them.

For Buganda to want to opt out of this random agglomeration of peoples might seem reasonable, but to accept that proposition would be to overlook many important consequences of British administration. In the first place, the Buganda of 1960 was not the Buganda of the 1890s, when the British made official contact with the kingdom. In the early 1890s Buganda's future was far from secure. In spite of its inner strength it could have fallen victim to one of its rivals. By co-operating with the British the kingdom ensured that its enemies became Britain's enemies. As a result of joint military action with the British against its threatening western neighbour, Bunyoro, Buganda was transformed from a tiny kingdom into a substantial power – in area, a quarter of the whole protectorate of the future; in population, one-third. Under the terms of the 1900 agreement, the imperial authority – which had been impressed by the highly organized character of the kingdom – was prepared to leave routine administration to the Ganda themselves, a practice which was to become famous (or notorious) under the title of indirect administration.

It is important to note that the British did not make the agreement with the *kabaka*, who at that time was a minor, but with a number of his officials. Under the terms of the agreement, 1,000 of those selfsame officials – who were prepared in future to work with the British – were authorized, for the first time in Buganda's history, to acquire freehold ownership of land. These men and their descendents became prosperous farmers and landlords by encouraging their tenants and others under their supervision to grow cotton to meet Britain's industrial needs. Further proof of their reliability as agents of Britain's purpose in East Africa was provided by their wholehearted participation in the protectorate authority's campaign against sleeping sickness, when they were instrumental in moving all their people away from the shore of Lake Victoria. Their behaviour, as much as the climate, contributed to Britain's decision to develop Uganda as an African country. At the same time, the officials themselves, acting as semi-autonomous civil servants – tax collectors, magistrates, police officials – on behalf of their British overlords, enhanced their standing, if not always their popularity, in the eyes of their people, while adding to their wealth by dabbling successfully in a wide range of commercial and minor industrial activities. This powerful group, by co-operating with the British administration, made it possible for Buganda, not the Bantu south, to become the hub around which the whole of the protectorate's economic system rotated, the centre from which all its communications radiated, and the seat of the protectorate government.

Simultaneously, a modified version of the Ganda system of administration, which had so greatly impressed the British officials, was introduced into the rest of the protectorate with the assistance of experienced Ganda agents. At this stage it might even have been possible to have made Luganda the common language of the territory, thus removing a divisive factor which was to have serious effects in the future. But the arrogance of many of the agents made them unpopular. As a result, the local leaders who were under instruction adopted the Ganda administrative system in the hope of deriving the benefits which Buganda seemed to have acquired, but clung ever more fiercely to their local identities. Accepting the situation, the British created smaller facsimiles of the Ganda state, using vernacular languages as the common factor, but with a British district commissioner rather than a local *kabaka* at the head. Gradually, with the example of Buganda to spur them on, these new mini-states began to develop a corporate identity in matters affecting relations between their inhabitants and the protectorate authorities. In so far as the routine of daily life was concerned, traditional, local loyalties were little affected.

While the rest of the protectorate was becoming more like the Buganda of its imagination, the kingdom itself was busy shedding that image. In the early days of Britain's relationship with Buganda, the central role of the *kabaka* had already been greatly diminished when a refractory holder of that office was replaced by an infant. Such of his powers as had not been assumed by the new overlords were then transferred to co-operative Ganda leaders, powers which further strengthened the demands this privileged group could make upon the loyalty of the Ganda people. Later, in the 1920s, some of the formerly influential Ganda, and in particular the clan heads, who had not been involved in the 1900 Agreement but who had acquiesced in what the British had done without recognizing its influence for good or ill, came belatedly to appreciate the disadvantages under which they now laboured in comparison with the active collaborators. They began to express their dissatisfaction, and soon afterwards they were joined by some of those who had benefited from the British presence but had become resentful of the restrictions which that presence imposed upon them now that their wealth and influence seemed assured. From this time, collaboration with the protectorate administration was increasingly condemned by many of the leading Ganda, who tried to consolidate support for their position by appealing to Ganda patriotism.

Not all the leaders were of the same mind, and the Second World War had the effect of brushing these disagreements into the shadows. But as soon as the war was ended they resurfaced with added strength, and in order to bind the people of Buganda still more closely to their cause the disaffected leaders set out to revive the mystique of the office of *kabaka*, but not the personal power of the man himself. In the previous forty years, the majority of Ganda had given little thought to constitutional matters and had not been profoundly concerned with questions of identity. They had been content to obey their immediate overlords and to share, albeit to a lesser extent, in the prosperity which British rule had brought. Now the tranquil tenor of their lives was to be sharply disturbed. They were told by some of their leaders that British rule was a threat to their integrity, and that to preserve their identity they must rally in support of their traditional ruler. The threat took what appeared to be tangible shape when, in 1953, the British withdrew recognition from the *kabaka* and drove him into exile after a dispute over the distribution of responsibilities between central and local governments.

That dispute greatly enhanced the fears aroused among the Ganda leaders by a rumour that there were to be closer political links with white-settler-dominated Kenya. If such links were forged, there appeared to be every likelihood that the privileged and prosperous position those leaders had for so long enjoyed would be sharply challenged. It was a possibility they could not contemplate, and to forestall it they accused the British authorities of threatening the integrity of the kingdom and of preparing to violate the 1900 Agreement. Collaborators were vigorously denounced, Ganda patriotism flourished as never before since the early days of British rule, and now it took hold of virtually the whole people, not just the leaders. Gone for ever was the ready co-operation which the British had formerly enjoyed from those leaders in the days when to co-operate was to enhance the position of Buganda. From this time, whatever plans the protectorate authorities might have for Uganda were looked upon as a threat to the kingdom's security.

Meanwhile, in the rest of the territory, the process of creating ministates – which transcended village or clan loyalties but fell short of establishing any feelings of Ugandan patriotism – received a further impetus in 1953, the selfsame year in which recognition was withdrawn from the *kabaka*. A move was made to incorporate elected representatives of the African population in the Ugandan legislative council, and the local governments – those modified versions of the Ganda model – were used as electoral colleges. When the franchise was later widened, those same administrative districts became electoral constituencies, and their distinct identities were still further emphasized because it was impossible for a candidate to seek election outside his own district owing to language differences. This situation, coupled with Buganda's growing insistence upon its separate identity and the jealousy that claim aroused in other parts of the protectorate, meant that would-be council members were forced to canvass support on the basis of local concerns, however hard they might try to focus attention upon issues affecting the whole country in the course of their debates within the legislative council. In this way the feeling of neo-tribal unity in each administrative district was further consolidated. Several districts even sought to assert their identity by asking for the creation of paramount rulers in emulation of the role of the *kabaka*.

In spite of the many divisive tendencies within the protectorate, and despite the reluctance of the Ganda leaders to become involved in promoting any campaign which promised to link Buganda with any larger unit, a small but lively group of Ugandan nationalists did emerge in the 1950s. They were not members of the elite, landowning bureaucracy of Buganda but were educated, younger men who were trying to fashion a political system capable of leading Uganda to independence. Their first attempt to create a formal nationalist movement by founding the Uganda National Congress (UNC) in 1952 was, however, bedevilled at once by the Ganda question. The founders of the Congress, though they had recruited in many parts of the protectorate, were themselves Ganda, and they were inevitably caught up in the campaign to resore the deposed *kabaka*. To have stood aloof at such a critical moment in the life of the kingdom would have condemned them to the political wilderness as traitors to their people. The non-Ganda members gave their tacit support to the campaign but this diversion from the main purpose of the Congress weakened its structure.

Undeterred by these problems, another nationalist political party, the Democratic Party (DP), also came into being. Once again, the founders were Ganda; this time Roman Catholics, who, because of the predominantly Protestant composition of the kingdom's hierarchy, had little prospect of advancement through Ganda channels. The party also won adherents in the northern district of Acholi, where Italian Catholic missionaries had been active for many years, and in the western kingdom of Ankole. After the return of the *kabaka* from exile, yet another party was formed when the non-Ganda members quitted the UNC to dissociate themselves from purely Ganda issues and to set up the Uganda People's Congress (UPC). This proliferation of parties was not the good thing which British observers thought it was. Far from guaranteeing a democratic future for Uganda it meant that the nationalist movement had no unified leadership, and no party or party leader could claim to be the undisputed champion of a united Ugandan people either in dealings with Britain or in opposition to Ganda separatism. This was to prove a damaging weakness.

Challenged by these competing nationalist movements, those Ganda leaders who were anxious to protect the privileged position they had acquired under British rule but who were now opposed to Britain's plans for Uganda, set up their own organization, *Kabaka Yekka* (KY), meaning 'The *Kabaka* Alone'. They then called upon all the Ganda people to demonstrate their loyalty to their national heritage by giving their support to the new movement. By this time a a large proportion of the Ganda people had fully imbibed the patriotic propaganda to which they had been subjected, and the campaign for Ganda separatism was in full swing.

In the early 1960s, with independence seen to be only months away, the Ganda, save for the relatively small number who had joined the DP or still clung to the shreds of the UNC, seemed wholly alienated from the rest of Uganda. Wedded to a system which, through its use and abuse, had brought them power and prosperity, their leaders could see no way of reconciling their own advantage with the society contemplated by the Ugandan nationalists. By playing upon the patriotism – or tribal pride as the English press would have it – which they had so skilfully built up, they were able to carry the majority of the Ganda with them into a position of isolation. It was a situation which threatened disaster to an independent Uganda. There was no prospect of a *rapprochement* with Ganda members of the DP or UNC who were simply regarded as traitors, willing to subordinate Buganda's interests to those of its neighbours.

By this time most of the prominent UPC members had lost patience with what they regarded as the selfishness and intransigence of the Ganda who, they believed, sought only to consolidate their dominant role in the economy. But Milton Obote, the leader of the UPC, a Langi from northern Uganda, clearly recognized that there could be no independent Uganda without Buganda, the geographical heartland of the country, and that Buganda could not be coerced. The British authorities had reached the same conclusion, and so agreed to the hybrid constitutional arrangement under which Uganda became independent in 1962 – with the seat of government, the members of which were predominantly non-Ganda, situated in a Buganda which was in a largely autonomous relationship with the rest of the country. The fact that the smaller kingdoms had been granted a lesser measure of autonomy was of no political significance because, after making their token bid to emulate Buganda, they had, for the most part, returned UPC members to parliament. The one potentially redeeming feature about the confused situation, and that an unlikely one, was that Obote had somehow manufactured an improbable alliance between his party and KY in order to defeat the DP.

The future did not look bright. With no genuine unity between the UPC and KY, with no generally acknowledged national leader, with no common language and with a mule of a constitution, even the thriving agricultural economy which the government had inherited could not avert disaster. Nevertheless, it should be recognized that revenue from agricultural exports did grow rapidly immediately after independence, offering reasonable prospects for all and modest prosperity for some. Unlike many other countries, Uganda had not suffered any loss in food production from the introduction of export crops, the soil in the areas where those crops were grown being sufficiently fertile to produce adequate subsistence crops – in addition to cotton, coffee, tea, and sugar – to supply the needs of the population. Nor was the country dependent upon the market for one crop alone. Coffee, for example, overtook cotton as the country's chief exchange earner, but the market in other crops remained buoyant. Uganda may not have been created to stand on its own, but there were certainly no economic reasons why it should not be capable of doing so. On the political side, too, the DP, much to the satisfaction – premature as it unfortunately proved – of liberal-minded observers in Britain, did begin to act like a constitutional opposition. Unfortunately, the role of the DP was to be far less significant than that of the obdurate Ganda leaders, and it was on the rock of that obduracy that hopes were to founder.

In an attempt to calm the situation, Obote – now prime minister of an independent country – arranged for the *kabaka* to be elected president of the whole territory. It was not a successful move, for it soon led to a dispute over the extent of the president's powers. At the root of the matter was the rejection by the Ganda of any suggestion that the *kabaka*, particularly in his own kingdom, should be subordinate to an outsider, and one who belonged to a people whom the Ganda, under British administration, had come to regard as less than their equals. The battle-lines were quickly drawn up, all the other peoples of Uganda forgetting their differences to unite against what they saw as the overbearing behaviour of the Ganda. Even the other monarchies forgot any separatist intentions they might have cherished to join in the condemnation of their powerful neighbour. Each side believed the other was working for its downfall. Plots feared and plots rumoured became plots in reality. Reluctantly, Obote came to the conclusion that action must be taken against Buganda if a Ugandan national identity was to be established. At the same time it was clear that the negative force stirred up by impatience with Buganda had overcome ethnic differences and had provided a powerful cement to bind the rest of the country together. A bungled attempt, under the military command of Colonel Idi Amin, to seize the person of the *kabaka* resulted in more violence than had been intended. The *kabaka* escaped and eventually found refuge in England, and the former resentment of the Ganda blossomed into open hatred of Obote's government.

The situation was in no way improved by the prime minister's decision to become executive president, to abolish the monarchical status of Buganda and, for uniformity's sake, to get rid of the monarchies in the other kingdoms. It was not a successful operation. As president, Obote had no more effective power than he had previously exercised; the Ganda were prepared to wage covert war against him, and he had lost the support of the other kingdoms which had formerly sympathized with him in his dilemma. Now Buganda no longer stood in isolation. It was the former kingdoms against the rest, the south-west against the north and east. Tribal and ethnic differences had taken on a new shape, focused upon support for, or opposition to, Obote.

Increasingly repressive measures by security police against known and imagined enemies of the government led to a steady breakdown of law and order. The seizure of power by Idi Amin in January 1971 was essentially a personal venture by one man who feared retribution for his own misdeeds, but its success owed everything to the divided loyalties engendered by the Ganda problem. An army mutiny soon after independence had been put down with the aid of British troops. Since then, Obote had been suspicious of many of the army's leaders but had trusted Amin because he was a northerner and because he was a member of a small ethnic group, the Kakwa, which had been divided by imperial boundaries and had had little influence upon Uganda's politics. His trust had been misplaced. Traditionally the army had been mainly drawn from the Acholi and Langi – the latter being Obote's own people. After the mutiny, however, Amin had recruited a considerable number of Kakwa, thereby creating an army within an army, a virtual tribe, loyal to himself rather than to the government which it was meant to serve.

Amin seized power by acting in collusion with the defence minister who sent the Acholi and Langi officers on leave, thus enabling Amin to turn his Kakwa soldiers on the other ranks. This was a first step, but once again it was Ganda intervention which determined the outcome. The joy of the Ganda at the overthrow of Obote set the seal of success on Amin's coup. It helped him to win the acceptance of the world outside Uganda and especially of Britain's Conservative government which had been worried by Obote's predilection for socialist policies. By the time the Ganda recognized that Amin was not simply a buffoon to be manipulated, he had crippled the army – the only group which, if properly led, might have challenged his position. Subsequently Amin carried out a systematic persecution of Obote's former soldiers. Those who were not killed fled, taking refuge in their own districts, far from the capital, Kampala, and the main roads along which Amin's armed ruffians travelled. Some took up residence in adjacent countries. Thus, a small tribe, created by the efforts of one man, but with the initial approval of the Ganda leaders, had disrupted the whole constitutional structure of the state. Amin then proceeded to hold on to power – not through tribal loyalty but because he was able to recruit a considerable armed following of scoundrels whose support he retained by letting them loot and pillage at will, and because some influential people deemed it expedient to go along with him.

The eight years of Amin's misrule ruined Uganda's export economy and made dishonesty the norm in everyday commercial operations. Paradoxically, it united most of the country, even if only in opposition to his tyrannical government. Unity in Uganda, it seemed, was doomed to be a negative force, and the superficial nature of this most recent unity was soon to be revealed when Tanzanian forces, accompanied by a group of armed Ugandans, marched into Uganda. The aim of the majority of the Ugandan invading force was to overthrow Amin and return to the status quo by restoring Obote's government. This was not the intention of ambitious political exiles who had met in Moshi, in Tanzania, to form a new government for Uganda and to appoint an executive committee of eleven men to assist in the administration of the country after Amin had been ousted. The group did not include Obote, because the members disliked the policies he had increasingly adopted when he was in office, and in any case, they wanted power for themselves. It was a dangerous omission in the light of the former president's experience and of the support he had in Uganda – even among his former opponents, most of whom could think of no one else capable of rallying the country. It was likely to create problems, too, because the executive committee set up by the Moshi exiles surprisingly contained a majority of members who sympathized with Obote.

The problems emerged soon after the government took office. The ministers had as their first objective the healing of rifts between the various peoples in Uganda. The appointment of Yusuf Lule as president seemed an inspired move, admirably designed to promote that aim. Lule was a man of high education and had had experience in important political and administrative posts both inside Uganda and in the international arena. He was a Ganda and although he had been a member of the DP he had never overtly criticized the *kabaka*. He was, therefore, grudgingly approved by the wary Ganda leaders who were at least relieved to see one of their people as head of state. The vast majority of Ganda had suffered so greatly under Amin that they had little spirit left at that stage to oppose the appointment, even had they wished to do so, and many did not. On the strength of his reputation, Lule was also acceptable to most of the remaining population of Uganda, though those who would have preferred Obote were watchful to see how this former member of the DP would comport himself. They were not too pleased to note that his fourteen-man cabinet contained no one from Lango, Obote's district, while of the two Acholi selected by Lule one was known to be hostile to the former president. On the other hand, the executive council – later to become the advisory and then the consultative council – contained five Acholi, while the commander of the National Liberation Army (NLA), Colonel Tito Okello, was also from Acholi and his chief of staff, Lieutenant-Colonel David Oyite Ojok, was from Lango.

The illusion of unity was destroyed mainly in consequence of a dispute over economic policy, but the disagreement also marked the beginning of a clear split between those who wanted Obote back and those who did not, chief among the latter being most of the leading Ganda. With the economy in ruins, Lule was anxious to take advantage of the western powers' apparent willingness to provide aid. In this he had the support of those who had controlled the wealth of the country in the early days of independence, who again were mainly prominent Ganda. Associated with Lule's policy was the desire to rid the country of the Tanzanian troops who had been instrumental in overthrowing Amin and who, it was feared, might be used by President Nyerere of Tanzania, a known friend of Obote and a supporter of socialist policies, to reinstate the former president. Believing that he did not have the unanimous backing of his cabinet in spite of the various precautions he had taken, Lule carried out a purge in June 1979. Among others, he demoted Paulo Muwanga, the one member of the cabinet who had shown a measure of support for Obote and who had been included in the executive council set up in Moshi on the insistence of President Nyerere. It was a rash step, for it encouraged rumours that the president was trying to appease the Ganda. The advisory (formerly executive) council at once condemned him for acting without consulting its members and passed a vote of no confidence requiring him to resign. Reluctantly Lule left the country, and with him went probably the best hope of uniting Uganda by peaceful means.

The fact that he was replaced by another Ganda but one with a very different record, was a clear indication that neither the Ganda leaders nor the pro-Obote faction was as yet geared for full-scale action.

Godfrey Binaisa had been attorney-general in Obote's government but had resigned after disagreeing with the president. He certainly did not now see his aim as being to keep the presidential seat warm for Obote, but he failed to convince the suspicious Ganda of his good intentions. These latter were further alienated when Binaisa accused Lule and others of having acted on behalf of the Ganda neo-traditionalists who, he said, were anxious to reassert their influence by introducing regional confederation. If they succeeded, they would keep the ethnic groups apart and give Buganda a dominant role in the country. He himself favoured integration.[1]

Binaisa's rise to power had the effect of uniting the Ganda leaders with Lule's party, the DP, which they had formerly distrusted because of its loyalty to the concept of a united Uganda and its strong links with the Roman Catholic church. The two groups then upheld the claims of the absent Lule. Binaisa's new cabinet included as minister of defence a man who, though not himself a Ganda, was to exercise great influence through co-operation with Buganda. Yoweri Museveni had grown up in Nkore in south-western Uganda and had led a small band of fighters in the war against Amin. He had previously been involved with Frelimo forces in the struggle for Mozambican independence. His personal following in Uganda was small, but his ambitions were great. For the time being, however, he acted with circumspection, though some months later he was sharply criticized when, together with eight other members of the cabinet, he suggested that a peace-keeping force consisting of Angolan, Mozambican, and Ethiopian troops should be brought to Uganda to replace the Tanzanian force.[2] Though the majority of the cabinet was anxious to rid the country of the Tanzanians, the proposal was rejected. Tanzania's version of African socialism might be unpalatable to the members of the government, but they found the overt Marxism of the countries mentioned by Museveni wholly repulsive. Neverthelsss they remained cautious because, according to Lule, Nyerere had admitted in May that he had not sent his army to Uganda in order to let the sharks continue to exploit that country as they were exploiting Kenya. He was keeping his forces there in order to create a climate in which the country could evolve into a socialist state.[3]

The cabinet was fully aware that Uganda's own troops were unfit to take over security duties and were a potential danger to stability. Though they had fought to overthrow Amin they were little more than gunmen in uniform and were totally lacking in training or military discipline. In accordance with Uganda's military tradition they had been recruited mainly from the Acholi and Lango districts, though

Museveni was beginning to augment their number by recruiting in Nkore. As northerners, the Acholi and Langi were known to favour the return of Obote and were consequently disliked by the Ganda and feared by those in positions of authority. Already the terrible years of Amin's misrule were being forgotten by the Ganda in their hostility to the return of Obote, who, in any case, was held to be responsible for providing Amin with the opportunity to seize power. Even Binaisa, though he was not to be trusted, was felt to be preferable to the dreaded prospect of Obote's return. But the president lost support when he appointed a National Consultative Council consisting of 127 members to replace the advisory council – on the ground, he said, that the latter had contained too many supporters of Obote. The Ganda pointed out at once that the new body had no mandate from the people and, discounting Binaisa's protestations, they suspected that, in reality, it was no more than an expanded version of its predecessor.

In spite of these ominous rumblings, it began to seem that Binaisa might yet be able to establish his authority on a firm foundation when the NCC endorsed a cabinet reshuffle which he carried out without consultation in November 1979. Among the victims of the change was Museveni, demoted from minister of defence to minister of regional co-operation. Binaisa had clearly sensed the presence of a rival, but Museveni, after first refusing the new post, agreed to co-operate because he shared the president's aim of keeping Obote at bay and he could not, at that time, envisage any other way of achieving his objective. To open a dispute within the cabinet might have risked intervention by Nyerere. In February 1980, however, Binaisa took a further step which threatened to undermine any success he might already have achieved. The removal of Paulo Muwanga from the office of interior minister was sound enough from an internal point of view. He was a schemer and, for his own purposes, favoured the return of Obote. But his dismissal brought thunder from without, for Nyerere intervened immediately to insist upon Muwanga's reinstatement to the cabinet in which he became minister of labour.

Binaisa's position was not restored by his capitulation to the Tanzanian president. There was now a sharp division in the NCC and the supporters of Obote's UPC were clearly in the majority. It was also becoming increasingly obvious that the sympathies of the Uganda National Liberation Army lay firmly in the same quarter. Of the 10,000 men under arms, barely 2,000 had been recruited outside the Acholi and Lango districts. Surprisingly, in the circumstances, Binaisa won a majority vote in the NCC in support of his proposal that in any future elections for either parliament or the presidency political parties would be forbidden to campaign. All candidates, it was agreed, must stand as representatives of the Uganda National Liberation Front. This success could only suggest that the northern leaders, though loyal to Obote, were even more anxious to avoid internal divisions. The Ganda members of the council saw the move as the best means of denying to the UPC the immediate prospect of taking over the government of the country. Obote, still in exile in Tanzania, challenged the decision and announced that he would return to Uganda on 27 May. The former members of the UPC were delighted by the news and planned a great welcome for their leader, but the interior Minister, Barnabas Kununka, threatened to use the police to break up any rally summoned to greet the former president. Throughout this period, party politics overshadowed both tribalism and ethnicity, though Ganda influence continued to make itself felt.

Alerted to the threat posed by Obote's imminent return, Binaisa sought to strengthen his own position by dismissing his army chief of staff, Brigadier David Oyite Ojok, on the ground that the brigadier's abrasive methods were harming relations between the armed forces and the civilian population. It was a dangerous gamble and it failed. Ojok refused to accept dismissal and he was supported by Muwanga who claimed that the president could not get rid of the chief of staff without the approval of the NCC. Binaisa maintained that, as commander in chief, he had a free hand in the matter, but the realities of power proved him to be wrong. A military commission, chaired by Muwanga and supported by the army, deposed the president and went on to dismiss a number of cabinet ministers who had supported Binaisa, replacing them with Obote's men. The absence of any protest from Tanzania was evidence of Nyerere's tacit approval. When he was appealed to by Binaisa to reverse the course of events, he replied that, while he regretted the manner in which things had happened, he did not feel there was anything he could do. The return of Obote to Uganda on 27 May was a further pointer to the direction events were taking, though pending elections Muwanga held the reins of power as chairman of the military commission.

Museveni now felt it was time for action. Early in June he announced the formation of the Uganda Patriotic Movement (UPM) to contest the leadership of the country with Obote. Ironically, in view of his own future actions, he announced that his party would not tolerate any dictator seizing power by military force. The Ganda leaders now turned hopefully to the UPM because the DP appeared to be no longer a credible ally after Lule had been refused re-entry to Uganda. The former president would not withdraw his criticisms of the role of Tanzania which the military commission insisted must be a precondition of his return. Time was to show that the DP was not a spent force, however, and that the Ganda leaders were quite prepared to shift their allegiance yet again if expediency demanded it.

To counter Museveni's initiative in the short term, and in an attempt to reunite the people of Uganda in the long term, Obote called for a government of national unity which would include the most able people regardless of which party might gain a majority when elections were held. Though his critics were sceptical the proposal was sincerely made. In 1962 Obote had been one of the few political leaders who had made positive moves in the direction of uniting Uganda, and he was still fully aware that without union there could be little hope of peace. But the prospect of union under Obote's leadership was anathema to most Ganda, who looked upon him as the author of all the kingdom's sufferings. Others, like Museveni, wanted power for themselves, and the opposition to Obote was further strengthened after a wave of killings took place in and around Kampala in August 1980, which were said to have been carried out by the army to intimidate those opposed to the UPC. From this time, the role of the army as potentially the most important factor in Ugandan politics began at last to be recognized. The army leaders were determined to ensure that whoever held office should not be allowed to interfere in their own pursuit of the spoils of power. The other ranks supported their leaders through a sense of loyalty to men from their own districts. Obote's hopes of uniting the nation were thus doubly threatened. On the one hand he faced the challenge of Ganda patriotism, whether genuine or simply based upon self-interest, and on the other the regional loyalties of his own self-styled supporters.

There was another more personal element to be taken into account. Behind all these other developments stood Paulo Muwanga, neither Acholi nor Langi but a renegade Ganda, who was trying to manipulate events to satisfy his own craving for power. It was he, backed by the army and the pro-Obote faction in the NCC, who began the train of events leading to the election of Obote to the presidency. The office was one to which Muwanga himself, a Ganda distrusted by his own people, could not aspire, but behind which he sought to become the *éminence grise*. His first step was to arrange for the passing of a bill to define the electoral districts in such a manner as to ensure that those which supported Obote would have a preponderance of seats in parliament. Next, he induced Paulo Ssemogerere, who had succeeded Lule as leader of the Democratic Party, to agree reluctantly that ballot papers should be unmarked and that each candidate should have a separate box for his voting slips. This made it easy for anyone who wished to do so to exert pressure on the voters. Then he took advantage of an opportunity offered by the invasion of the remote West Nile district by supporters of the former president, Amin, who had drawn most of his military recruits from that region. The army, consisting of peoples who had suffered heavily at the hands of Amin's forces, took vigorous action against the invaders, leaving the countryside in turmoil. Treating the district as a disturbed area, Muwanga was able to cancel elections and to ensure the uncontested return of candidates who supported Obote. Needless to say, Obote would not have been successful in Amin's territory if the elections had been free. To add the final touch to his plans, Muwanga engineered the dismissal of the chief justice, William Wambuzi, whose duty it would be to call upon the leader of the party victorious in the elections to form a government. Wambuzi's proven honesty caused Muwanga to doubt his suitability as an agent of his plans. The new chief justice was of a more compliant disposition.

Against such a background of plots and schemes, and with the state radio and government and army vehicles put at the disposal of UPC candidates, the presence of a team of commonwealth observers during the elections held in December 1980 could have little impact on events. Yet even with the scales weighted so heavily in favour of the UPC, Muwanga had a moment of doubt. When the first returns appeared to favour the DP he intervened to insist that he alone should announce the results. This meant that, even if the UPC triumphed fairly, their opponents would never accept the validity of the result. In the event, the UPC claimed to have gained seventy-three seats. Seventeen of these were said to have been uncontested, though the commonwealth observers were sceptical of that statement, and the UPC's position was still further strengthened by the nomination of ten members to represent the army. These included Major-General Tito Okello and Brigadier David Oyite Ojok. The Democratic Party won fifty-one seats and the UPM one. The Ganda had voted tactically, giving their support neither to the UPM – as they might have been expected to do in the light of their earlier response to the formation of the party – nor yet to the Conservative Party of Joshua Mayanja Nkangi, former chief minister of Buganda, which had advocated devolution and a federal form of government. These two parties, the Ganda believed, had little prospect of defeating the UPC, and the best hope lay after all in supporting the DP. The leaders of the DP might favour a united Uganda, but they were moderate in their political views and the Ganda regarded them as the least of the immediate evils.

If any party had grounds for dissatisfaction with the way the elections had been conducted it was the DP, and its leaders at once challenged the result. When it became clear that Obote's accession to office was inevitable, however, they agreed to act as a constitutional opposition. It was an honourable decision and one which gave promise of more orderly government in the future. Obote, meanwhile, had preached reconciliation throughout his campaign and he now tried to make his cabinet representative of the whole country, including Buganda. He was happy to accept the DP as the official opposition and the DP functioned vigorously in that role. But two developments made the arrangement ineffective. First, Museveni, whose party had never looked capable of offering a challenge to the UPC or the DP and who himself had failed to gain election, decided to pursue his vendetta against Obote by military means. He took to the bush early in 1981 and tried to rally the disgruntled Ganda to his cause, taking his stand in the region immediately to the north of Kampala. From his base there he conducted a series of attacks on government, police and army buildings and personnel.

These operations were initially only small-scale undertakings, but they became more frequent and more extensive as the guerrillas were able to seize arms, ammunition, and equipment. They also began to be levelled against civilians with a view to forcing them to support the anti-government campaign. In spite of their leaders' hatred for Obote, the majority of the Ganda were reluctant to become embroiled in civil war yet again. Considerable force had often to be used to ensure their acquiescence to, and involvement in, the guerrillas' activities. But the government troops, with their long-standing distrust of the Ganda, made little distinction between active and passive supporters of the guerrilla movement.

The second disruptive factor followed inevitably upon the first. Although the government had a duty to suppress acts of terrorism, the army was not a suitable instrument for the purpose. The soldiers' animosity towards the Ganda was fuelled by their memories of the rejoicing in Buganda when Amin had seized power, and they knew how strongly the Ganda opposed Obote's return. Ill-disciplined and unpaid, due to shortage of funds in the treasury, they were only too ready to turn anti-guerrilla operations into an excuse for looting and for taking reprisals against their hated opponents. Regrettably, their senior officers appeared to have little inclination to restrain them, and as a result the Ganda were once again induced to form the core of the opposition to Obote, but this time as guerrillas led by non-Ganda.

From this point, guerrilla violence and army excesses – both fired by ethnic animosity – made a peaceful solution impossible. In essence, armies drawn from two allied ethnic groups – the Acholi and the Langi – too remote from their own peoples to claim their direct support, were at war with a third group, the Ganda, which claimed to be a nation. But the situation was confused by the fact that there were by this time some 3,000 Nkori in the government's army, recently recruited by Museveni himself. Moreover, though not directly involved in the struggle or represented significantly in the armed forces of either side, the peoples of eastern Uganda favoured Obote's government, while the peoples of the south-west were inclined to sympathize with Museveni. The division between north and east on the one hand and between south and west on the other, which Obote had created when he abolished the monarchies, had been obscured by a common hatred of Amin, but it was beginning to reappear.

Yet the Ganda were not the only ones to suffer the indiscriminate hostility of an army whose minimal discipline gave way before the temptations of revenge and loot. In the extreme north-west of the country a campaign of devastation was being waged against the Kakwa and Lugbara, Amin's people and their near neighbours. In the north-east the Karamojong, many of whom had seized arms from the arsenals of Amin's defeated army, had developed their traditional pursuit of cattle raiding into a technique for survival. Against the whole Karamojong people, irrespective of whether they had been engaged in cattle raiding or not, the army turned its fury. Restraint was cast aside, and the task of restoring order was converted into a campaign of wholesale brutality. Villages were destroyed and their inhabitants were forced to seek refuge in less accessible parts of the district or over the Kenyan border.

In June 1981, Museveni visited London where he made common cause with Yusuf Lule. It was a strange alliance – between a conservative, essentially pacific politician and a guerrilla leader whose sympathies inclined towards socialism. Museveni himself justified his move by pointing to Lule's influence in Buganda, where he was still seen as the only leader who might unite most of the peoples of Uganda behind him. It was in Buganda he was fighting, Museveni said, and it was among the Ganda that he, as an outsider, needed help. He got it, too, by co-operating with Lule, in the shape of substantial financial assistance from Ganda exiles in Britain who henceforward supported him throughout his campaign.[4] The army's excesses had fanned the Ganda leaders' hatred of Obote to an even greater intensity and now they looked to Museveni to rid the country of their arch enemy. The alliance also won for Museveni the backing of the Roman Catholic

Church in Uganda which had, for so long, felt that its members had little prospect of attaining high office either in Buganda or on the wider Ugandan stage. Ironically, it was about the same time that Museveni turned to Muslim, socialist Libya in search of arms and military training for his guerrilla forces.

Obote was fully aware that the only hope of restoring order – and that a meagre one – lay in a swift and massive improvement in the country's economy. Only the fertility of the soil had enabled the people to survive so many wasted years. Corruption flourished among higher ranking officials, accompanied by petty dishonesty among the population at large. This was a legacy of the Amin era and was still encouraged by the anarchic conditions prevalent throughout the country, but especially in the towns where shortages of essential commodities were most acutely felt. It was a state of affairs which could not be countenanced by any government which was trying to create stability, but it was difficult to eradicate. Britain and other western powers, as well as the International Monetary Fund (IMF), were willing to give support and some improvement was achieved. South-eastern Uganda staged a fair measure of recovery, but the income derived from renewed coffee exports frequently did not reach the people who most needed help. At the same time, the stringent measures recommended by the IMF in return for its assistance, though economically sound in the long term, weighed heavily upon people who had suffered privation for many years and who were unwilling to endure further impositions. The situation was not helped by threats from Museveni's National Resistance Army (NRA), as he now called his guerrillas, to blow up coffee-processing plants, or by his demands that coffee growers should not sell their produce to the state marketing organization. The effects of this policy were quickly seen in Buganda, where many farmers ceased to grow coffee – primarily from fear but perhaps in some cases from the satisfaction it gave them to oppose Obote. This only strengthened the army's conviction that the Ganda were bent upon subverting the state.

Drastic steps were taken by the government to counter these developments. In May 1983 hundreds of people were taken for questioning in the Kampala area in a search for the guerrillas and their supporters. A little further north, in what became known as the Luwero Triangle where the guerrillas had their main base, government troops rounded up villagers in thousands and put them in camps. It was hoped that under these conditions they would be unable to give help to the guerrillas either willingly or under duress, but in practice the camps became the scene of suffering and privation. It was not a policy calculated to warm Ganda hearts, even though it was accompanied by the announcement of large increases in the prices to be offered to farmers for their cotton, coffee, tea, tobacco, and cocoa in the hope of stimulating production.

Yet, in spite of these problems, an acute observer, Charles Harrison, reported in July 1983 that for the second year in succession Uganda had met its coffee quota, laid down by international agreement. He also said that the DP was still free to operate as an active, critical opposition in parliament and that the press was at liberty to report killings by the army as well as by the guerrillas.[5] Gradually, too, government forces were beginning to gain control in the Luwero Triangle.

Responding to the changing circumstances, the guerrillas switched the centre of their activities westward, into the Bunyoro and Masaka districts, and intermittently they also carried the struggle into Kampala itself. In its turn, the army carried out a sweep in Bunyoro in March 1984 after a successful attack by NRA guerrillas on military and police barracks in the western town of Masinde. Thousands of civilians were rounded up and roughly interrogated, and the resentment aroused by these measures among people hitherto only mildly committed to Museveni's cause meant that the Ganda ceased to be the only overt opponents of the government in the southern half of the country. From this point, Museveni was able to establish his base firmly in the south-west.

Obote also faced growing dissension nearer home. In December 1983 Brigadier Oyite Ojok was killed in an air crash. The leading contender for his appointment as chief of staff was Lieutenant-Colonel Basilio Okello, commander of the troops in Buganda. But Okello, like his namesake, Tito Okello the army commander, was an Acholi, and Obote, to please his own people, was anxious to appoint another Langi. His candidate was Lieutenant-Colonel Smith Opon Acak, a much less experienced soldier than Okello. Obote was conscious of the opposition to his proposal among senior officers and, characteristically, he sought to avoid any confrontation with his own supporters, behaviour which had already done him grave disservice during his first presidency and was to do so again. On this occasion he waited until August 1984 before appointing Opon Acak. In the interval the rivalry between the two contenders and their supporters had time to grow still more acute. Ever since Obote took office, the Acholi officers had been of the opinion that the Langi had occupied a disproportionately large number of senior posts in the army. The appointment of Opon Acak reinforced their view that the Acholi were

getting less than their desserts in the light of their considerable
contribution to Amin's overthrow and their subsequent loyalty to the
government. This division between two groups of soldiers who had for
so long been allies against the Ganda and their consolidation into
assertive ethnic units, were further signs of the corrosive effect of civil
war, of the lack of a national identity, and the absence of any focus of
loyalty higher than that provided by a common language. The
probable outcome had been foreshadowed by the murder of at least
eighteen Langi officers by their Acholi troops in the seven months
before a new chief of staff was appointed.

While these jealousies festered in the army, the guerrillas had been
regrouping. Their switch to the west, officially announced in June
1984, convinced many Nkori soldiers in the government's army that
the guerrilla movement was not, after all, limited to the Ganda, with
the result that many defected and joined Museveni. On the civilian
front, the DP continued their criticism of the government, twenty
seven of their number walking out of parliament at the beginning of
Obote's 1984 budget speech in protest against the killing of so many
people in the course of the fighting. About the same time, in mid 1984,
Amnesty International accused the army of having tortured thousands
of people since Obote became president. Then, as a climax to the
whole series of confrontations, the army dispute came to a head in
July. Acholi troops stationed in Jinja refused to go into action against
the guerrillas, claiming that they had done more than their share of
campaigning while the Langi had been kept out of the battle. Fighting
between the two groups broke out in the barracks, and the army
commander, Tito Okello, hastened to Acholi with some of his forces
and refused to return. On 27 July, Acholi troops under the command
of Brigadier Basilio Okello took over the government and Obote fled.
Okello then attacked Kampala, where he met with little resistance, the
demoralized Ganda inhabitants joining the hitherto hostile soldiers in
looting shops, offices, and private houses.

Museveni was in Sweden when the coup took place but he had been
in touch with the disaffected Acholi for some time and his immediate
reaction was to welcome Obote's overthrow. He was not so happy
with subsequent developments, for on 29 July Tito Okello was sworn
in as head of a nine-member military council which was to govern the
country and which contained no less than five Acholi. The NRA had
not been consulted at any time prior to the formation of the government, and when they learned that Paulo Muwanga was to be executive
prime minister they refused to join the council. Muwanga had con-
veniently abandoned Obote, just as he had abandoned Binaisa, but

the criticisms levelled against him were now too much even for his remarkable powers of survival and he was dismissed before the end of August. This opened the way for talks in Nairobi between the new government and the NRA. The latter claimed that they had played as important a role in encompassing the overthrow of Obote as had the Acholi troops, and that they should therefore be integrated into the army and be given a large share of seats in the military council. Museveni also insisted upon a number of measures to deal with corruption.[6] After a 6-week truce, fighting broke out between the remnant of the army and the NRA, and while the negotiations were still continuing in Nairobi the NRA seized the western Ganda town of Masaka.

The talks in Nairobi continued intermittently until December. To strengthen its claim to become part of a future government, the NRA announced that it had set up formal administration in Western Uganda. On 17 December an agreement was signed under the terms of which Okello's forces and the NRA would each have seven members in a twenty-member military council. Other groups who had opposed Obote would also be represented and Tito Okello would be chairman. Although an immediate ceasefire was declared, the Acholi soldiers were out of control. They looted Kampala and their officers could do nothing to restrain them. By the third week of January 1986 the agreement had still not been implemented and the truce came to an end. Museveni's forces moved against Kampala and on 26 January they occupied the city. Okello's troops fled in disarray, heading first into Eastern Uganda then turning northwestward towards their Acholi homeland. Wherever they went they looted property and molested the civil population. Their depredations did not cease until they were back in their own territory.

Museveni was sworn in as president on 29 January 1986 and also took the portfolio of defence. He chose as his prime minister Samson Kisekka, an elderly Ganda doctor who was a friend of former-president Lule. Though recent events had taken place without the active involvement of the Ganda they had been at work in the background on Museveni's behalf. Kisekka himself had acted as external co-ordinator for the NRA in Nairobi for five years. Museveni then announced that his government would uphold human rights and try to put an end to tribal factions. He added that he was prepared to support a mixed economy, a statement which undoubtedly pleased the leading Ganda who might have been made wary by the new president's earlier commitment to Marxism.

Initially, the minister of finance, Professor Ponsius Mulema, was the only member of the cabinet who had not taken part in the liberation struggle. He had been DP spokesman on financial affairs. In due course, however, Museveni fulfilled his promise to form a broadly-based government by appointing four more DP members, including Ssemogerere as minister for internal affairs, a post which, to the dismay of many of the party faithful, he had previously agreed to hold in Okello's government. Three former UPC members were also added to the cabinet, as was Joshua Mayanja Nkangi, former leader of the Conservative Party, and representatives of two small guerrilla groups which had fought against Obote. Significantly, no less than thirteen posts were allocated to Ganda ministers. The peoples of northern Uganda were scarcely represented. Now the country was no longer divided along simple ethnic – and still less upon overtly tribal – lines but rather between the predominantly Nilotic but completely disunited North and the Bantu South.

By early March the NRA had advanced into Acholi and had seized the principal town of Gulu. From there it continued its advance into the West Nile district – the land of Idi Amin – completing the conquest of that area, against minimum resistance, by the end of the month. Museveni then announced that, after five years of war to restore peace and democracy, reconciliation must begin. In April he appointed a commission to investigate charges of corruption against high-ranking officials in previous governments. Farmers were promised better prices for their produce and Asians expelled by Amin were offered compensation for the loss of their property. Another commission was set up to look into the atrocities and contraventions of human rights which had taken place during the previous fifteen years.

The good intentions of the government met with a minor setback when Ganda elders began to press for the restoration of the *kabaka*. Museveni replied that the civil war had not been fought to restore the kingdoms and that national unity demanded there should be no change in the constitution for at least four years. Twenty-five members of the monarchist group were arrested and charged with plotting a coup against the government. Fortunately for Museveni, their views were not representative of the rest of their people – although Ronald Mutebi, son of the former *kabaka* who had died in exile, was rapturously received by thousands of people when he visited Buganda for the first time for twenty years at the end of August. The fact was that the Ganda, for the time being, were mainly anxious to re-establish their economic prosperity which had been so disastrously affected by the recent strife, and co-operation with Museveni seemed the obvious way of achieving their objective. Tribal exclusivism must be relegated to the background.

About the same time, the first of what was to become a series of intermittent, but increasingly severe, attacks against government troops and strategic communications in the north-west was thought to have been inspired by members of Okello's former liberation army. This was the reverse of the coin minted by Museveni himself when he began his own guerilla campaign against Obote's government. A guerrilla attack on the northern town of Kitgum in late September was followed by the arrest of Muwanga and three ministers, all of whom were believed to have been involved in a plot to overthrow Museveni. The charges against Muwanga and one of the ministers were later dropped. An announcement that the NRA had itself killed sixty-two people in raids against cattle rustlers in October was a reminder that it was acts of this sort by supporters of Obote's regime which had been so heartily condemned by Museveni.

By the end of the year, rebel activity supported by the local civilian population in Acholi had increased markedly, and there were reports that government troops were showing considerably less restraint in handling civilians now that they were no longer operating among friendly peoples. In January 1987 an important battle took place between the NRA and a group of rebels. The NRA was victorious but casualties on both sides were heavy. In Teso, Langi supporters of Obote attacked the town of Soroti in February,[7] about the same time as a further attack was made by Acholi on Gulu. Yet neither the Acholi nor the Langi peoples were positively contemplating secession. They were not opposed to the idea of a Ugandan government. What they did not want was government by Museveni, and their view was only strengthened by the actions of the NRA, which was becoming increasingly brutal in dealing with its opponents, killing many of its prisoners as well as some of the wounded guerrillas who fell into its hands. At the beginning of November, Amnesty International published a report which gave details of human-rights abuses by the NRA, including the torture of prisoners and civilians. The abuses may not have been on the scale of those carried out earlier by Obote's troops, but the guerrilla movement in Acholi was still relatively in its infancy, and the population of Acholi was not so tightly packed as that of the Luwero Triangle. Again, the fact that the NRA excesses took place in areas remote from the capital – where journalists mainly congregated – meant that they attracted less attention than did those further south, where the press and the parliamentary opposition had access to news of what took place.

In August Museveni offered an amnesty to the guerrillas, but added that any who were guilty of crimes would have to stand trial. Nevertheless, a new anti-government group emerged, headed by an Acholi woman, Alice Lakwena, who claimed to have been ordered by God to overthrow Museveni. Lakwena had been collecting her 'troops' for 9 months in northern and eastern Uganda but her main support came from the Acholi, who felt humiliated by their treatment at the hands of the NRA. These people were civilians, not former soldiers, a clear indication that opposition to the government was spreading. She had little success in recruiting among the Langi, however, because they now thoroughly distrusted their neighbours and former allies. The quest for a Ugandan national identity in a region where hopes had once been high now seemed hopeless. Lightly armed, Lakwena's supporters were no match for the NRA, but in spite of a number of heavy defeats they continued their advance through eastern Uganda until they began to threaten Jinja, the second largest town in the country. By November, however, the rising was at an end and Lakwena herself escaped capture by taking refuge in Kenya where she was arrested for illegal entry. The brutal tactics employed by the NRA to defeat Lakwena's rebellion further tarnished its image as a peace-keeping, disciplined army. Disgusted by what they saw, many young eastern Ugandans joined the pro-Obote guerrillas.

It now seemed that two groups, the Acholi and the Langi, each relying upon ethnic loyalty yet lacking the central political focus to be described as either a tribe or a nation, were independently opposing a government which had the tentative support of most of the rest of the country except Karamoja. But that support was less than whole-hearted because the people were anxiously watching to see if Museveni could achieve the overall control which his predecessors had so patently failed to establish and without which there could be no security. Eastern Uganda, which had prospered under Obote's rule and with which Museveni had hitherto had little contact, could only wait and judge him by his performance. But many of the people distrusted him, and the behaviour of the NRA did nothing to win them over. Though many of the Ganda had supported Museveni both militarily and financially they, too, were wary of a man who was not one of themselves. They were reassured to some extent by the presence of a large number of their fellow Ganda in the cabinet, but there were too many non-Ganda in positions of the greatest importance for them to feel wholly at ease. Tribal pride, closely linked with economic self-interest, exerted a powerful influence, and Buganda could still present problems to the new government. Ugandan Roman Catholics, however, have been delighted by Museveni's success. In his government they dominated several key ministries and exercised a measure of influence in the country which they had never previously enjoyed,

save in the evanescent period between self-government and independence. But even they are on the lookout for signs of instability in
the new regime.

Though Buganda was no longer the main focus of political activity,
its role had been central to everything that had taken place since
independence. Buganda's opposition to Obote had created a feeling of
instability in the late 1960s, which had encouraged repressive measures
by the government and paved the way for Amin's seizure of power.
The kingdom's initial support for Amin had helped him to gain
general acceptance. Ganda opposition to Binaisa had weakened his
position and had made it easier for Obote's supporters to ensure their
leader's return – a result the Ganda had certainly not intended.
Finally, Museveni's guerrilla movement would never have succeeded if
it had tried to establish a base other than in Buganda and without the
financial aid which leading Ganda provided. Throughout the whole of
the previous century the central location of Buganda,[8] its economic
strength and its educational pre-eminence, had made its assimilation
into a united Uganda a virtual impossibility. It would have taken a
remarkable personality to lead the whole country to union, and no one
of that calibre had emerged. The particularism of the Ganda leaders
and their economic strength – drawing when necessary on the support
of the majority of the Ganda people – had also made it difficult for
the other peoples of Uganda to accept Ganda leadership. It has been
on that rock that attempts at unity have foundered again and again.
Probably the most effective solution would have been to separate
Buganda from the rest of the country and to set up an independent
state as the Ganda leaders themselves had wished. To do this,
however, would have been to reverse the whole history of the British
period in Uganda and would have meant the creation of a new communications network, a new capital, and new national facilities of
every kind. These were expensive measures which Britain, blown
along by the wind of change in the late 1950s, had neither the time nor
the desire to contemplate. Nor would such an arrangement have been
acceptable to the other inhabitants of Uganda, who had witnessed
Britain's attempt to unify the country and believed they could only
benefit from perpetuating that unity.

Today the restoration of Uganda's economy has the same overriding importance that it has had since the ruinous days of Amin, but
internal divisions still distract attention from that vital objective. Talk
of a north/south division temporarily obscures the more fundamental
conflict which has its roots in the desperate search for security and
which, because of the country's history, manifests itself as tribalism or

ethnic exclusiveness. But that search goes on, and tribalism and ethnicity are still factors which cannot be overlooked – even though their focus seems to have shifted for the time being from Buganda to the north. Uganda's future still depends upon whether Museveni can convince all the peoples of the country that he is strong enough to resist the pressure from any one group while working successfully for the prosperity of all.

The hostility to the hegemony of any one tribe, or alliance of tribal or ethnic groups, which is the fruit of bitter experience, could work to his advantage. In the early days it had been Buganda's sense of superiority and its overt economic prosperity which had aroused a spirit of emulation and encouraged the development of individual ethnic loyalties among the other peoples of Uganda. It had transformed them into something akin to proto-tribes which appeared to institutionalize the existing divisions within the country. But it should not be forgotten that at the time of independence most of the peoples of Uganda, the Ganda excepted, had been prepared to join together provided the union took place on equal terms and local interests were safeguarded. Buganda's obduracy, springing from the anxiety of its people to protect their strong economic position, an anxiety which was powerfully reinforced by the revival of ancient feelings of patriotism, encouraged that spirit of unity in the rest of the country. It also provided the rock upon which union foundered.

Yet, despite the troubled years which have intervened, and despite the desperate state of the country's economy, Museveni's task is in some ways easier than Obote's was. Unlike Obote he has, for the time being, the support of the Ganda. If he can continue to reassure them, chastened as they have been by the tyranny of Amin and the ravages of Obote's troops, that it is in their interests to go on supporting him – which Obote as a northerner could never hope to do – he will have laid important foundations. He has, too, the backing of the Roman Catholics, though once again this is dependent upon his continuing ability to satisfy their long-felt desire to share in the exercise of power. His main troubles lie among the peoples furthest from the centre of affairs and these can be dealt with outside the glare of publicity which in Obote's day shone on events taking place mainly in Kampala and its immediate vicinity. In addition, he is operating from a base in the economic heartland which is vital to Uganda's recovery, and for that reason the role of Buganda and its relations with the government are again all-important. It is essential that Museveni should handle with the greatest delicacy the patriotism of a devastated but still proud people and cherish the still strong economic position of their leaders without arousing the envy of the rest of Uganda's peoples. If he does all this, he might succeed in uniting a country which has the resources and the manpower to prosper, and in this respect Uganda is more fortunate than many other African countries which seem doomed to poverty.

Meanwhile, rampant inflation is creating horrific problems for everyone except the blackmarketeers who thrive on the country's economic uncertainty. This cannot augur well for Museveni's continuing popularity, however much sympathetic outside observers might wish to cast him in the role of his country's saviour. Moreover, he may already have created implacable enemies among the proto-tribes of the north, as Obote did in Buganda. It is not a promising situation, and Uganda's history has shown that, when difficulties arise, tribalism and neo-tribalism can become powerfully destructive forces – not so much as the originators but rather as the instruments of groups determined to pursue some local advantage, or as a defence against the machinations of alien bodies. Tribalism is the volunteer reserve, enlisted by those intent upon extending or defending their interests.

In spite of Idi Amin's uncoordinated attempt to extend the use of KiSwahili, the peoples of Uganda are still separated by their languages. President Museveni is trying to create a nation out of people whose loyalties are still predominantly local because their experience of central government has often confirmed their fear of remote control. Their chief concern is not with nationhood but with peace and security and they are far from confident that Museveni can guarantee either. But their tribalism is not essentially atavistic. It resembles in many ways the suspicious nationalism of post First World War Europe, when small states, recently created and lacking many of the cardinal features of nationhood, survived in uneasy juxtaposition with larger, older, more self-conscious peoples who were determined to preserve their identities and their pre-eminence. So, anarchy and strife have been the order of the day. Nationality/tribalism has asserted itself, with alliances of expediency following upon each other to protect local interests as best they could.

In this chapter the recent history of Uganda has been covered in some detail. The aim has been to illustrate the variety of factors which contribute to the problems of one contemporary African nation state. Using Uganda as a model, it will not always be necessary to look at other countries in quite such detail, but one must be wary of drawing conclusions in respect of any country without looking carefully at the sequence of events both immediately before and then subsequent to the achievement of independence.

3   Ghana: a confederation of regions?

To what extent has Uganda's experience of the effects of tribalism been reflected in other African countries? Ghana, for example, roughly equal in area to Uganda, but lacking the overall fertility of its East African counterpart, relied heavily, under British rule, upon the export of cocoa for its foreign exchange. This seemed reasonable while the country was assumed to be a perpetual member of an imperial economy. Since independence, however, with little prospect of finding any alternative to cocoa in the event of a price failure, and having been tempted into becoming an importer of food by the prospect of profits from the sale of cocoa, Ghana is clearly not cut out ecomonically to stand alone.

None the less, like Uganda, the country embodies a number of ancient polities, some of them formerly had centralized forms of government, others having been more loosely organized. Like Uganda, too, it has been unable to rid itself of its political past simply by becoming independent. 'We labour' said Chairman Jerry Rawlings early in 1987, 'under historical constraints which do not always allow us the elbow-room we want.'[1] More positively, Mr Justice D.F. Annan, a member of the ruling Provisional National Defence Council (PNDC) and chairman of the National Commission for Democracy (NCD), the government's 'think tank', dismissed the so-called popular democracy of the Workers'/People's Defence Committees, the People's Border Guards, the People's Army, the People's Tribunals and the National Investigations Committee, which had been in vogue from 1982 to 1984, as no longer relevant. What Ghana needed, he said, was a political system rooted in the country's history and cultural tradition.[2] Professor Kofi Awoonon, Ghana's ambassador to Brazil, added his own version of the same theme in a lecture delivered to the Political Science Student's Association at the University of Legon. A nation's ability to run its own affairs, he said, depended upon its grasp of its own historical personality, not on a simple-minded document setting out a model of government.[3]

All these statements seem strangely at odds with Rawlings's appeal to the Press on 1 January 1982, the day after the PNDC seized power, to act as the vanguard of a Holy War and to become part of the revolution by helping to convey the government's policy to the masses.[4] Yet, in response to those critics who accuse him of reverting to Ghana's feudal past, Rawlings firmly denies that the government is changing its policy. It is learning, he says, to assess what can be attained at a particular point in time with the resources available to it. He is not the first would-be reformer to be forced to that reluctant conclusion. The revolutionary doctrine enunciated by Ghana's founder, Kwane Nkrumah, has its attractions still. But Rawlings has come to recognize that, whether he likes it or not, ancient practices cannot be ignored. Moreover, the influence of Ghana's customary authorities, whether traditional or neo-traditional, which Nkrumah tried to destroy, is still alive, and with careful handling might even contribute to the achievement of Rawlings's aims. Mishandled it could only serve as an impediment to progress.

Nkrumah took a different view. He resurrected the name 'Ghana' from West Africa's medieval past as a symbol of his anti-imperialist plans for his country's future, not with a view to reviving what he considered to be outmoded practices. Regardless of the scarcity of natural resources – a weakness he hoped would be overcome in due course through co-operation with other African states – he had always proposed that Ghana should develop as a modern state which refused to be tied to the apparatus of the past. Customary authorities, in his eyes, were an obstacle to the creation of a united country and a society based upon socialist principles. As leader of government business he had tried to deprive them of their powers and wealth by his local government legislation of 1951. More recently, and long after Nkrumah's departure from the political scene, the 1979 constitution also attempted to debar these former rulers from taking an active part in politics. Neither enactment was wholly successful in attaining its objective. So Rawlings, learning from past failures, now seeks to use traditional authorities and customary practice to promote his aim which, he says, is to establish a national consensus on the basis of informed debate. Whether this is a practical proposition, or whether it is simply another example of the political rhetoric which, since independence, has so often been used as a substitute for planning, must depend, as it has in Uganda, upon the assessment of the advantages or disadvantages of co-operating with the central government made by those who could summon traditional loyalties to their aid. Rawlings says that he wants their help, but is he really dependent upon it? Is the Ghana of Nkrumah's dreams no more than a confederation of regions in which tribalism is still a decisive force, as Professor Adu Boahen has recently claimed?[5]

There is little doubt that, even after thirty years of independence, the instinctive loyalty of most Ghanaians is to their family, or village, or clan, or to whichever social unit they know they must ultimately answer to for their behaviour. It is, perhaps, even more significant that educated Ghanaians continue to address each other in vernacular languages and only use English when speaking with a member of another ethnic group. In the early days of Ghana's independence, Nkrumah's young pioneers arrogantly used their muscle to defend the unifying slogans of the Convention Peoples' Party (CPP). But even in their heyday their private behaviour did not always match their public bravado. In their daily lives there were traditional rules which could not be casually jettisoned in response to nationalist propaganda. Nkrumah, with all his powers of leadership, could not ignore history completely.

Ghana, like every other former British dependency in Africa, was compounded of a great variety of peoples whom the British had done nothing to unite and may even have confirmed in their differences. As in Uganda, there were those who feared that a united, independent country might not serve their interests. Their fears, like those of the people of Buganda, sprang mainly from economic considerations, but they often encouraged tribal or ethnic solidarity and a concern to preserve customary authority as a defence against insecurity, even in societies where such characteristics had not previously been greatly in evidence. The Ewe, for example, in British-administered Togoland, had never been noted for their internal unity. But the prospect of being united with an independent and alien Ghana aroused unexpected feelings of affinity with their relations in French-administered Togoland. Such a small group, lacking political cohesion, could not pose a serious threat to Nkrumah's ideal of unity, even though its members might have preferred secession. But it remained as a grumbling appendix.

The Ga, too, a mainly urban people living round Accra, possessed, in many cases, a level of education which fitted them for employment of a sort which, under British rule, they were unable to find. They might have seemed likely recruits for the CPP in its protest against the evils of imperialism, but they did not rally to Nkrumah's call. Though lacking any tradition of joint action they formed a non-political association to protect their interests even before independence. When they discovered that the protection of those interests did not feature prominently in Nkrumah's plans, their association at once took a more political form as a defence against any threat posed by the central government. Like the Ewe, they lacked a strong tribal organization upon which to focus their political energies, so that, although they could create problems for the central government, their protest was less dangerous than it might have been. Unlike the Ewe, they never contemplated secession.

A greater threat to Ghana's future as a united country was posed by an alliance cemented between some of the country's most highly educated people and a group of prosperous farmers, many of both elements being closely linked to traditional authorities. The farmers had been angered by the decision of Nkrumah's pre-independence government to fix the price which they would receive for their coffee, a price which seemed far below its market value. The reason for fixing prices, the government said, was to enable it to use the reserve built up when world prices were high to guarantee farmers a reasonable return for their efforts in leaner years. In the meantime, any excess funds could be spent on projects of national importance. The cocoa farmers resented such paternalism and strongly objected to the seizure of what they regarded as their own hard-earned profits. The intellectuals, for their part, had watched with dismay the bullyboy tactics employed by Nkrumah's younger followers to compel the people to support the CPP. They were justifiably sceptical of the qualifications of the party faithful to put into effect the ever more grandiose plans of their leader, and they regarded Nkrumah himself as an incipient dictator.

For these reasons, the two groups formed themselves into the National Liberation Movement (NLM), challenging Nkrumah's claim that his CPP represented the unanimous voice of the Ghanaian people who wanted immediate independence, and calling upon him to prove his assertion by agreeing to hold national elections before making the final move to independence. The NLM then campaigned in favour of a federal constitution, justifying their proposal on the ground that the peoples of Ghana belonged to a number of tribes possessing divergent social structures which were at different levels of adaptation to western democracy. This meant that their sense of national identity was too weak to make united, democratic government possible. The Asante, for example, owed allegiance to the golden stool of their paramount ruler, while other peoples were loyal to a variety of political identities.[6]

The reference to the Asante was revealing and also, from the point of view of the NLM's hopes of success, unfortunate. It only served to emphasize what was becoming increasingly evident – or so the rest of the population believed – namely, that the membership of the party was mainly drawn from Akan-speaking peoples even if not solely from the Asante, and that Asante traditional rulers had played an important role in the party's formation. This view was strengthened when an attempt by Nkrumah to interfere in the activities of the Asante paramount, the *Asantehene*, led to rioting in the Asante region and made it impossible for him to set foot in the area for more than two years. The Asante leaders, it would seem, were acting in much the same manner as the Ganda leaders were doing in Uganda. Both possessed a strong sense of tribal identity, yet had prospered as a result of co-operating with Britain's plans for the economic development of their respective regions. Both were prepared to exploit that identity to protect the privileged positions they had attained.

In fact the Asante lacked some of the advantages which made Buganda such a formidable obstacle to national unity. Their territory, for example, did not occupy quite as important a strategic position as did Buganda in Uganda. Nkrumah, too, was a far more dominant figure than Obote could ever aspire to be. Not only had he organized a large personal following throughout most of Ghana but he was also widely regarded, inside and outside the country, as the most significant African leader in the whole continent. He therefore seized upon the growing concern about the intentions of the NLM with alacrity, and it was not difficult for him to convince many of the other peoples of Ghana that the Asante were aiming to dominate the whole country. The cocoa farmers he castigated as selfish capitalists who were trying to undermine his great concept of a socialist society. The intellectuals he accused of acting as allies of the imperialists by retarding the country's united advance to independence. The traditional rulers, he said, were obviously trying to hold on to outdated systems of authority in the face of an overwhelming liberation movement.

In these circumstances, it is not surprising that the CPP had a convincing victory in the elections held in 1956, even though it was the NLM that had asked for them. The heady call for freedom from imperial rule and the hopes of prosperity which it was believed that freedom would bring proved an overwhelming incentive to many Ghanaians to support Nkrumah, whose powerful personality singled him out as the leader, not only of his own country but of the whole of Africa. The CPP gained 71 seats in the assembly to the opposition's 35. Moreover the NLM collected only 30 per cent of the total votes cast, but the distribution of those votes made it clear that one region at least, Asante, still wished to distance itself from the rest of the country.

This was not due primarily to feelings of tribal or ethnic exclusiveness, though such feelings were enlisted in support of the action taken by the NLM, which feared and detested the socialist policies proposed by Nkrumah and the CPP.

It was, however, disappointment in a quarter other than Asante that brought Nkrumah's government its first problems. In August 1957 rioting broke out in Accra among the Ga, who resented paying taxes which did not have the immediate result of bringing the jobs and accomodation they had looked to the victorious party to provide. Nkrumah was wary of any movement which might threaten his dream of a united country and it was in response to these troubles that he enacted his Avoidance of Discrimination law which made illegal any tribal, racial, or religious groups organized for political purposes. In an attempt to avoid any charge of tribalism, the NLM proceeded to merge with other opposition groups on 3 November 1957 to form the United Party (UP), which was led by Dr Kofi Busia. Busia, as a distinguished professor of sociology and a member of one of Western Asante's ruling families, embodied two of the leading elements opposed to Nkrumah. Moreover, in his person and in his participation in the new political alliance, Busia demonstrated the difference between the leaders of Asante and those of Buganda. The Asante leaders had no wish to dissociate themseleves from the rest of Ghana. It was against Nkrumahism that they took their stand.

Nkrumah was quick to react to the new challenge. The Preventive Detention Act of 1958 empowered him to deal with opponents who became too threatening, and Busia was one of those who was forced into exile. But among those who were opposed to Nkrumah, the traditional rulers – and not only the traditional Asante rulers – proved to be more resilient than the president had anticipated, and the loyalty of their people was not easily diverted either by the threats or the promises of the CPP. He quickly discovered that direct confrontation aroused endless difficulties. He therefore tried to minimize the influence of the rulers by using pressure through his party machine to ensure that when vacancies occurred in traditional offices, complaisant men were chosen to fill them – men who would carry out his wishes. But in spite of his efforts, opposition in one quarter or another grew steadily year by year.

Responsibility for Nkrumah's overthrow after nine years of increasingly dictatorial and extravagant rule was proudly claimed by many Ewe as the work of their people. Three of the five leaders of the coup which unseated Nkrumah, including the most senior officer involved, Colonel Emmanuel Kwasi Kotoka, had indeed been Ewe. But it was not an ethnic revolt which led to the government's downfall. It was a movement which transcended ethnic or tribal disaffection. The plot was, in fact, crystalized in Kumasi, the Asante capital, but its success was due in the first instance to the support it gained in the army, the only body possessing the weapons to carry it out effectively. But the Ghana coup bore no resemblance to Idi Amin's seizure of power in Uganda. Whether or not there was any truth in Nkrumah's retrospective claim that the two senior policemen involved (both Ewe) were about to be accused of diamond smuggling,[7] their role could scarcely be compared with that of Amin. The military leaders in particular had been educated in the belief that the army was the servant of the government, and their intervention in politics took place only because they were convinced that the vast majority of the people were desperately looking for a change of government. Their opinion would certainly seem to have been borne out by the widespread satisfaction with which the coup was greeted. Grievances had been felt in virtually every section of the community. Throughout the country the slogan 'Freedom and Justice', so proudly proclaimed at the time of independence and so boldly engraved on the triumphal arch in Independence Square, had developed a hollow sound. Nkrumah, the potential leader of the whole of Africa, had beggared his country in pursuit of his great dream of a continent free from external domination.

The army had been starved of equipment and even of clothing. In the meantime, Nkrumah had built up an independent presidential guard which he armed with the latest weapons from Russia. While army pay failed to rise with the cost of living, the presidential guard was seen to fare exceptionally well. Money which might have been used to rescue the army from despair was openly spent in support of freedom movements in other parts of Africa. The police, like the army, had had more than enough of dictatorship. The Press had been reduced from thirty-three newspapers at the time of independence to four in 1966, all of them supporting the CPP. Trade union leaders had become increasingly irked by their total subservience to a Trades Union Congress which not only controlled their purse strings but also seemed more concerned to mouth party rhetoric than to fill the mouths of the working classes. Leaders of opposition parties were in self-imposed exile or in prison under the Preventive Detention Act. Former supporters of the CPP, who had seen the cost of living rise many times faster than their incomes, had begun to lose faith in their leader. Even stalwarts of Nkrumah's government, when forced to witness the healthy reserves in hand at independence being squandered on projects about which they had not been consulted – or on which their views had been unheeded – now looked for change. The president had utterly failed to maintain contact with the people he ruled and upon whose support he depended, while the CPP had been transformed into a corrupt bureaucracy instead of being the mass movement it had set out to be. Above all, Nkrumah's search for the political kingdom he had so much coveted had led to the adoption of economic policies which brought bankruptcy to a once precariously prosperous country, and disillusionment to those who had given him their unstinting support.

It would be untrue to suggest that Nkrumah had no achievements to his credit. The introduction of universal primary education, now abandoned for reasons of economy, was a triumph which other African countries emulated only many years later. The creation of better communications and the building of good urban houses were other areas in which he showed the way to his country's neighbours. And, greatest achievement of all, he had led his country to independence, and by his example he had inspired similar movements all over Africa. But he had failed to use to the full the human resources at his disposal. He had kept power in his own hands and, as a result, the management of the economy had been grievously neglected. That, coupled with the fall in the world price of cocoa, left him defenceless when his opponents sought to destroy him. Like every heir to imperial rule he had been expected to provide in full measure the benefits for which his people looked as the prize for those who gained their independence. At the very least he had been expected to prevent their situation from deteriorating. In spite of his vaunted invincibility he had done neither. The fact that his errors had been compounded by the readiness with which nations and individuals had helped to conceal the shallowness of Ghana's economy by offering credit on terms highly beneficial to themselves reflects adversely on the creditors, but it also underlines Nkrumah's own lack of economic understanding as the willing recipient of such loaded gifts.

The military leaders of the coup had no desire to prolong their rule unduly. They had neither tribal nor personal ambitions to gratify and they were in no way anxious to destroy whatever unity Nkrumah had achieved. They were not seekers after power and they were not sectarian in their allegiance. As an earnest of their good intentions they invited the country to return to civilian rule as soon as a democratic constitution could be agreed upon and elections arranged. With Nkrumah, the dictator, in exile, tribalism as a defence against his unwelcome policies lost its importance and all thoughts of a federal type of government were dismissed. All the party leaders were agreed that, if democracy were to flourish, the new government must be seen to represent the whole country. The Progress Party, formed under Busia's leadership in May 1969 to contest the elections later in the month, set out deliberately to enlist candidates representative of each area of the country. So, too, did its main rival, the National Alliance of Liberals (NAL). But high ideals at the national level were not sufficient to overcome regional fears and suspicions. Perversely, the political parties and their supporters saw in each other the defects each of them claimed to want to avoid. The NAL quickly became identified, in the eyes of the rest of the electorate, with the Volta Region and with the Ewe-speaking peoples. Lesser parties met with a similar fate. The National Party (NP) was widely thought to be the party of the Ga, while the People's Action Party was seen to draw its strength mainly from the Nzima and the All People's Republican Party was believed to express the views of a disgruntled section of the Akan-speaking peoples.[8] As in Uganda, this situation was reinforced by the virtual impossibility of any candidate standing for parliament in a con-stituency where he was not a member of the dominant ethnic group.

The problem was that, after their experience of Nkrumah, many of the members of different ethnic groups, like the people of Uganda today, were genuinely afraid that their interests would be overlooked by any central government. They consequently believed that their only hope of making their voices heard effectively in parliament was by voting for candidates presented by parties composed exclusively of people drawn from their own districts and speaking their own language. To play a minor role in a party claiming to represent the whole country seemed pointless. This meant that the larger parties found difficulty in recruiting candidates to stand on their behalf among the smaller ethnic groups. The fears of those groups both contributed to, and were in due course reinforced by, the problems arising from the introduction of the Westminster system of govern-ment upon which the makers of the new constitution, with the best of intentions, had insisted.

Initially the system seemed to work very well. Campaigning on a platform of liberal democracy, welfarism and private enterprise, the Progress Party aroused a powerful response from an electorate deprived of all those desirable features for nine years. Winning 105 seats in the new parliament, out of a total of 140, the party appeared to have captured the support of the bulk of the population. But, in spite of all their efforts before the elections, they had won only two seats in the Volta Region, the homeland of the Ewe. Moreover, because the more able Ewe politicians had supported the NAL, neither of the victorious candidates seemed suitable for ministerial office. This meant that, under the Westminster system, not only were members of defeated parties – which in the circumstances meant members of minority ethnic groups – automatically excluded from office, but even where some members of a minority ethnic group had agreed to co-operate with a major party they were unable to represent their people in positions of importance. When, in addition, the leader of the NAL – himself an Ewe – was denied a seat in parliament because he had been an office-holder in the CPP, in accordance with one of the few provisions insisted upon by the military leaders when the constitution was drafted, the Ewe wrongly but understandably concluded that they were being subjected to deliberate discrimination.

Worse was to follow. Though Busia did his utmost to minimize the impact of his pruning of Nkrumah's wildly inflated civil service, there were those who argued that Ewe civil servants suffered dispropor-tionately in the process. It was not enough for the Progress Party to make every effort to show tolerance for the opposition. The latter groups quickly united to form the Justice Party under the leadership of an Asante, Joe Appiah, in an attempt to demonstrate that they, at least, were able to transcend ethnic differences. Paradoxically, their motive for uniting was to protect regional interests. In response, the PP did its utmost to show its own impartiality by allowing the opposition to be represented on the council of state, on whose advice the head of state acted, and on all committees of the national assembly. Appiah was even invited to attend cabinet meetings,[9] while the press was encouraged to act as an informed critic of government policies.

In spite of these measures, the Progress Party was still regarded by opponents of the government as an Asante party, or at best as repre-senting the interests of the Akan-speaking peoples. Among the urban population of Accra especially, this view was reinforced by Busia's decision to introduce a national-development levy on the salaries of urban workers in order to develop the rural areas neglected by Nkrumah. It did not escape adverse comment that the income was to be used to assist the cocoa-growing regions, the stronghold of the PP.

If regional, and particularly Ewe and Ga, fears provided the spark to kindle the opposition to Busia's government, the opposition was fuelled by grievances of a wider or alternatively of a more personal nature. Nkrumah had left the country heavily in debt, and foreign creditors who had suffered as a result of pandering to his economic incontinence were slow to rally to the assistance of his successor. This factor could well have been the most significant in Ghana's recent history. If the western powers, in particular, had acted with generosity immediately after Nkrumah's downfall, and had either waived or postponed repayment of their debts, the Progress Party might have been able to reassure even the most mistrustful of its ethnic opponents. So widespread, too, was the realization that the heroic days of Nkrumah were long since past, that even the former president's supporters were reluctant to press for the revival of his policies. But the creditors pursued their demands and Busia was left in an impossible position.

Economic recovery, even if it were feasible, could not come as swiftly as people had hoped, and it was this that led to the overthrow of the government. Though prices offered to farmers for their cocoa were raised, the Asante growers – until now supporters of Busia – were still dissatisfied, and began to criticize the PP for not being sufficiently responsive to their needs. Students became indignant when it was proposed that they should take loans to finance their education so as to reduce the demands on national resources. Nkrumah's former supporters regained some of their confidence and represented Busia's legislation to abolish the authoritarian TUC, popular though this was in many quarters, as a covert attack upon the railway workers who happened to be on strike when the measure became law. The act, Busia's critics maintained, was evidence of the reactionary bourgeois tendencies of the government. Even his efforts to restore some of the rulers destooled by Nkrumah and to re-establish their authority were seen by his opponents as an attempt to enlist a popular, traditional force as part of a government machine which was being operated solely in the interests of the Progress Party. Busia's insistence, as a Christian, that the best means of ending apartheid in South Africa was through dialogue, proved to be the final factor in losing the support of even some of his most trusted friends. As a climax to his problems, he was forced by a fall in cocoa prices – from £330 a ton in 1970 to £230 in 1971 – to devalue the currency by 49 per cent in December 1971. This caused an immediate increase in prices inside Ghana of between 30 per cent and 40 per cent and was disastrous to Busia's hopes of establishing a stable, democratic government.

Although they aroused ethnic, regional, political, and economic opposition, these many difficulties did not, to a detached observer, suggest that Busia and his ministers had thereby surrendered the right to govern the country. There was, it is true, widespread dissatisfaction, but the government's overthrow came as the direct result of a second intervention by the army on 13 January 1972. The army itself had grievances. Since the overthrow of Nkrumah it had been considerably weakened, initially at least by its own choice. The military members of the National Liberation Council, which had been responsible for the downfall of the previous regime, had retired voluntarily from the army after dismissing several other senior officers whose loyalty to the coup had been suspect. In addition, however, Busia had found it necessary to remove a number of other officers in a manner which, to his critics, again suggested that he was obsessively suspicious of the Ewe. But the second coup was certainly not exclusively motivated by the concern of the Ewe members of the armed forces. It was the product of personal ambition and of more general military discontent. The leaders were, in fact, all Asante, but the proposed coup had wide support among the army officers because for the first time, and as their special contribution to the country's rehabilitation programme, they were to be required to pay a part of the cost of electricity and water in their billets.

The leaders of the coup had other, more personal, reasons for acting as they did. Lieutenant-Colonel Ignatius Kutu Acheampong, the main figure in the plot, even boasted that he had started to plan the government's overthrow only a few months after it took office. He was not a well-educated man and he had difficulty in passing his promotion examination. But the NLC, by their earlier coup, had shown him a swifter means of getting to the top. Three of his four main assistants were majors faced with dismissal from the service after failing their promotion examinations, and the fourth, Brigadier Alphonse Kadzo Kattah, was being prosecuted for alleged fraudulent activities.[10] Once he had seized power, Acheampong quickly dispensed with the assistance of these four lest they should in any way pose a threat to his position.

Though it would have been difficult for the people to resist the take-over, there is little indication of any widespread desire to do so. Disillusionment with Busia's government had grown rapidly because expectations were unjustifiably high, and as a result there was a strong if illogical undercurrent of opinion in favour of the restoration of Nkrumah. The latter's death in exile shortly after the coup took place put an end to these hopes, but it had important repercussions. Nkrumah's shortcomings were not forgotten by those who had rejoiced in his overthrow only six years earlier. But, for all its good intentions, Busia's government had failed to capture popular support, and the memory of Nkrumah's flamboyant leadership shone brightly by comparison with the earnest endeavours of his successors. Acheampong maintained initially that Busia had been displaced because he had adopted Nkrumah's oppressive methods.[11] But when he saw the trend of popular opinion he quickly changed his style and claimed to be a disciple of Ghana's first and greatest leader – the man who had united the country in the face of those who stood for faction and had led the peoples of Ghana to independence. By strong government, Nkrumah had made the country's black star a symbol of African pride and self respect and an inspiration to the entire continent. By similar methods, Acheampong set out to restore what had been lost.

By adopting this stance, Acheampong hoped to give the impression that the coup had made possible a reversion to the sort of Ghanaian nationalism which the people, tired of factionalism, had forced their leaders to pursue, but the people were not deceived. Though he echoed the rhetoric, he had few of the leadership qualities which Nkrumah had so amply demonstrated. Nevertheless, he did begin by taking the important and internally popular step of revaluing the currency, to do which it was necessary to repudiate those of his country's debts which, for various reasons, he deemed to be invalid. His National Redemption Council – which later changed its name to the Supreme Military Council – also claimed, as the NLC had previously done, that it was anxious to put an end to corruption and to allow freedom of expression. Hopes of better things were quickly extinguished, however. In June 1973 a new law was passed which took away the liberties which the Press had enjoyed under both the NLC and Busia. Addressing the board of directors of the information services secretariat in June 1974, Acheampong stated categorically: 'Your loyalty to the government and state should be unquestionably absolute'. This was the voice of Nkrumah in its most authoritarian vein. There must be no divisions inside the country and no hostile criticism of the government's actions. But the speaker was only a shadow of the former leader.

Towards the end of 1975, Acheampong claimed that he had uncovered a plot to stage a coup. All eight of those charged were Ewe, and it was alleged that they had been severely tortured to extract confessions.[12] Four soldiers and one civilian were found guilty and sentenced to be executed. Two other officers were given long prison sentences and one soldier was acquitted. Several of those found guilty claimed that their interrogaters had abused them because of their ethnic origins – an indication that, justifiably or not, the Ewe were still suspected of harbouring disruptive sentiments and of exercising a dangerous influence in the armed forces.

A further problem arose in January 1977. The supreme military council had set up a committee to test opinion about the best form of civilian government for Ghana. In response, the restored Trades Union Congress, seeking to recapture the authority it had wielded under Nkrumah and fearing the influence the cocoa-growers were believed to exert upon government policy, called for a 'union government' with a mass movement as its base, an 'unperverted socialist form of government'. Acheampong was not pleased with the proposal. He replied that Ghana was searching for a Ghanaian way of returning to civilian rule. The people wanted a form of government suited to their particular needs rather than something transplanted with little modification from abroad. But his intentions were far from clear, and although he eventually came to accept the principle of a union government he refused to set a date for the restoration of civilian rule.

The Times of 14 January 1977 said there was more freedom of trade-union organization in Ghana than in any other African country, and the fact that there had been several strikes indicated that there was little intimidation of the unions. The Press, too, though mainly state-owned, seemed reasonably free. But in the background there remained the threat of preventive detention. The government may have been reasonable in its intentions, but it did not appear to be good at getting results. Its 'Operation Feed Youself' brought an increase in the amount of food produced in Ghana, but a great deal of food had still to be imported. With better organization this would have been unnecessary. Inflation was still very high and an attempt to control prices by limiting the sale of goods to certain shops at a fair price only led to long queues of would-be buyers. In April 1977 a comprehensive five-year development plan was launched – but it came at a bad time. Inflation was adding greatly to the price of food and shortages in some areas created severe tension.

In May of the same year there was an another attempted coup, this time by a handful of former supporters of the government, both military and civilian, who were disillusioned by its incompetence. It posed little threat, but the government tightened security still further by publishing a new decree making the publication of rumours punishable, on conviction, by imprisonment for from 5–10 years. In the same month, the University of Legon was closed after students had taken part in anti-government demonstrations. In June, doctors, engineers, bankers, chartered accountants, veterinary surgeons, and surveyors all threatened to withdraw their services if the government did not resign in July. A week later, Ghana's lawyers threatened to stop work if the government did not immediately initiate moves towards a return to civilian rule. They rejected Acheampong's idea of a union government and demanded a return to party politics.

None of these protests was aimed at destroying national unity. The lawyers, like most of the members of the other professional classes, had been educated in European fashion. They abhorred tyranny, but they wanted to establish a western-style democracy, not a society divided along traditional, ethnic lines. An ultimatum drafted by the professional bodies' association on 23 June said that the government had proved by its recent acts that it was incapable of governing the country. It had placed people who were corrupt or incompetent, or both, in positions of trust. It had made it almost impossible to voice criticism and had sought out scapegoats – arresting people like the chief justice, the governor of the Bank of Ghana, and the commissioner for income tax.

In response to this pressure from the professional sector, Acheampong reluctantly announced on 1 July that he had called upon the committee which was studying the future form of government for Ghana to report within three months. A referendum would then be held within six months from that date, to decide which form of government the people wanted. Thereafter, depending on their choice, a constituent assembly would be set up to draft the relevant constitution under which elections would be held and the transfer of power effected. The professional workers were not impressed. On 8 July they went on strike to support their demand for civilian rule. The government responded by making strikes by medical officers illegal, but the doctors ignored the order to return to work within twenty-four hours. On 14 July 1977 the government announced that it would hand over power to a civilian government on 1 July 1979. A commission to draft a constitution would be appointed by 19 April 1978 and a constituent assembly would consider the draft by March 1979. Elections would then be held on 15 June 1979. Having achieved this measure of success, the professional bodies brought their strike to an end.

In November 1977 Acheampong took a backward step when he announced that Ghana would not return to party politics to suit the whim of a few people who thought they had been born to rule. Union government, he said, involving all sections of the people, was best for the country. He did not make any reference to socialism. Towards the end of 1977 he made it clear that he was not anxious to surrender power – by announcing that if the country wanted him to become president he would have to consider the idea. In the following year, he decided to hold a referendum about the desirability of union government – in the hope of crushing the claims of those who were calling for the revival of political parties. The People's Movement for Freedom and Justice was immediately founded to campaign against the referendum. Former opponents joined together to promote the movement, including General Akwasi Afrifa, formerly one of the leaders of the National Liberation Council, and Komla Gbedema, who had been prevented by the NLC from taking his seat in parliament after the 1969 elections. But Acheampong persisted, and the referendum was held on 31 March 1978. The vote was officially claimed to have gone in favour of one-party government by 54 per cent to 46 per cent. The People's Movement for Freedom and Justice was banned, together with two other groups which announced their opposition to dictatorship. A few days later, thirty-five people alleged to have been plotting to overthrow the government were arrested.

On 5 July 1978 Acheampong was forced to resign as head of state. He handed over to Lieut.-General F.W.K. Akuffo, who was Chief of General Staff, and retired from the army. The main support for Acheampong's union-government proposal had come from former supporters of Nkrumah, and this had worried the more conservative members of the armed forces who distrusted the CPP. Nevertheless, the decision to overthrow the government was based upon more fundamental grievances – of which galloping inflation and food shortages, together with the referendum and the arrests which followed it, were the most important. For a regime that had come to power to redress the economic situation created by its predecessor, the lack of success of Acheampong's government had proved a damning indictment. It is true that there had been years of drought in the early 1970s, but the 1977 cocoa crop had been good, as too had the world price for cocoa. Regrettably for the government, 80 per cent of the crop had been sold forward at low prices because of bad management. Oil prices, too, had soared, thereby creating further problems for a government which had to import all its petroleum.

Akuffo began by ordering the release of all those arrested for opposing the referendum. He also dismissed Joe Appiah, Busia's leading opponent, who had been special adviser to Acheampong. He enlarged the supreme military council by introducing politicians from the CPP and the Progress Party (Busia himself had died some little time before), he proposed a return to civilian rule in 1979, and he went on to devalue the currency by 38 per cent. In spite of these changes, the military members of the SMC still favoured a national government rather than the revival of political parties – at least for an interim period of up to five years. To reassure possible critics, therefore, Akuffo demonstrated his desire to satisfy reasonable demands by creating a permanent negotiating body to arbitrate in disputes between the civil servants' associations and the government. This brought a rapid end to a series of strikes, among which action by electricity workers had been the most serious in its impact on the general public. In November 1978 the constitutional committee recommended that there should be an executive president who, together with the vice-president, should be elected by direct ballot. In spite of qualms among the military, the ban on political parties was lifted early in January 1979, and at once two parties were formed, to be followed within days by eight others.

Akuffo had no wish to hold on to power for long, but he was given no time to step down voluntarily. Many younger people longed for a return to the idealism which they firmly believed had characterized Nkrumah's rule. Of greater practical significance was the fact that the younger officers of the armed forces had grown tired of seeing their seniors using their positions of authority within the government for their own profit. On 4 June 1979 Akuffo's government was overthrown by an Armed Forces Revolutionary Council, led by Flight Lieutenant Jerry John Rawlings, which took over temporary control. Acheampong was executed by firing squad after being found guilty of corruption by a military court. For many, he had been the chief representative of a group of senior officers who had held lucrative civilian jobs in addition to their military commands, and in that capacity he had won no sympathizers.

The proposal to restore civilian rule was now put into effect, but as the political parties took shape to contest the elections, old divisions reappeared. The Peoples National Party (PNP) proved to be little more than the rump of Nkrumah's CPP, while its opponents were the residue of Busia's Progress Party. The PNP did, however, make an attempt to give itself a national flavour by appointing as its leader a northerner, Dr Hilla Limann. Limann was an honest man and had had a good education, but he had had little political experience. He was even believed to have approached the rival party with a view to joining it and had been told to obtain northern sponsorship in order to make himself a useful recruit. His acceptance of the leadership of the PNP was consequently seen by many to be little more than opportunism. Certainly it brought him no great personal benefit, although his party won the elections held on 18 June and he himself became the country's president three months later. In the meantime, General Akuffo, together with General Akwasi Afrifa and four other senior officers of the armed forces, had been executed by firing squad as part of Rawlings's efforts to rid the country of corruption. This had done nothing to strengthen foreign confidence in Ghana, however. Nigeria, for example, cut off oil supplies. Nevertheless, the return to civilian rule was regarded as a hopeful sign.

Unfortunately for the new government, Acheampong – like his predecessors – had left the economy in chaos, and Limann and his new cabinet had no clear idea how to tackle the problem. Limann himself was too weak to control his more politically experienced and notably less idealistic supporters. Even before the elections had taken place the party had been accused of extensive corruption, and the corruption became worse and more blatant when the PNP took office. Exasperated, Rawlings and his junior-officer group again took charge on 31 December 1981, not with the efficiency of the NLC but with that mixture of idealism and intolerance characteristic of young, inexperienced men suddenly thrust into a position of absolute power. The constitution was suspended and the civilian members of the government were accused of being criminals motivated by corruption and greed. A Provisional National Defence Council (PNDC) was set up, with Rawlings as chairman, to take responsibility for the government of the country. A period of anarchy, in which old scores were paid off while soldiers robbed and looted at will, was followed by the announcement of revolutionary policies intended to restore strong government based upon the popular will. This would be expressed through workers'/people's defence committees, the new rulers believing that this was the type of government that Nkrumah, whom they had not known but whom they idolized, had fought to establish until factionalism and vested interests had destroyed his work. Nkrumah, in their view, was the one man who had eliminated the wasteful divisions of traditional society and had rebuffed all attempts at interference by foreign powers.

The workers'/people's defence committees were greeted with enthusiasm by a population which had suffered from greed and incompetence in high places and whose views had been ignored for so long. It was hoped that, in due course, a national assembly would be elected which would represent the committees and that a 'front' would be created embracing all patriotic and democratic organizations and individuals. To bring about the national revolution which was the goal of the new government 'all organs of popular power were given the task of destroying oppressive power relations and institutions'. Workers and peasants, being in the majority, would ultimately take charge of their own destinies.[13]

Foreign observers considered Rawlings's plans naïve and there was sporadic opposition to the government from inside the country. Many of the early decisions of the PNDC were wildly inappropriate. For example, the wage and salary structure was compressed to a ratio of 1.80 : 1.00, with the result that at least half of the top professional people left the country to seek employment elsewhere. Teachers, craftsmen, and other skilled workers also left in their thousands – to the great and immediate detriment of Ghana's development. Then, not long afterwards, when Nigeria forced hundreds of thousands of immigrants to leave, Ghana was suddenly overwhelmed by the unexpected return of its own emigrants.

Not surprisingly, there were a number of attempted coups in the first 18 months of the PNDC's rule, each involving some members of the armed forces. One that took place in May 1983 was attributed by the government to the machinations of the American CIA. In the same month, the University of Kumasi was closed after student clashes with townspeople. This was followed a week later by the takeover of the University of Legon by the Accra workers' defence committee whose members had been angered by student demonstrations against the government. Educated in the tradition of free expression, the students were to be a constant source of opposition to Rawlings, an opposition which, because of its idealism and inexperience, was slow to recognize the change which was later to come over the government. Meantime, in spite of these difficulties, the defence committees achieved some positive results. Thanks to Rawlings's efforts the inflation rate was brought down from 120 per cent in 1983 to 20 per cent in 1986, while over the same period the GDP rose steadily and the price given to cocoa growers for their crop increased sevenfold.

As he became better acquainted with the realities of government and the problems of stabilizing the economy, Rawlings admitted that he must amend his original plans. Productivity and reconciliation became the slogans which replaced the more ideologically dogmatic statements of his early days in office. In December 1984 he devalued the currency for the third time in that year; and that, together with his involvement with the IMF, did not please his more radical supporters. He was accused of having abandoned the ideals of the revolution and of following instead the directives of the IMF and the World Bank. But, as Rawlings himself was later to recognize: 'drought, bush fires, the enforced return of over a million of our citizens from Nigeria, destabilization attempts by powerful foreign interests, all these have taught us lessons that no text book in political theory can offer.'[14]

Nevertheless, there were lavish celebrations in March 1987 to mark the thirtieth anniversary of independence. Rawlings seized the opportunity to challenge the nation to think seriously about the direction it had been taking. In his anniversary speech, broadcast over the radio on the evening of independence day, he said: 'We must admit to ourselves that the political institutions that we have tried to run in our nation have remained largely irrelevant to the reality and expectations of the majority of our people.' Referring to the political freedom achieved on 6 March 1957, he asked: 'When are we going to translate this political independence into economic freedom as well?' These were not sentiments which appealed to many of those who still held to Nkrumah's ideology, while those of a more conservative outlook — who might have been expected to give their support — had too vivid memories of the turbulent early years of Rawlings's government to trust this apparent change of heart. Writing for *West Africa* early in 1987, Yao Graham remarked that the way forward must:

> be built on a framework and principles that enable the people to analyse and select which strands of the nation's thirty years experience are worthy. . . . In the past, when given a genuinely free choice, they always opt for the vision with which Kwame Nkrumah galvanized the working classes to overthrow colonialism thirty years ago.[15]

The tragic experiences of Ghana since Nkrumah's overthrow have, indeed, blinded many of the people to weakneses in Nkrumah's policies, particularly in the economic sphere. It is against this naïve idealism that Rawlings is beginning to campaign.

Two groups were particularly critical of the government's negotiations with the IMF and the World Bank. University students protested against the decision to remove subsidies at all levels of education because, they claimed, it would place an intolerable burden on parents. They also argued that the government's massive retrenchment of workers in the public sector was depriving many of them of any prospect of employment on graduation. In 1985, public sector employment was reduced by 27,000 — 19,000 of these being in the Cocoa Marketing Board — and the hope that the private sector would expand to accommodate the loss was not fulfilled. Clashes between soldiers and students, after protests on academic campuses, increased the tension between the government and the universities. Eight members of staff of the University of Science and Technology in Kumasi, including the pro-vice-chancellor and the registrar, were accused by the under-secretary for higher education of having been involved in stirring up distrust among the students. They were told that in the event of further unrest they would be held responsible. The eight denied the charges, and claimed that they were being discriminated against because they were all Asante. This, however, was the only overt reference to ethnic issues in what was essentially a dispute over economic policies and their social implications.

The TUC was also critical of the government – in particular, of its devaluation policy and its plan to cut down on overmanning. It demanded to see the details of all agreements with the IMF and World Bank and other external creditors to ensure that Ghana's interests were being protected, and it called for a limit of 10 per cent on the disbursement of foreign-exchange earnings for debt servicing. Above all, it claimed that the people were not convinced by reports of the country's economic recovery and that, in order to gain their confidence, they should have a voice in determining who should govern them and how they should be governed.

Popular doubts about the economy were reinforced by the fact that the price of most commodities had risen beyond the reach of ordinary people. Yet the government could scarcely be held entirely responsible for this state of affairs. By following a policy of economic pragmatism – in conjunction with the IMF and the World Bank – from 1984 to 1987, it had succeeded in implementing a programme of radical economic reform. It had achieved a more realistic exchange rate; it had introduced new financial incentives to encourage cocoa producers; and each year there had been an impressive growth in the GNP. There had been a startling decrease in inflation; exports had risen sharply; and the 1987 budget had increased the daily minimum wage. All this, however, had taken place against a background of increased oil-import costs, with a consequent rise in transport prices and in the price of food and other produce. The stern measures required to run the country more economically had caused widespread if temporary suffering, and the IMF was warned of the social consequences of these developments and the opposition they would arouse. Nevertheless, Ghana had achieved an unaccustomed measure of economic stability.[16]

In response to various criticisms, the government tried to disseminate more widely an explanation of its economic policies and to involve more people in decision taking. On 1 July 1987 it announced that two pamphlets would be issued, the first a *National Programme for Economic Development* and the second entitled *District Political Authority and Modalities for District Local Elections*. The elections, it was proposed, should produce two-thirds of the members of district assemblies, the other third being nominated by the government from representatives of traditional authorities and of other organizations involved in the productive life of the districts. The assemblies would have deliberative, legislative, and executive functions, and would be chaired by one of their members. They would submit budgets for approval by the central government, and their deliberations might include issues of national concern about which they could make recommendations – again to the central goverment. There would be executive committees, chaired by district secretaries, with the duty of carrying out the policies of the assemblies and acting on their behalf when the assemblies were not in session. What the government hoped to do was to draw upon local, traditional forces as a source of support for its policies. In this way, local loyalties, instead of acting as a divisive factor, would help to strengthen the state while providing some assurance that local interests were not being ignored.

The government's critics were not impressed. They pointed out that, far from being the decentralizing process it was claimed to be, the scheme would still leave Ghana as a unitary republic with a strong, centralized administrative system. Of what political edifice did the district assemblies form a firm foundation, they asked? The PNDC had not made any suggestion about the ultimate form which government would take. Rawlings replied that this was only the first stage of a programme to restore democracy. He insisted that voting on its own did not guarantee the achievement of that goal. The electorate must educate itself first in local problems and potential and then, when the elections had taken place, it would still have to ensure that an interest was maintained in the performance of its chosen representatives. Only by starting at the grass roots could there be genuine participation in government.

When registration for the district elections took place in 1987 there was initially little overt enthusiasm for the proceedings. The absence of political parties meant that there was no automatic stimulus to local interest. Older voters, having been disillusioned so often in the past, were sceptical of the outcome. Traditional authorities, however, played an active part in urging people to register. The reason for their intervention is not wholly clear. They were aware that, constitutionally, they only held office as long as they had the approval of the central government. But they may also have seen in Rawlings's approach a hope that the government had at last begun to appreciate the considerable influence which they still exercised. As one traditional ruler pointed out, if the government's concern for participatory democracy was to have any meaning, it must, for example, take into account the linguistic differences which existed among the illiterate people who formed the majority of the population. Unless local languages were permitted at the meetings of the district council, many devoted people would be excluded from taking part. Traditional rulers, he went on, had always managed to carry out their functions satisfactorily through the medium of local languages and the central government must take cognizance of that fact.[17] Ethnic differences must still be taken into account even if they were no longer aggressively assertive.

Rawlings himself had already taken this warning to heart, but he still found difficulty in obliterating the memories of the days of violence which had followed his second seizure of power and which still troubled the more conservative elements in the population. At the same time, the spokesmen for democracy insisted that he had no mandate to speak for the people. They claimed that the only basis upon which he held office was the support given him by the army – in particular by his private guard which consisted of a few hundred chosen men. Recollections of years of military rule did not make for contentment in a country with a relatively large proportion of people whose education laid emphasis upon the importance of democracy, even if they had had little opportunity to put it into practice.

On the other hand, Rawlings's negotiations with the IMF and the World Bank, and his growing willingness to recognize the power of tradition, have not endeared him to the sons and daughters of Nkrumah's revolution – for whom such behaviour constitutes a betrayal of the true faith. Though authoritarian rule is not in itself unacceptable to them, like most ideologists they are quick to withdraw their approval when it is used to promote policies which are in conflict with their own views. For them, participatory government is all very well when it means the participation of the TUC and the workers. It is less desirable in the form presented by Rawlings, which would include the participation of intellectuals, professional people, farmers, and traditional rulers.

Because of these criticisms from two widely differing angles, Rawlings is in a difficult position. He is depressed by his people's uncritical acceptance of standards of irresponsibility which damage the nation's well-being. The easygoing tolerance which characterizes so much of Ghana's political life has its outward attractions but also has its disadvantages. The liberal attitude to politics adopted by one section of the people may not, he fears, be an end in itself, but rather become an instrument to remove restraints upon making money. Such self-seeking might provide an impetus for economic growth but could impede the orderly development of the economy which Rawlings seeks. At the same time he cannot accept the Marxist view that history is determined only by the masses and by inexorable economic laws. The Marxists, he says, failed to offer any solution, let alone a realistic one, to the problems which confronted the country in 1982. A more pragmatic approach is essential. Military government may be a temporary measure, but it has a clear task to root out both the self-seeking which leads to corruption and injustice and the ideological dogma which has little foundation in the reality of the Ghanaian situa-.tion. With those tasks before him he cannot waste time considering when he should relinquish power, but so long as he retains it he will remain a target for his numerous critics. Professor Boahen speaks the truth in claiming that Ghana is effectively a confederation of regions, for linguistic reasons certainly, and because the economy has not yet been so organized as to ensure the protection of all local interests. Perhaps most of all because the country is divided: between an educated minority associated with the economically better-organized section of the population, all of whom clamour for democracy and freedom of action, and the rest of the people who long for firm leadership coupled with clear direction. While both groups continue to feel dissatisfied, they tend to rely upon the local authorities which they feel they can understand and, in some measure, control. Those authorities traditionally have an ethnic flavour but, paradoxically, few Ghanaians would wish to attack the government on purely ethnic grounds. Fear of an oppressive central government remains, and it is that – as it was in the years immediately preceding independence – which helps to highlight ethnic differences. Yet the benefits of unity are not casually dismissed, and, although traditional loyalties remain strong, no one appears to want to undermine that unity by emphasizing them unduly.

4 Nigeria: federation by consensus

Nigeria differs from both Uganda and Ghana, and from all the other countries dealt with in this book, in its large population and its considerable wealth. The latter comes mainly from oil revenues and it has not been used to develop other facets of the economy. The wealth is unevenly distributed among the people, with the result that, in urban areas particularly, corruption has become endemic, while in rural districts agricultural output has not kept up with the country's rising population and the production of export crops has not shown the improvement which the judicial investment of capital could have achieved. The current military government, with the approval of western aid donors, is working hard to control and stabilize the economy, and at the same time is endeavouring to restore democratic, civilian rule on a sufficiently firm base to enable it to withstand the divisive forces which have already induced the army to seize power on several occasions. When the army last handed over to a civilian government, it did so on the basis of a constitution which many still regard as admirable in most respects. The problem then – and it is one of which the military leaders are fully appraised – is that too many influential people were unwilling to observe the spirit of the constitution. How to avoid a repetition of that previous failure is the present government's main concern.

Nigeria's history since independence does not give grounds for optimism, unless it is believed that the country's leaders have learnt the searing lessons of earlier disasters. If Ghana's rallying cry 'Freedom and Justice' is still in search of fulfilment, then the slogan 'We are now in charge of our destiny' – with which Nigerians celebrated independence on 1 October 1960 – echoes with equal sadness down the years during which two brief attempts at civilian rule have been punctuated by an assortment of military coups. The fact that the federal system of government adopted at independence has subsequently been accepted without serious contention by civilian and military leaders alike offers grounds for hope, though it originated in apparently irreconcilable differences of opinion between the constituent parts of the nation. It does, however, give warning of latent danger. Federalism may have been adopted by consensus, but it has arisen from an awareness that conflict still persists.[1] Nigeria's current military rulers are determined to ensure that the unity of the country shall not be jeopardized, but they acknowledge that local loyalties still survive and that legitimate local needs must be satisfied. Fortunately, after the bitter lessons taught by the civil war of the late 1960s, few Nigerians would contemplate secession for their own region. The main question which remains to be resolved is whether local interests are so strong that only an authoritarian central government, drawn from or supported by the army, can retain control.

The problems which have bedevilled Nigeria since independence do not, however, have their roots in ancient tribal or ethnic loyalties in quite the same manner as they have in Uganda, or even in Ghana, although there have been and there still remain many traditional centres of loyalty within the country. Since the early nineteenth century, wider loyalties have appeared which have increasingly superseded those more ancient loyalties without entirely obliterating them. The *jihad* proclaimed by Usuman dan Fodio towards the end of the eighteenth century welded the Hausa/Fulani north into a self-consciously Muslim community, clearly distinct from the non-Muslim south. But the religious homogeneity of the north is not an entirely seamless garment. Members of other religions are still to be found in the area. The political unity of the region has also proved unreliable, though at times it may have seemed menacing to the rest of the country. The diversity of ancient loyalties in southern Nigeria has also been overlaid by more recent political formulations. The much vaunted 'common culture' of the Yoruba-speaking peoples of the south-west was only discovered as a result of new experiences in the nineteenth century, and did not find expression in joint political action until the twentieth. Loyalty to more localized units persists in the south-west, as it does in the north, unless united action appears to offer greater benefit to the Yoruba as a whole. The same has been true of the Ibo speakers of the south-east, while the numerous minority ethnic groups in both northern and southern Nigeria also have their own centres of loyalty.

Out of this fluctuating mixture of identities, three main units – which were already beginning to take shape as a result of internal factors – became institutionalized by the introduction of British administration at the beginning of the twentieth century. The core of each of those units was provided by one of the three main ethnic groups: the Hausa/Fulani; the Yoruba; and the Ibo. In the north, the widespread influence of Islam persuaded the British overlords of the need to treat the region as wholly distinct from the south. Christian missionaries were discouraged from working in the area, with the result that the spread of European education was also restricted. But the sense of unity which this arrangement might have been expected to encourage among the northern Muslims was weakened by the decision to retain the existing rulers in the role of local government officials, wherever possible, because it was cheaper to do so. While those rulers were willing enough to act in unison when it suited them to do so – not least to keep the alien, non-Muslim south at bay – they were not averse from pursuing their own interests, even at the expense of their Muslim neighbours. As far as the people in general were concerned, their loyalty, as always, was focused in the first place upon their local rulers, and only if those rulers called upon them to support the Muslim north did they widen their horizons to embrace that wider loyalty.

An attempt was made to introduce a version of indirect administration – the technique of using indigenous authorities to act as local officials under European supervision – into the south-east, with a view to achieving uniformity with the northern system. It proved to be a totally artificial venture because of the absence of any suitable indigenous structure of government upon which to base it. Nevertheless, though the effort was abortive there were a number of Ibo with the foresight to recognize that participation in a British administrative system, alien though it might be to traditional practice, could provide them with a range of opportunities of which they had previously been unaware. In the first instance, those opportunities were mainly economic, but in time they encroached into the political field. This did not result in the development of quite such a distinctive regional society as was emerging in the north, but it did encourage the growth of an Ibo identity among the better educated section of the population, less self-consciously perhaps and certainly less aggressively than among the Hausa/Fulani.

The south-west developed in a manner that lay somewhere between the patterns laid down in the north and in the south-east. British rule may not have been welcome, but opposition to it offered little prospect of success. Acceptance of a cosmetic version of indirect administration served both to restrict British intervention in the internal affairs of the people and to reinforce the authority of traditional rulers. Many of the latter had memories of Yoruba resistance to Muslim invasion from the north in the nineteenth century. Now, as they became increasingly involved in the political life of the country, they grew to appreciate that concerted action by the Yoruba people might have its merits, not least in keeping the power of the North within reasonable limits in the future. This twofold and often contradictory effect of British intervention – the strengthening of the hand of traditional rulers in their dealings with their own people and the encouragement of regional unity – was to influence political developments in Nigeria long after the country became independent of Britain.

These administrative arrangements were convenient to the British officials who supervised them, but they did nothing to encourage the development of a Nigerian identity among the ordinary people. The latter remained loyal to their traditional rulers while acknowledging the existence of some sort of regional responsibility which did not extend to the recognition of Nigeria as a political unit. Meantime, enterprising members of all the larger ethnic groups were happy to exploit whatever advantages might arise from the consolidation of a variety of local loyalties into larger regional units. Each of those units was, by African standards, large enough and populous enough, as well as possessing the economic potential, to exist as an independent state – yet another factor militating against the easy acceptance of a unitary Nigeria. Each, however, contained minority ethnic groups whose relations with the dominant group were not always friendly.

The problems which might arise from the development of these new administrative divisions were of no great significance as long as the British remained in control. In the last resort, the administrators had the power to ensure that their will prevailed. Nor were those first Africans with a European-style education who began to take an interest in the government in Nigeria in the early twentieth century unduly worried by a system which had not yet shown its potential for encouraging disruption. In any case, from the foundation of the Nigerian National Democratic Party in 1923 – in response to the grant of the franchise to the inhabitants of Calabar and Lagos – Herbert Macaulay, one of the first Africans to become involved in his country's politics, had ignored regional divisions and set his sights on African participation in the government of Nigeria as a whole. The Nigerian Youth Movement was founded in 1938 with the same objective. Dr Nnamdi Azikiwe, Macaulay's successor, an Ibo, did not think in regional terms, and his oratory won him the support of another aspiring politician, Obafemi Awolowo, a Yoruba. But the first steps towards independence for Nigeria undermined their plan for a united country. The Richards constitution of 1946 and the Macpherson constitution of 1951 both advocated regional assemblies which effectively converted the three hitherto administrative units into political entities.

British administrators were not solely responsible for this development. In the northern region there had always been a deep-seated fear of rapid change, which became still more acute when it was demanded by a southerner, Azikiwe. Northern leaders believed that the Ibo, who had taken particular advantage of the educational opportunities offered by the British, were planning to seize control of the whole of Nigeria. The creation of the National Council of Nigeria and the Cameroons (NCNC) in 1944, under Azikiwe's leadership, and its call for nationwide support, did nothing to lesson that fear, though Azikiwe's aim was Nigerian independence, not Ibo domination. Awolowo, also, was disturbed by what he believed to be Azikiwe's growing reliance upon Ibo financial support. The *Egbe Omo Oduduwa*, the Association of the Children of Oduduwa, founded by Awolowo in 1948, though initially only a cultural movement, was nevertheless meant to stimulate a feeling of identity among Yoruba-speakers. When it later developed into the Action Group (AG) it did so with the clear aim of encouraging cultural nationalism among the Yoruba, to counter what Awolowo saw as the growing political influence of the Ibo. The founding of the Northern Peoples' Congress (NPC) in 1951 was also a defensive measure, taken by suspicious northern leaders in response to recent constitutional developments and to the political activities of the southerners. Membership of the NPC was restricted to people of northern descent – a clear pointer to the way in which political parties would develop in the future.

Awolowo defended his attempt to unite the Yoruba speakers against the charge that he was dividing the country by arguing that at least the federal unity of Nigeria would be assured if the members of each ethnic group felt happy among themselves – if they were free, within prescribed limits, to order their own lives and advance their own culture, and if the solidarity and devotion they felt among themselves were sublimated to the cause of building a Nigerian nation. His conclusion seemed to demand a remarkable number of preconditions, however, and it appeared even more open to question when he admitted that, although the Yoruba were a highly progressive people, they were badly united on the sole basis of the lip-service they paid to spiritual union and to the idea of being descended from a common ancestor.

Awolowo may well have been correct in maintaining that the Yoruba had something unique to contribute to the common pool of Nigerian nationhood. Equally, that contribution could scarcely be of benefit to the country as a whole if his people were reduced to the state of impotence into which, he claimed, they were rapidly degenerating.[2] But his protestations were only an attempt to mask his real concern. What he feared was that a unitary state would make it possible for power to be used to promote the interests of whichever group gained the upper hand, and he was not confident that the Yoruba would be that fortunate group. In Nigeria, as everywhere else in Africa, to wield power was the only means of guaranteeing wealth and gaining more power, and Nigeria had so much more wealth to offer than had any other of the recently independent African countries. For Awolowo, federation was an insurance against exclusion from both power and wealth. In a federal state the Yoruba could at least hope to control the region in which they were numerically dominant. It was to achieve that end that he strove to transform the nineteenth-century myth of a community of spirit into a political reality.

The Lyttleton constitution of 1954 made the immediate federal future of Nigeria certain. In the atmosphere of the time any other solution was impossible, but the immediate outcome was that the former administrative regions, rather than the capital, Lagos, became the foci of political activity. Each of the main political parties at once set out to assert total control over one of the regions, and from that base to defy, and if possible to erode, the power of their rivals in the other regions. Because of the Lyttleton constitution's insistence upon the employment of locally-born people wherever possible, it became difficult for anyone to make progress in his profession or occupation outside his own region. As a result, the opportunities open to educated people to attain prominence on the national stage were further limited. It was no surprise, therefore, when the NPC won all the seats in the northern region and the NCNC all those in the east in the federal elections held in 1964. Only the Action Group failed to win complete domination in its own region, and it quickly set out to protect its position in the future by dissolving the local councils in those areas which had supported the NCNC.[3]

The grant of internal autonomy to the eastern and western regions in 1957 reinforced the ethnic, as opposed to the tribal, basis of political power still further, though regional loyalties were temporarily forgotten in the surge of interest in the prospect of national independence when the north also became self-governing in 1959. The various party leaders enjoyed a brief period of apparent consensus, but the moment of euphoria was short and the sentiment which provoked it was false. The leaders were at one only in their mutual desire to capture the spoils of independence, and the interests of minority groups in particular were forgotten as each party strove once again to assert its sovereignty in its own region.

The federal elections of 1957 set the pattern for the future. The NPC won 134 seats, the NCNC 89, the AG and its minority-party allies 73, and 16 independent candidates were elected. The NPC thus established itself as the dominant partner in any alliance which might subsequently develop. Henceforward, the north's domination could be only slightly modified by any influence a partner might be able to exert. Even its initial alliance with the NCNC soon became unnecessary. The regional focus of the NPC became only too apparent when the party leader, Alhaji Sir Ahmadu Bello, who knew where his strength lay, chose to remain as premier of the northern region and sent his deputy, Sir Abubakar Tafawa Balewa, to be prime minister in the federal government.

Chief Awolowo, by contrast, having failed to form a coalition with either the NPC or the NCNC, abandoned his firm ethnic base in the western region, to become the leader of the opposition in the federal assembly. It was a dangerous move from every point of view. As leader of the opposition he could not hope to command sufficient support to challenge the government, even by rallying the disgruntled but wholly disorganized ethnic minorities. Meanwhile, in the western region, the Yoruba had not yet become the united people he had wanted them to be. In his absence from the immediate scene of action his rival for the leadership of the AG, Chief Samuel Akintola, made a bid for power and accused Awolowo of plotting against the federation. It was rather as if the Scottish National Party were suddenly beset by a revival of the enmity between the Macdonalds and the Campbells, with the leader of one faction charged with attempting to undermine the British constitution, and it was every bit as disastrous for the AG as it would be for the Scottish Nationalists. Awolowo was sentenced to 10 years' detention and a state of emergency was declared in the western region. In the context of this book, it was not without significance that both contestants for the leadership of the party bore the title 'chief'. The title itself was introduced by the British, but in this instance, as in so many others, the authority of the office holders derived as much from their traditional status as from any powers conferred by the British. The Yoruba still set great store by traditional status, and although the AG was a twentieth-century phenomenon those who sought to lead it could not ignore more ancient loyalties.

The NCNC seized the opportunity presented by the internecine struggles of the AG and successfully pressed for the west to be split in two. Anxious to escape Yoruba domination the inhabitants of the mid-west were happy to support the NCNC and a new region was created in 1963. As a counter measure, the NPC immediately offered to ally with Akintola and the rump of the AG – now renamed as the Nigerian National Democratic Party (NNDP). The alliance called itself the Nigerian National Alliance (NNA) in an attempt to conceal the dominant position held by the north, but the significance of what had taken place was not lost upon the imprisoned Awolowo and those Yoruba who had remained loyal to him. These latter joined with the NCNC to form the United Progressive Grand Alliance (UPGA) to challenge the NPA, but the new alignments and the divisions which had appeared among the Yoruba made very clear the fragility of political loyalties based upon ethnic solidarity when wealth and power were at stake.

The census of 1962 also provided irrefutable proof of the extent to which those seeking the spoils of office – or fearful of being excluded from sharing in those spoils – were prepared to play upon ethnic divisions and local greed to promote their ends. The population of each region was grossly exaggerated by the regional governments, and so blatant was the falsification of the results that the 1962 census was annulled. The results of a further census taken the following year simply reaffirmed the northern domination claimed in 1962 – with the figures still further inflated. The eastern region protested, but the NNA was able to resist the challenge and the east was forced to acquiesce. Against such a background of distrust and dissension, the elections held in 1964 could not fail to produce disputes. The UPGA sought to avoid defeat by organizing a boycott of the elections but could only muster support in the eastern region. Instead, the participation of the UPGA in the government was engineered by means of a far from noble deal arranged by Azikiwe and the chief justice.

It was at this point, on 1 January 1966, that a number of junior army officers decided that government was being conducted in a wholly unacceptable fashion and tried to seize power. They claimed that the army was the only group in the country which was not pursuing sectional interests, but the claim was soon questioned when it became clear that the young officers did not even speak for the whole of the army. It was, however, almost certainly a coincidence that those involved in the coup which overthrew the civilian government were mainly Ibo-speaking. It is still more certain that they sincerely believed in the honourable nature of their motives. But there were other, northern, officers who doubted both these premises. When Major-

General Johnson Ironsi, another Ibo, seized power after the young officers had mishandled the coup, the northerners were convinced that their suspicions – already inflamed by the assassination of their two leaders, Ahmadu Bello and Tafawa Balewa – were now fully confirmed.

The counter-coup, launched by northern officers in July 1966, was motivated by resentment against what was widely believed to have been an Ibo takeover. The extreme violence employed in the northern region against all non-northerners, and against Ibo-speakers in particular, was clearly inspired by the fear of domination by an alien ethnic group, although it did not indicate positive solidarity among the Hausa/Fulani. The army, it appeared, was just as capable as the civilian population of succumbing to paranoia. However unacceptable the factionalism of the civilian government had been, it was now clear that it was the possession of offensive weapons, rather than the justice of its cause, which gave authority to military government

The government of Major-General Yakubu Gowon, a non-Muslim northerner belonging to a minority ethnic group, nevertheless tried to break down the large ethnic power centres which seemed only to create friction. Retaining the federal concept, it divided the country into twelve states which also offered greater representation to ethnic minorities. But the move came too late to prevent civil war. So great was the horror aroused by the slaughter of the Ibo in the north that it was not difficult for the ambitious Lieutenant-Colonel Odumegwu Ojukwu to persuade his fellow Ibo that they were becoming the victims of a federal campaign of genocide. The only road to salvation, he said, lay in seceding from the federation and establishing the independent state of Biafra. The desire for power, and more particularly the fear that others might gain control, had converted the hitherto scarcely-acknowledged ethnic unity of the Ibo into assertive, twentieth-century nationalism – or, as the British Press would say, tribalism. Totally overlooked were the wishes of the small ethnic groups who had no desire to exchange the rule of the federal government for domination by the Ibo.

Nothing in the conduct of the army under Gowon's leadership during the war which resulted from Biafra's secession justified the charge of genocide. In the event, the main effect of the war was to convince the majority of Nigerians that secession must be avoided. If federation had its disadvantages, then secession – whether of larger groups embracing their own disgruntled minorities, or of smaller, more homogeneous units incapable of standing on their own feet economically – could be disastrous. It was a conclusion which Gowon's post-war policy of 'Reconciliation, rehabilitation, reconstruction' did much to justify. The Ibo had little about which to complain in the treatment they received in the aftermath of the fighting.

There were, however, other serious problems which did not spring directly from ethnic unease. The sudden acquisition of apparently limitless wealth from oil production was providing unexpected temptations both for those in power and for those who now more than ever wanted to seize power. The army, too, having expanded enormously during the war, was reluctant to return to a smaller, more tightly-disciplined shape. Many senior officers, now engaged in administering the country, had access to sources of wealth and patronage which neither they nor their dependents were willing to surrender. Others, who had not yet had a share of the spoils, were anxious to make up for lost time. Whatever his other qualities, Gowon was not, unfortunately, strong enough to control the corruption which had so swiftly become a feature of military rule. Nor had ethnic suspicion been completely eradicated. Even some of Gowon's closest supporters were anxious lest, through lack of experience, he should come to rely too heavily upon a civil service dominated by southerners. Most important of all, outside the government there was a widely shared desire to rid the country of military rule. When it became obvious that Gowon was incapable of fulfilling his earlier promise to restore civilian government by 1976 his overthrow was inevitable.

Yet it was the army, not the people at large, that engineered the palace coup which got rid of Gowon. For there were still men of integrity in the army, and only the military had the weapons needed to eject a military government. Major-General Murtala Muhammed, who succeeded Gowon, was a stronger character than his predecessor and did not readily submit to pressure. His first act was to appoint a panel to investigate whether it was desirable to create still further states in order to reduce feelings of ethnic insecurity. As a result of the panel's recommendations, five additional states came into being and at the same time greater emphasis was placed upon local government. In this latter context, due deference was to be paid to traditional rulers, but ultimate authority would reside in elected local councils. Conservative elements were dissatisfied with these proposals and Muhammed was assassinated. But it was his second in command, Lieut.-General Olusegun Obasanjo, not the plotters, who succeeded him and who pressed on with the implementation of Muhammed's plan to return power to a civilian government as quickly as possible. A committee appointed to draft the constitution completed its work in August 1976. The new units of local government provided the bases upon which elections to a constituent assembly were held and the assembly reported before the end of 1977. The government accepted the recommendations with only minor amendments, and in 1978 political parties were once again seeking to win support.

Under the terms of the new constitution it became the responsibility of the state to promote unity. Paradoxically, it might seem, the way recommended to achieve that unity was to emphasize the federal character of the republic. It was a practical solution to ethnic rivalries and an attempt to quell the fear that local interests might be overlooked. Offices must be distributed in such a way as to involve all sections of the people, and political parties must demonstrate that they had support in enough regions to prove they did not represent only one ethnic group. The cabinet must include one indigenous member of each state. The composition of the officer corps must reflect the federal character of the country. No Nigerian must feel excluded from national life because of his ethnic origin, any more than on grounds of religion or sex. Finally, although the house of representatives would be elected on a population basis from single-member constituencies, the states would have equal representation in the senate. The satisfaction of local interests, which often meant ethnic interests, had obviously been high on the constituent assembly's list of objectives.

Sadly, the best intentions were incapable of preventing ethnic confrontation if there were people who wished to encourage it. With so much wealth at stake there were, indeed, persons who believed that to play upon ethnic mistrust was the sure way to seize power and wealth for themselves. The northern leaders, too, though generally happy with the new constitution because they believed that for reasons of demography it would guarantee their dominant position, were critical of the tardiness with which it was implemented. Southern leaders disliked it for the same demographic reasons which won for it the approval of the north, and they also pointed out with some justification that it would prevent men with high educational qualifications – of which there were proportionately more in the south – from achieving office on merit.[4]

In the circumstances, it was unfortunate that the victor in the subsequent presidential election should have triumphed only by what might be described as a legal nicety. It was a remarkable achievement for Alhaji Shehu Usman Aleyu Shagari to gain a significant majority of the total votes cast, and at least 25 per cent of the votes in twelve out of nineteen states. But to have to rely upon the claim that he had gained two-thirds of 25 per cent in a thirteenth in order to meet the requirements of the constitution, laid him open to criticism from a jealous rival – and in Obafemi Awolowo jealousy was strong. Considerations of personal profit aside, Awolowo firmly believed that he was the best man to be in charge of the country's affairs. Nor did it help Shagari that his National Party of Nigeria (NPN), though winning more seats than any other party in both houses of the assembly, had failed to gain an overall majority in either. Awolowo's party, the United Party of Nigeria (UPN), had, in spite of its title, been victorious only in Yoruba-speaking states. However, that did not deter Awolowo from appealing to the supreme court against the electoral commission's intepretation of the constitution with regard to the presidential vote, nor from calling for the resignation of the chief justice when the supreme court rejected his plea. Awolowo condemned the chief justice, who was himself a Yoruba, for having, he said, betrayed his own people, and he also attacked Obasanjo, another Yoruba, for having so arranged the constitution that the north was bound to be the dominant region.

The extent to which thwarted ambition and a genuine fear of the northern domination had warped Awolowo's judgement could be seen from the election returns. The northern voters had clearly demonstrated that they were not slaves to any monolithic, conservative, Muslim party, nor to their traditional rulers. In both Kano and Kaduna states, members of the comparatively radical People's Redemption Party (PRP) had been elected as governors in competition with candidates from the NPN. In Kano, electors had voted overwhelmingly in favour of the PRP candidate for the presidency, Alhaji Amino Kano, who had always opposed the more gradualistic policies espoused by the leading northern families. At the same time, the NPN had clearly met the constitutional requirement that it should be capable of winning support in most areas of the federation. In no less than nine states Shagari polled the highest number of votes and he came second in nine others. The NPN itself won seats in the House of Representatives in sixteen out of nineteen states, and in seventeen for the senate, while winning control of the legislatures in eight states. Perhaps the most significant factor was the success achieved by the NPN in states where it could command no ethnic majority. In the states of Cross River, Rivers, and Benin the party clearly benefited from the unhappy memories of Ibo domination shared by ethnic minorities. By contrast, the NPN lost support among the ethnic minorities in states such as Niger and Bauchi where there were fears of Hausa domination.

Both the UPN and the Nigerian People's Party (NPP) emerged as essentially ethnic parties. Awolowo's electoral slogan 'What is ours is ours' probably appealed to the ethnic loyalty of the Yoruba who, in any case, were disturbed by memories of the northern domination of the first republic. Without question, the UPN polled exceptionally high percentages of the votes cast in Ondo, Ogun, Oyo, and Lagos – over 80 per cent in every case – but won House-of-Representative seats in only nine states and Senate seats in ten. The NPP was similarly successful in the states of Anambra and Imo – where ethnic considerations triumphed over all others when a party split arose over a dispute as to who should be leader. Recognizing that the NPP was unlikely to win an overall victory, Nnamdi Azikiwe concluded that he could create a stronger basis for negotiation with the victors by getting the solid support of the Ibo than from leading a looser coalition which might have conflicting objectives. He therefore deliberately converted the NPP into an Ibo party and entered into an alliance with the NPN which ensured a majority for the coalition in both houses of the assembly. The PRP, the only party with any claim to a political ideology, won practically no support outside Kano and Kaduna.

It could be argued that the NPN was virtually certain to be the majority party because of the distribution of the population and that the support it gained from minority ethnic groups was due to their dislike of Ibo or Yoruba domination rather than to any positive liking for the Hausa/Fulani of the North. But the genuine attraction which the party had for many sections of the population should not be ignored. The NPN had stressed its determination to develop Nigeria along customary lines, giving scope for individuals to pursue their own interests whether in farming or business. This had appealed to both conservatives and progressives alike. Farmers were attracted by the promise of more mechanization, of better rural housing, and of encouragement to livestock developers. Businessmen looked forward to having a government which promised to seek foreign investment to assist in the expansion of Nigeria's economy. To many prosperous community leaders this was a far more attractive programme than the promise of increased state control implicit in the manifesto of the UPN, a manifesto which also underlined the ethnic exclusiveness of the party. Moreover, while the leaders of the Yoruba and the Ibo might be forgiven for their frustration at the apparent inevitability of a northern victory, it was clear that they had lost support of minority ethnic groups as a result of the unfavourable treatment they had meted out to them.

Perhaps the most interesting feature of the elections was the ease with which the leaders of the UPN and NPP had been able to enlist the almost unanimous support of their own ethnic groups. People whose day-to-day loyalties were much more localized had somehow been convinced that their interests within the republic could only be protected if they supported a large, ethnically-based party. It was almost as if the Yoruba and Ibo were beginning to think of themselves as nations. But not quite, because the Ibo who, for historical reasons, would seem to have most cause to fear the northerners, were prepared to follow Azikiwe into a coalition with the NPN. The conclusion would appear to be that ethnic loyalties were being stimulated and manipulated to suit the ambitions of political leaders. A similar conclusion might be drawn from the disunity, rather than the unanimity, to be found in the NPN. The first National Party convention, held in Kaduna in June 1980, broke up without ratifying the party's constitution because of the scramble for office among rival claimants whose eyes were fixed on the benefits which preferment would bring them.

The shallowness not only of party but even of ethnic allegiances became apparent in the November debate in the house of representatives over the revenue allocation bill. The bill proposed that the government should control 55 per cent of the funds available, with 34.5 per cent going to state governments and 8 per cent to local governments. Local opinion had already found expression when the state governors urged that federal spending power should be reduced. At the same time, those states which produced oil had argued that their share of funds should be commensurate with their contribution to revenue. In the event, the house of representatives voted to cut federal funds and increase the money available to the states. The senate reversed the decision and its conclusion was supported by a joint vote of the two houses. But an appeal to the courts by opponents of the bill was successful and the proposed legislation was left in the air. What also became clear was that the accord between the NPN and the NPP no longer had any meaning. It was quickly dissolved, although the NPN leadership was willing to reinstate NPP ministers and officials who had made a significant contribution to the country. The important thing was that the NPN had already won enough support in the legislature to command a majority except when issues affecting significant local interests proved too divisive.

While the disposal of millions of pounds was causing rapid realignments among the country's political spokesmen a tribal dispute of a much more traditional character briefly disturbed the unity of one section of the Yoruba. The struggle for the succession to the office of *Oni* of Ife, the senior *Oba* (ruler) among the former Yoruba kingdoms, appeared to outside observers to be a strangely anachronistic phenomenon. But the rancour which marked the rivalry between the three families from among whose members *Onis* were normally chosen, made it clear this was not simply a desire to take part in ancient pageantry. The crowds who came to witness some of the installation ceremonies of the successful candidate also testified to the instinctive attachment of the Yoruba people to traditional forms which was more deeply rooted than the loyalties stirred up by politicians, whether for their own advancement or for what they believed to be the good of the country.

The motives of politicians cannot easily be categorized. When the minister of industries, Malam Adamu Ciroma, publicly criticized the governor of Bornu state for appointing what the minister described as foreigners to the state offices of chief justice, chief secretary, and attorney-general, he could well have been moved by a conviction that local pride had been unfairly flouted. To Awolowo, the minister's objection was a clear case of a northerner wishing to dominate every available office of state, a view no doubt reinforced in his eyes by the fact that the three appointees were all Yoruba. Awolowo's intervention inevitably provoked a reaction from the NPN in support of the minister, who was then emboldened to repeat his accusation and to claim that the UPN wished to appoint only Yoruba.

As has already been suggested, even the Yoruba were not united over every issue and old loyalties died hard. In mid April 1981 violence broke out between the inhabitants of the towns of Ile-Ife and Modeke, the latter believing that, under existing local government arrangements, their interests were being subordinated to those of their neighbours. Modeke had been founded in the 1830s by refugees, driven from Old Oyo by the Fulani during the latter stages of the *jihad* which had established the Muslim empire in northern Nigeria. After a century and a half these more northern Yoruba still felt ill at ease among Yoruba of another kingdom, and even the intervention of the *Oni* of Ife was insufficient to calm the violence until it was ended by riot police. Only an external threat could arouse a sense of ethnic identity between two peoples whose differences were so deeply rooted.

Ancient loyalties made their presence felt in Kano, too, when rioting broke out after the governor of Kano State, pursuing the PRP's policy of trying to weaken the influence of the traditional rulers, challenged the Emir of Kano to show reason why he should not surrender his office. For the Muslim electorate, the emir embodied the culture of the region. Nevertheless, the governor maintained that the riots were not spontaneous but had been orchestrated by opponents of his party. The sympathies of the ruling NPN were, implicitly at least, with the emirs, but in this instance it would be difficult to separate political rivalry from traditional loyalty in seeking an explanation for the disturbances. By contrast, it was quite clear that the failure of the Nigerian Labour Congress to sustain the general strike it called in May 1981 over the level of the minimum wage, and its acceptance of terms which it had originally rejected, meant that the unions for their part could not muster the enthusiasm aroused by more local concerns.

Another problem, and one which, like the Labour movement, was likely to make a greater impact in the future than it could hope to do immediately, was that resulting from the emergence of a fundamentalist Islamic movement. Rioting took place in Kano in December 1980. It was the work of Muslim zealots who were trying to purge their backsliding co-religionists, and before it was put down by the army more than 200 people had been killed. The movement won no support from the people of Kano, and similar outbreaks in Bauchi, Plateau, and Imo States, in January of the following year, met with equal hostility and were quickly suppressed. Less than two years later, there were further serious troubles in Bornu State, and when the police intervened some of those involved fled to Kaduna to stir up trouble there. These outbreaks had no direct political content, though in banning the sect believed to be responsible the government was doubtless mindful of the possibilities of *jihad*. In a situation where dissatisfaction with the government was more widespread, such a movement could provide the nucleus of a revolutionary upsurge.

The government's performance in the economic sphere was certainly one factor which might have fuelled such dissatisfaction. Although by the end of 1980 Nigeria was producing 70 per cent more rice than it had done three years earlier, it was not enough to meet the rapidly growing demand resulting from the population explosion. It became necessary to buy rice externally and the government issued licences to would-be importers. Opposition members claimed that the licences were being given to government supporters as a reward for their services, and demanded that anyone who wished to import rice should be free to do so. The government replied that licences were necessary to control imports in the interests of indigenous growers but many believed that they were being used as a means of creating false shortages so as to increase profits for importers. These critics were jubilant when the Press published the findings of an inquiry on behalf of the national assembly, which demonstrated that the list of importers contained a number of fictional names as well as those of some assembly members. Corruption of this sort was becoming an increasing problem and was undermining public confidence in the government, irrespective of ethnic or tribal interests, and not only among those who were politically committed to criticizing the NPN.

The government's popularity was not enhanced by a series of restrictive measures against the Press. Nigeria's tradition of free speech had encouraged critical elements to err on the side of licence, and the Yoruba Press, in particular, had freely referred to Shagari as a usurper. Such extravagance was not, however, an unusual feature of Nigerian journalism, and it was contrary to tradition when senior staff of the *Nigerian Tribune* were charged with sedition in August 1981, after the newspaper had accused the president of bribing opposition federal legislators to gain their support for government measures. A few days later, the editor-in-chief and editor of the *Standard* were also arrested, having been accused of exciting hatred between classes, and of publishing a press release which had charged the NPN with planning to assassinate its political opponents in Gongola State. Other, similar, accusations against the Press, though clearly not unjustified, gave colour to the picture of an insecure government adopting repressive measures to silence criticism. It was not in Shagari's nature to be repressive, but many of his supporters were intolerant of opposition, especially when voiced by members of ethnic groups regarded as being innately hostile to a northern government. By contrast, the invitation to former president Gowon and former general Ojukwu to return from exile displayed both confidence in its position and a degree of magnanimity on the part of the government which was only marred by the suggestion that the return of a compliant Ojukwu would provide a useful counter to Azikiwe's leadership of the Ibo.

In spite of the problems it had faced during its first term of office, the government approached the 1983 elections in good heart. Characteristically, when the electoral commission announced the numbers registered, there was a clamour of protest and allegations from various quarters that the figures were inflated to suit party interests. When the elections themselves took place, there were immediate accusations of ballot-rigging from unsuccessful contenders. Shagari's resounding victory over Awolowo in the competition for the presidency was greeted with suspicion by the Yoruba, although the exceptionally heavy voting for Awolowo in Yoruba-speaking states might have appeared to justify counter-accusations. During the elections for state governors, feelings in Lagos, Ibadan, and Abeokuta ran high, and culminated in outbreaks of violence. In Oyo State, the victory of the NPN candidate was attributed by many voters to the machinations of the electoral commission, and this again caused disturbances. Finally, the announcement by the chairman of the commission that all allegations of malpractice would be carefully investigated was nullified when, within twenty-four hours, he declared himself satisfied with the results. In view of the strength of party dissatisfaction in Oyo and Ondo, elections to the Senate in those two states were postponed. In Anambra, Ojukwu's home state, Ojukwu himself failed in his campaign to gain election. The strength of Ibo feeling was such that his defection to the NPN could not be forgiven. In the rest of the country, however, voting was light – the turmoil and discontent among the party leaders having served only to encourage feelings of apathy in the electorate. Overall, the NPN won fifty-five of the eighty-five senate seats – with ten still to be contested – and 263 of the 385 seats in the house of representatives.

The extent of this victory may have owed something to malpractice at the polls. More probably it represented the influence of two factors. First, there was no tradition in Nigeria of permanent, constitutional opposition to a government. Opposition to individual measures was demonstrated from within the ruling group rather than by staying permanently outside it. Now that the NPN had established itself as the dominant party, it would be natural for anyone on the fringe to join it. In support of this contention, one might point to the criticisms levelled by some NPN members of the senate against a number of Shagari's nominations for his new cabinet. Second, the material benefits available to supporters of the government provided a strong incentive to all but the most committed opponents to forget their differences. At the same time, the strength of the opposition parties indicated the extent to which political leaders, by skilful propaganda, had induced the members of ethnic groups to forget their traditional local loyalties and assume an identity which must, if it were to achieve its purpose, be at enmity with other ethnicities. This was not a permanent state of mind among either the Yoruba or the Ibo, but an election was an invaluable opportunity for their leaders to stir up such feelings.

Shagari's main problem did not lie with the opposition, and still less with ethnic concerns. Though his personal integrity was never in doubt, during his first term of office he had not dealt firmly with his less honourable colleagues and he had allowed the economy to crumble. As a result, he had been unable to prevent the erosion of popular confidence in the honesty of anyone who held public office. During the oil boom which had marked the opening years of his first term of office, widespread corruption had meant that profits, instead of being used for the good of the country as a whole, had been channelled into the pockets of the few. Now, because of the fall in prices offered for oil and the levelling off in production, an intelligent development programme formulated on the basis of the income available in the expansive years was no longer capable of realization. Sudden economies were disastrous to schemes which had already been started and popular expectations suffered a serious setback. Shagari was not blind to the predicament. He could not change the pattern of the world economy but he knew that urgent reforms must somehow be made in Nigeria. He therefore called hopefully for an ethical revolution and created the new post of minister of national guidance with the sole task of ridding the country of corruption. Fortified by his victory in the 1983 elections he also carried out a fundamental revision of his cabinet.

It was too late. His critics saw all too clearly that the measures he was taking were inadequate to stem the inflation which was hitting every member of the population. Perhaps he was not given enough time to test the efficacy of his policies, but the army, having intervened on a previous occasion, had come to regard itself as the ultimate conscience of the nation and had, for some time, been watching with growing concern the direction in which events were moving. On 31 December it seized power, apparently with the general approval of the civilian population. That the coup was greeted with such popular acclaim was a measure of the despair felt by most Nigerians at their leaders' failure to formulate a workable, democratic system of government. It was a failure due to mutual distrust, resulting from the misuse of power and the acquisition of wealth by those in office, compounded by the cynical or defensive manner in which they and their opponents had manipulated ethnic rivalries to serve their ends.

A nineteen-member supreme military council, under the chairmanship of Major-General Mohammed Buhari, was sworn in on 3 January 1984. Buhari began by promising to put an end to corruption and to try to solve the economic problems which beset the country. It was a programme which had a widespread appeal, but to recognize Nigeria's problems was not to solve them. Southerners, for example, noted with apprehension that among the nineteen members of the supreme council there were only three Yoruba and three Ibo. Awolowo was among the first to stress the need to return to civilian rule as soon as possible, delighted though he may have been by Shagari's departure.

In the first place, however, the government needed to build up the sort of momentum which alone could make reform a possibility. At the same time, it must satisfy both the expectations of the civilian population and the criticisms of junior officers – whose own plan for a more violent military takeover had been deliberately forestalled by their seniors. This was no easy task, despite the goodwill it enjoyed. Religious zealots, undeterred by the presence of a military government, created a number of new disturbances, first in Gongola State in February 1984, then in Bauchi state in April 1985. The army had to be called in to suppress the violence which caused hundreds of casualties on each occasion, though once again the dissidents found little support among the population in general. It was, in fact, an inopportune time to raise the standard of religious purity. The people were much more immediately concerned with economic issues and were looking to the new government to rid the country of its burdens. Only if the government failed would the religious zealots have a genuine hope of winning support.

It is not without significance that, in an announcement made after holding office for three months, Buhari claimed that his government had given a new impetus to national unity by putting an end to party politics. It was a statement which might not have had the approval of the party leaders, but it undoubtedly reflected the wishes of a people tired of the endless struggle for advantage. He also said that he had launched a campaign to purge the civil service of 3,000 members deemed to be 'undesirable, partisan, and unproductive' and that a twenty-five-man tribunal had been set up to try political detainees – more than 500 in number – accused of 'economic sabotage, corruption, and unjust enrichment'. The latter announcement was received with markedly less enthusiasm. Although the public were anxious to see offenders in those categories brought to justice, they were appalled by the mandatory sentence of 21 years' imprisonment without appeal, and by the news that judges would only act as advisors to the military tribunal. Lawyers were particularly alarmed when they discovered that the tribunal would sit in camera, and they declared a boycott to demonstrate their disapproval. Not all those arraigned before the tribunal were found guilty, however, though it did not go unnoticed that some of the first to be charged had been state governors. Perhaps the most spectacular proof of the government's determination to bring offenders to justice was provided by the kidnapping of the former minister, Umaru Dikko, in Britain in July 1984, and the unsuccessful attempt to smuggle him back to Nigeria drugged and in a goods crate. There was concern, too, at the severity of the economy measures introduced by the government. These included a cut of

15 per cent in the budget proposed by Shagari's government only two days before its overthrow, a rise in interest rates, and a ban on raising overseas loans by state governments. Stern measures were also taken to restrict criticism by the Press, measures which made the actions of the Shagari regime seem lenient by comparison.

As the task of reviving the economy proved increasingly difficult, younger officers grew restive. Buhari himself suffered from ill health and much of the work was left to Major-General Tunde Idiagbon, whose popularity declined rapidly. On 28 August 1985 there was another bloodless coup and Major-General Ibrahim Babangida, chief of army staff and a member of the supreme military council, was sworn in as president, the first military head of state to claim that title. Effectively, there had been a change in ultimate authority rather than a revolution. Babangida, from Niger state in the Middle Belt, had broadly-based support in the armed forces. He made few alterations in the higher ranks of the army and, while the supreme military council was replaced by a twenty-eight-man, armed-forces ruling council (AFRC), nearly half the members of the new body were drawn from its predecessor.

One of Babangida's first acts was to repeal Buhari's anti-Press decree, but his attempt to declare an amnesty for 'political saboteurs' met with strong opposition. To his credit, although he is a very determined man he is prepared to listen to advice – from the civilian members of his council as well as from the military. It is a characteristic which does not please some of the Hausa/Fulani officer elite who have grown accustomed to having a dominant voice in the government under both Shagari and Buhari. They were disturbed by Babangida's announcement of cuts of from 2.5 per cent to 20 per cent in army and police salaries, the heaviest cuts to be imposed on the most senior ranks, but their attempt to stage a coup in December 1985 proved unsuccessful.

It has been in his handling of the country's economic problems, exacerbated by the continuing fall in oil prices, that Babangida has demonstrated most clearly both his responsiveness to public opinion and his strength of character. Conscious of the suffering which a strict implementation of the measures recommended by the IMF would bring upon the people, he has had the courage to reject the IMF's advice, coupled with the good sense to introduce a 'structural adjustment programme' (SAP) which has called upon Nigerians to rebuild the economy by their own efforts. It is a policy which would not work in a country less well endowed with natural resources, but it has impressed the IMF which is now prepared to support the programme.

Babangida's efforts have been rewarded to the extent that, with an increase in oil prices – though the market remained uncertain – and with the promise of support from European financiers, he was able to introduce a budget early in 1987 which, though still contemplating strict control of the economy, looked to the future with growing confidence.

If Babangida is winning support for his economic programme he is not without problems from other sources. There was violence in a number of universities in 1986 after several students were shot by police in Ahmadu Bello University in Zaria during disturbances thought to have arisen from disciplinary problems between students and university authorities. An attempt by the Nigerian Labour Congress to attract attention to itself by protesting in sympathy with the students was abruptly stopped by police. More serious was an outbreak of rioting in Kaduna state sparked off by a clash between young Christians and Muslims. Babangida, in a public statement, said that although the disturbances had originated in a religious disagreement he believed the subsequent violence was the work of evil men, intent upon overthrowing the government. He went on to call upon the country to recognize that Nigeria was a multi-ethnic and a multi-religious society. If it were to survive, people must learn to live together in peace and concord. The president himself clearly did not believe that local interests had been set aside in the pursuit of economic recovery.

One development in particular was thought by some to provide grounds for Babangida's concern. In January 1986, following upon the president's announcement of a return to civilian rule in 1990, a group of former leaders of the banned NPN and NPP – traditional rulers, retired generals, and civil servants – had set out to provide a forum in which, ostensibly, to discuss common ideas and aspirations, and to forestall a repetition of the disputes of a religious, tribal, ethnic, and political character which had created problems for the constitution drafting committee in 1978. All the participants were northerners, and most became members of a new committee of elders which came into being in June 1987.[5] Once again, the committee claimed to have as its aim the prevention of disharmony and conflict in the northern states, but there were acute observers who believed it had a more sinister objective. The committee, they argued, because of its members' entrenched position in the feudal and economic life of the country, was anxious to get rid of a president who held such independent views and whose rise to power owed nothing to their support. It was these men, some said, who had been behind the recent religious disturbances, and their aim, whatever their overt statements, had been to stir up ethnic rivalry. In calling for the creation of still more states, they were only trying to weaken the federal government by encouraging people to pursue local interests at the expense of national programmes.[6] This could be no more than surmise. As the commission of enquiry into the disturbances was subsequently to point out, many elements had been involved. It was easy for any contending parties to enlist the support of disgruntled minorities in southern Zaria, where there were any number of people who believed they had grievances against the majority Hausa/Fulani majority.[7]

The death of Obafemi Awolowo in May 1987 opened the prospect of a new orientation among the Yoruba, with the possibility of ending the confrontation between the major ethnic groups. For forty years Awolowo had encouraged the Yoruba to insist upon their ethnic identity, believing that this was the only way to protect their interests against the threat of northern, Muslim domination. Although he had not been in the forefront of Nigerian politics since 1983, he had always made it clear that he was available if needed, and the influence of his death upon the political scene is not yet resolved.

Against a background of covert and sometimes more open dissent, Babangida has persisted with his policies. A political bureau – set up to identify the problems which had prevented previous governments from creating a stable society, and to sound out public opinion concerning the form of government which should be adopted when power was handed to civilian rulers in 1990 – completed its task in September 1986. It took until July 1987 for the government to consider the bureau's recommendations, and when it announced its conclusions it did so together with the warning that to carry out the programme effectively would mean the postponement of the handover of power until 1992. The basic problem, in the opinion of one commentator, was 'to find institutional means to enable ethnic groups to live together in some degree of equity and mutual security'.[8] He might have come nearer to the point if he had suggested that what was needed was to find means of controlling the lust for power and wealth, or the fear of the misuse of them by others, which had been displayed by some of the traditional rulers, politicians, and entrepreneurs who had manipulated ethnic differences – in the belief that to do so was the most effective means of achieving their ends. It was they who had encouraged assertive ethnicity and had stirred up confrontation between peoples whose instinctive loyalties were of a far more localized and usually less aggressive character. If consulted, there might have been many who would have supported the plea made by the *Alake* (traditional ruler) of Egba, a former Yoruba kingdom – i.e. that one way out would be to allow traditional rulers, operating within their more limited traditional spheres, a more active role in politics than had been granted them by the 1979 constitution.[9]

The political bureau and the government were agreed that Nigerians had been far too susceptible to manuipulation by a power-seeking elite. Their recipe, however, was not a return to traditional forms. They could see no justification for giving traditional rulers any political role. Such persons, far from contributing to the unity of the country were thought to have been in competition with the nation for the people's allegiance and to have acted as a reminder of differences which it was essential to forget. The government may have been at odds with popular feeling in holding this view, but it was determined to achieve its objectives. To do so, it was decided that a 'comprehensive, coherent, and sustained programme of social mobilization and political education for the country' should be launched immediately. The transition to a democratic form of government would then be a broadly-based process of political learning, beginning with local government elections, which would take place on a non-party basis, and continuing with the introduction of political parties in 1989, arriving ultimately at the federal elections of 1992. To avoid the ethnic clashes inherent in a multi-party system, it was decided that only two parties should be permitted – though it was recognized that this might lead to a north–south or a Muslim–Christian split. A forty-six-member constitution review committee, appointed in September 1987, was given, among other responsibilities, the daunting task of suggesting 'ways by which religious intolerance and tribalism may be curtailed through constitutional provisions'. As a final concession to what was deemed to be justifiable 'tribalism', however, two new states were to be created: Katsina, from part of Kaduna, the scene of numerous disturbances; and Akwa Ibom, from Cross Rivers state.

The chairman of the constitution-review committee did not underestimate his responsibilities. Like many others, he believed there had been nothing seriously wrong with the 1979 constitution. The problem had been to get the people to observe its spirit because it had been difficult to check the abuse of power. The political bureau and the government had foreseen this difficulty, and two proposals were made to overcome it. First, there must be a code of conduct for those holding public office, enforced by code-of-conduct tribunals. This, unfortunately, seemed unlikely to guarantee the transformation of leaders into the 'shining examples of accountability and discipline' which the bureau hoped they would seem to be in the eyes of the public. The second proposal, however, was more draconian. It disqualified three categories of people from seeking elective office or from holding any position within a political party. The first category was predictable. It embraced all those politicians and former officeholders, civilian or military, who had been found guilty of any offence since independence, together with non office-holders guilty of corrupting public officials. The second and third were more open to question. They were, in the second group, all high office-holders under previous government, and in the third, all senior officers in the armed forces of the present government. The exclusion of the two latter groups would be enforced only up to and including the elections of 1992. Babangida stressed that the administration had no intention of succeeding itself.

It was a noble sentiment, aimed at ensuring that people who had enjoyed office should be unable to perpetuate their power, but it meant that any future government would be deprived of an invaluable fund of experience. Nor was there any certainty that their successors would be any less self-seeking. The local elections, too, which took place in December 1987, showed little sign that there was a new spirit abroad. Numerous charges of malpractice were made at the time of the registration of voters. Some of these may have arisen because an unexpectedly large number of people came forward, and the workings of the electoral commission were consequently thrown into disarray. But the elections themselves were marred by the inefficient distribution of voting papers and ballot boxes and by violence in some areas, sparked off by frustration or intimidation. It was a depressing start to Babangida's transition programme, though lessons could be learned before the full sequence of elections was launched with political parties taking part.

What was clear was that the government, with the aid of the political bureau, had identified most of Nigeria's problems, whether they arose from religious differences, the survival of ancient, local loyalties, or the emergence of newer, ethnic loyalties under the pressure of political competition. There was, too, the difficulty of controlling an economy which, while potentially rich, was subject both to external fluctuations and to internal self-seeking. Above all, there was the temptation to use power for purely personal ends, and it was that which exacerbated all the other problems. Ancient, traditional loyalties were still strong, but they no longer exerted a critical influence upon the country's affairs, even in the conservative north. For most people, as elsewhere in Africa, those loyalties provided a refuge when the pressures of political life became too great or incomprehensible. It was Nigeria's great wealth, even after the income from oil was sharply reduced because of a fall in world prices, that simultaneously offered great possibilities for the future and tempted ambitious people to enlist any forces, no matter how divisive, to help them to seize a portion of that wealth. Among those forces, religion, greed, ethnicity, fear, and want were the elements which possessed the greatest emotive power. All were readily available and any of them could be harnessed by unscrupulous persons to serve their ends.

For more than a generation it had been skilfully stage-managed ethnicity, bordering at times upon neo-tribalism and fuelled by the prospects of great wealth, that had created the greatest problems for the government. In the future, with opportunities of both wealth and advancement more restricted, it could well be that those in search of power might enlist religious extremism as the instrument most likely to help them to achieve their goal. If that were to happen, it might be tempting for the country's leaders to divide Nigeria into its three main ethnic regions. The political motivation would have to be strong, because the breakup of the country's economy would weaken the north in particular – a weakness underlined by the region's dependence upon its southern neighbours for its main trade links with the outside world. Then, too, there would be the problem of ethnic minorities which the federal state has done much to eliminate. It is not a tempting proposition, as the Biafran War so clearly demonstrated, and if it is not feasible in Nigeria it could scarcely be possible elsewhere.

5 Kenya: the president's country

Opinions about the state of contemporary Kenya are sharply polarized. Twice the size of Uganda but with far less agricultural potential – either as a food producer or as a marketer of export crops – for many western observers it is, nevertheless, the one stable country in Eastern Africa, characterized by a sound if modest economy and a moderate, pro-western government. To its critics, it is the prime example of co-operation between a fortunate few and the world of capitalist exploiters who have battened upon the emergent nations of Africa. On the one hand, Kenya's admirers believe the main threat to stability could come from the machinations of an educated minority steeped in Marxist–Leninist theory and encouraged by the USSR. Tribalism, they consider, can also sound a discordant note, but any link between the two, if it exists, is not made clear. On the other hand, Kenya's detractors feel that the only hope of salvation for the incoherent majority lies in the social concern of an ideo-lologically-motivated minority among the educated elite. Is there any truth in either of these extreme opinions, for there seems little prospect of reconciling them?

The violence which preceded independence in Kenya, and the relative tranquillity that followed it, were the reverse of events in neighbouring Uganda. There was, in Kenya, no counterpart to the powerful local patriotism of Buganda and there were no traditional or neo-traditional authorities with influence and wealth such as there were in Uganda, Ghana, and Nigeria. But there were divisive forces of an ethnic nature which, had they possessed leaders minded to split the country, might have caused havoc. The Mau Mau rebellion may have retarded rather than expedited the achievement of independence, but it was no Kikuyu equivalent of Buganda's attempt to dissociate itself from its neighbours. Nor did it bear any resemblance to the ethnic struggles which occurred in Nigeria. It is true that the Kikuyu were the largest linguistic group in Kenya Colony and, like the Ganda in Uganda, they occupied the geographical and economic centre of the country. Similarly, some of the more educated among them took the lead in whatever political activities Africans organized during the period of British administration. However, the fact that the rebellion was limited to the Kikuyu and their cousins – the Embu and Meru – was due to the lack of leadership and resources among the guerrillas, and to the military control exercised by the British, rather than to any tribal designs emanating from the Kikuyu themselves.

It was a sense of common deprivation which alone bound even the Kikuyu together in their revolt. They had a common language and a common culture, but they had no tradition of loyalty to one political head. Until the British authorities created an administration based on linguistic groups, clan elders and village headmen had controlled the destiny of the various units into which Kikuyu society had been divided. Even under British rule, this state of affairs had not changed in so far as most areas of everyday life were concerned. It was frustration akin to desperation, rather than local patriotism, which led so many Kikuyu to take up their primitive arms against an alien administration.

The educated Kikuyu elite, whether remaining loyal to the British authorities or demanding their removal, feared that violence would only delay any prospect of their participating in the government, and still more of their taking total control of it. It was a belief they shared with the elites of other language groups in Kenya, which were divided in the same way between loyal officials who sought a gradual progression towards self-government and nationalist politicians who wanted immediate independence. The nascent nationalists sought to promote their aims and to demonstrate their right to do so by organizing political parties, but the popular support they gained was due to the prospect they held out to the public of greater prosperity and freedom from white domination rather than to the appeal of political programmes.

If the nationalists agreed over objectives there was, nevertheless, a division of a superficially ethnic character between the two main political parties which emerged to demand independence. The Kenya African Democratic Union (KADU) was formed among the smaller ethnic groups which feared that the Kenya Africa National Union (KANU) might pursue the interests of the larger groups – the Kikuyu, the Luo, and the Kamba – at their expense. The British administrators shared that fear, and insisted upon a constitution for independent Kenya which vested considerable authority in regional councils.

KANU, however, triumphed in the 1963 elections, and it was the policy decisions taken by KANU with regard to the economic and administrative future of Kenya which made it possible to change the constitution in 1964, and by doing so to lay the foundations of a united country.

Jomo Kenyatta's pre-eminence as the undisputed leader in Kenya at the time of independence may, as some claim, have been exaggerated.[1] His adoption as leader by KANU may, in the eyes of KADU supporters, have branded him as the spokesman for the dominant ethnic groups, if not of the Kikuyu alone. Even within KANU itself there were some members of other groups who saw him as, essentially, the leader of the Kikuyu. But they had to accept his leadership, because Kenyatta was the only person who could arouse sufficient unity of purpose to win the 1963 elections and so enable them to inherit power from the departing European government. Kenyatta's contribution to events in Kenya was, therefore, of paramount importance. For Kenyatta and KANU alike, it appeared vital that they should win those elections, because they were convinced that the regional constitution insisted upon by the British would have a permanently divisive effect upon the country. Once in power, they could amend it to meet their needs.

Although KANU was indeed victorious in the elections which led to self-government in May 1963, KADU continued to press for a federal system of government and did so even after independence was achieved in December of the same year. As a result, Kenyatta's role in shaping affairs grew in importance to meet the challenge to his dream of unity. His insistence upon magnanimity towards former opponents encouraged European businessmen, and even a number of European landowners, to stay in Kenya, and to maintain continuity with the existing economic system. Of one thing he was certain, and that was that Kenya needed external assistance if it were to survive as a politically-independent country. The confidence which his attitude inspired also facilitated the transfer of land from white settlers to African ownership without the acrimony which might otherwise have occurred. His decision to retain the existing system of provincial and district administration reassured those Europeans who contemplated staying in Kenya. At the same time, it won for Kenyatta the support of the newly emerging generation of African career officials as well as of the old guard of chiefs and headmen who had been appointed by the former British rulers.

The acceptance of all these trappings of an imperial system was probably the only practical solution to the problem of administering

Kenya. However, it marked the abandonment of revolutionary change and it did not please the more radical elements in the country who resented their continuing dependence upon outside, and particularly western, aid. Nevertheless, it had the advantage of forging an alliance between the former imperial loyalists and the new KANU party leaders, which, in time, was to ensure both unity and stability in the country. That the militant members of Mau Mau also accepted such a conservative settlement owed everything to the influence which Kenyatta's reputation exercised over them. His conviction by the British of managing Mau Mau – a cause he never seriously espoused – and his forced exile in northern Kenya may, as some have claimed, have undermined his links with the political scene. But it was this 'martyrdom' which enabled him to become the hero *sans peur* and – because of his forced removal from the political infighting of the time – *sans reproche* among the Mau Mau activists.

In January 1964 Kenyatta further consolidated his position. Forewarned by mutinies in Tanganyika and Uganda, he unhesitatingly sought British military assistance when a battalion of the former King's African Rifles attempted a similar rising in support of a claim for higher pay and better prospects of promotion. The trouble was quickly suppressed, but Kenyatta recognized that he must take action to prevent any future attempt by the military to exert pressure on the government. In the first place it was essential to reduce the dominance of two groups – the Kamba and the Kalenjin peoples – who made up the greater part of the army. By a process of selective recruitment, the percentage of Kikuyu officers was raised to something approaching that of Kamba officers, and it was further increased in the 1970s. As a further insurance against trouble, a number of British officers were retained in the army – even if only, after 1966, in an advisory capacity. The last of them left in 1975. Meanwhile, Kenyan officers continued to be trained in Britain in the apolitical tradition of the British army. The government also created a General Service Unit (GSU) in the late 1960s – distinct from the army and with an officer corps in which Kikuyu predominated – with the duty of dealing with internal disorders. The creation of the GSU did not mean that the army would be powerless to intervene in politics, but it did reduce the likelihood of any popular protest reaching a pitch at which the army might feel justified in intervening.

An armed struggle of a more directly nationalist character did begin soon after independence and flared up from time to time over the next quarter of a century. The discontent of the Somali of north-eastern Kenya had its roots in the boundary decisions taken by Britain and

Italy in the early days of East African partition. Cut off by an arbitrary boundary from their kinsmen in Somalia, and by culture, language, and geographical distance from the other peoples of Kenya and from the government in Nairobi, they had looked to independence to provide an opportunity to redress the errors of a bygone age. They were prompted to indulge in that hope by the government of Somalia – which was already pursuing a policy of expansion at the expense of another neighbour, Ethiopia. During the negotiations preceding independence, the Kenyan Somali asked to have their land transferred to Somalia. When they failed to gain this concession, they boycotted the elections in May 1963 and, with support from Somalia, they attacked a number of police posts and trading centres. Only the declaration of a state of emergency in the region and strict military measures by the Kenyan government over a period of years, reduced the rebels to submission. Subsequently, sporadic outbreaks of banditry made it clear that the Somali, though chastened, were far from content to accept what they regarded as alien rule. This was, however, the only separatist movement of an ethnic character to trouble the newly independent state of Kenya.

Fortunately for the Kenyan government, the Somali troubles took place on the country's periphery, and to that extent were less disturbing than they might otherwise have been. Nearer the centre of affairs, both KANU and KADU, whatever their differences over the importance of regional administration, embraced a variety of ethnic groups – none of which showed any inclination to break away from the rest. Kenyatta's tendency to rely heavily upon his immediate circle of Kikuyu supporters may have caused misgivings, but it was no indication of any desire on his part to establish Kikuyu hegemony, still less to set up an independent Kikuyu nation. He chose his closest associates mainly, but not exclusively, from among the Kikuyu of Kiambu district – because he knew them, and because they were men upon whose support he believed he could rely – in his struggle to create a united country. He recognized, nevertheless, that other peoples must have a share in building the nation – and in any spoils which might accrue in the process.

In December 1964, a year after independence, Kenya became a republic, and Kenyatta was able to reduce the powers promised to the regions – powers which he still firmly believed would militate against the creation of a national identity. He also ensured that, although parliament was deemed to be sovereign, true power resided in the office of the president – a situation which was reinforced by the fact that the president of the country was also president of the ruling party,

KANU. In addition, the president was empowered to appoint all ministers – including the vice-president – and all office holders were, in practice, his nominees or those of his ministers. Candidates could only stand for parliament if nominated by a political party and, in view of the patronage exercised by office holders, opposition parties would inevitably find themselves at a disadvantage when elections took place – unless there was overwhelming discontent with the government. In these circumstances, the days of KADU as an effective opposition movement were numbered. An official opposition with the obligation to challenge the government on every issue was, in any case, a concept alien to the traditions of the Kenyan peoples. To be part of the government was obviously a more effective way of protecting the interests of those one wished to represent than to be permanently content with the role of critic. So KADU was absorbed by KANU at the end of 1964.

With the country's political leaders at least nominally united under the KANU banner, Kenyatta took further steps to consolidate his position. While continuing to allocate the main cabinet posts and a significant proportion of senior administrative appointments – and the patronage and prospects of wealth they carried with them – to Kikuyu who had demonstrated their loyalty to KANU, he distributed offices to members of other ethnic groups in such a way as to ensure that all parts of the country enjoyed some of the benison of patronage. In this way, he hoped to gain widespread support for the government from people whose interest in politics was minimal but who were desperately in search of greater prosperity. His two most important appointments were those of Charles Njonjo as attorney-general and Oginga Odinga as vice-president.

Njonjo was the son of Senior Chief Josiah Njonjo, a leading Kikuyu who remained loyal to the British when they were in power. The younger Njonjo had received his university education in South Africa and had read law in England. The position of attorney-general was a potentially powerful one. As a civil servant, Njonjo had no need to strive for the popular support so vital to politicians. At the same time, he had access to a great deal of information about a large number of people – many of them in positions of responsibility – and he was in a position to use that information to the detriment of the people concerned if they did not act in accordance with the president's wishes. As the official guardian of the constitution, he could pounce upon any attempt to subvert it. As a member of the cabinet, he was the all-important link between the civil service and the politicians. Yet, by the nature of his office, he could have no popular following, and he was wholly dependent upon the president for the powers he exercised. Kenyatta thus had, in Njonjo, an extremely powerful agent from whom he had little to fear provided he kept a watchful eye on his activities.[2]

The office of vice-president was largely an honorary one. By appointing Odinga, Kenyatta honoured the Luo people of western Kenya, many of whom regarded Odinga as their spokesman. At the same time, it helped to assuage Luo fears of Kikuyu domination while attempting to muzzle one of Kenya's most vigorous politicians who, at the head of a ministry, might have tried to pursue policies which did not accord with those envisaged by Kenyatta himself. Odinga, however, was not easily silenced, and it was not long before he became involved in bickering with other members of the cabinet. Though his supporters were virtually all Luo, his criticism of the government was always of an ideological character and he had no wish to promote ethnic interests. If he could be accused of sectionalism it was on behalf of the poor of Kenya that he spoke, rather than for his Luo kinsmen. It was the government's preference for a capitalist system that he condemned. He believed that Kenya's leaders were being manipulated, willingly perhaps, by western interests which had no concern for the people of Kenya. His ideal was a form of socialism tailored to the needs of Africa, and although he denied any attachment to Communism – on the ground that it was as much a European creation as was capitalism – he preferred to accept aid from eastern-bloc countries because he believed that to do so would involve less commitment to alien ideologies.[3]

The differences between Odinga and Kenyatta came to a head in 1966 and the powers available to the president to suppress opposition were immediately brought into play. Odinga planned to challenge government policy during the party conference in March, but his attempt was foiled because of Kenyatta's control of the party machine. By skilful manipulation, the president induced the conference to divide the office of party vice-president, held by Odinga, among eight people, thereby reducing the power wielded by each of them. Odinga responded by resigning from the party, taking twenty-nine supporters with him. He then formed a new party, the Kenya People's Union (KPU), but won little support, except from his ever-loyal Luo. Nevertheless, Kenyatta gave him no respite. At once, the president induced parliament to pass a bill requiring MPs who quitted their party to seek re-election at the end of the parliamentary session. When the by-elections were held in conformity with the new law, Odinga himself was elected by his loyal constituents. But because of the influence exerted by members of the provincial administration, all of them nominees of the government, KANU won twenty-one of the remaining twenty-nine seats made vacant in conformity with the recent legislation. Kenyatta now had no need to rely on the power of his own personality to enable him to control events. The powers of the president's office were unassailable so long as the government was able to satisfy the reasonable expectations of the population at large.

It was in striving to fulfil those expectations, rather than from ethnic disaffection, that the government faced its main challenge. Odinga's claim that the interests of the poorer people were being neglected was reinforced in 1966, when a serious drought – which led to the failure of the maize harvest – meant that 250,000 people needed famine relief. Rumours of corruption in the maize industry were, it is true, quickly followed by an investigation into the operations of the West Kenya Marketing Board, but confidence in the government was shaken. Fortunately, aid was soon forthcoming from Britain, Canada, and Australia, and the famine-relief organization worked well. Odinga maintained that what had happened was a foretaste of more serious troubles to follow, which could only be averted by adopting socialist methods. Kenyatta, however, set out to demonstrate the hollowness of that claim by distributing to thousands of African smallholders land made available by an agreement with Britain to buy out a large number of European settlers. By the end of 1973, some 12 million acres of land had been systematically converted into more than 650,000 holdings. Large areas of the former white highlands had become African-owned farms which were gradually beginning to be productive. Thousands of small farmers were growing crops for export – coffee, tea, and tobacco. The quality of livestock on small farms was improving and, in addition, more than half the land formerly held by Africans under various forms of customary tenure had been converted into freehold. Many Africans were prospering and the incomes of some of the smallholders had more than trebled in real terms.[4]

Not everyone was successful. Many Africans were unaccustomed to modern methods of farming and virtually all lacked capital. The fluctuations occurring in world markets alternately raised and depressed the farmers' hopes. In 1967 the high prices paid for coffee in previous years resulted in a record crop which seriously exceeded Kenya's internationally agreed quota, and a proportion could not immediately be sold. In an attempt to avoid a repetition of the error, the government urged farmers to grow more tea. But advice of that sort, sound though it may have been, only led to over-production of tea while undermining confidence in coffee growing. This was partly due to a serious shortage of agricultural officers to instruct the farmers in the best ways of managing their output. The same lack of middle-ranking officials to act as channels of information and instruction was responsible for the failure of the people to implement other policies enunciated by the government.

The steep rise in the price demanded for oil in the early 1970s created further difficulties for the government, and it became increasingly important to ensure that the persuasive eloquence of Odinga should not be allowed to stir up discontent. Fortunately for the government, his departure from KANU meant that he ceased to be vice-president of Kenya. He was succeeded briefly by Joseph Murumbi, a veteran KANU man, who, however, resigned in September 1966. Kenyatta then made a well-planned move, appointing in Murumbi's stead Daniel arap Moi, who was not a man of outstanding ability but was an indefatigable worker. Moi had been a prominent figure in KADU, and he was a member of the Kalenjin group of peoples. There was little likelihood of his posing any challenge to Kenyatta's leadership, but his appointment encouraged the smaller ethnic groups to believe that the government was concerned for their well-being.

The campaign against Odinga was prosecuted as unremittingly as ever. So persistent was the government's manipulation of the local elections in August 1968 that every KANU candidate was elected, while KPU candidates were disqualified for allegedly filling in their nomination papers incorrectly or for various other technical reasons. In January 1969 Odinga was forbidden to address the students of Nairobi University College, as it then was, whereupon the students boycotted their lectures in protest. Kenyatta at once ordered the closing of the college, though later all but five of the students were allowed to return after giving an apology to the government and pledging their total obedience to college rules. These events marked the beginning of a rift between the government and the university which, for a variety of reasons, was to pose a growing threat to the country's stability.

For the moment, however, it was Odinga who was singled out as the government's most dangerous opponent – a role in which he seemed to be more firmly cast after the assassination of the minister of economic planning and development, Tom Mboya, on 5 July 1969. Though a Luo like Odinga, Mboya's devotion to KANU had been unshaken, and, again like Odinga, though pursuing a different course to achieve his goal, he was committed to Kenyan unity. Even before independence, he had told the Kenya National Farmers' Union: 'True, we have tribal differences and sensitivities. So often people point at the Congo[5] and warn that Kenya is doomed to become another Congo. I do not share this view. We have passed the stage when this could have happened.'[6] It was an opinion from which he refused to deviate. He had consistently opposed Odinga, a fellow Luo, because he disagreed with his politics. He had frequently been called upon to defend the government's case when criticism was strongest, because he was one of the ablest spokesmen for the party. Yet, from 1966, his position had been threatened from within the party, where ethnic hostility from some of the Kikuyu who enjoyed Kenyatta's patronage reinforced their jealousy of Mboya's talents and of the popularity he enjoyed among all sorts of people both inside Kenya and in the wider world. Even Kenyatta had been briefly concerned lest Mboya's influence with the trade unions should cause them to become centres of unrest. As usual, however, the president had acted quickly to avoid the threat, and had later given every support to the able young man who had contributed so much to the success of the government.

There were others who were willing to undermine Mboya's position, and fears that Kenyatta's failing health might lead to his withdrawal from politics created a sense of urgency about the succession, which was only rendered more acute by the anxiety among some of the Kikuyu leaders to ensure that Mboya should not be the successful candidate. Overt attempts were made by his opponents to revise the constitution – which Njonjo and Mboya had changed in 1964 to ensure that, in the event of Kenyatta's death or resignation in mid term, the vice-president, at that time Odinga, should not automatically succeed him. Kenyatta himself now intervened to prevent any untoward action, but it was eventually agreed by parliament that the vice-president, Moi, should, if necessary, succeed for 3 months, pending an election. Thus, Mboya's hopes of the presidency, if he had any, were thwarted. Nevertheless, his assassination, though it was said to have been carried out by a man of no political standing, was widely believed to have been the culmination of a campaign against him on the part of leading political figures.

The effect of the assassination was to stir up defensive ethnic solidarity in a form which had not been encountered since independence. The split which had previously existed between the southern Luo supporters of Mboya and the central Luo Odinga loyalists was forgotten. The Luo were now firmly united in a positive protest against what they saw as the threat of Kikuyu domination. This was not yet a tribal separatist movement, but the Luo were determined to defend their interests. The fact that Mboya had never spoken as a Luo was now of no importance. The car in which vice-president Moi travelled to pay his respects to the dead man was stoned by Luo mourners. Odinga, who had respected Mboya while still seeing him as a powerful political opponent, called for restraint in the expression of communal anger, but he called in vain. A crowd of 20,000 – mainly Luo – was also present outside Nairobi cathedral, where a requiem mass was to be said. There were shouts of disapproval when President Kenyatta arrived and his car was stoned. Further demonstrations took place when Mboya's body was carried in procession to Nyanza – his home district – for burial, and the interment was accompanied by scenes of intense emotion. Ethnicity, if not tribalism, had suddenly become a force to be reckoned with.

Kenyatta's first reaction was to try to appease the Luo by promoting some of their representatives in the government, but they were not easily mollified. They firmly believed that a Kikuyu plot was afoot and that oath-taking – similar to that practised in Mau Mau days – was secretly taking place among the Kikuyu of Kiambu District. There is independent evidence to show that their suspicions were well founded – the aim of those involved being to ensure that Kenyatta should be succeeded by a member of the group already closely linked with him – but there was nothing to suggest that Kenyatta himself was implicated. The president had no intention at that stage of handing over power to anyone.[7] In parliament, Odinga demanded to know if there was any truth in the rumours, to which Moi replied that there was none. However, Kenyatta himself visited Kisumu, the main town in Nyanza, in October 1969, and there accused Odinga of stirring up trouble, adding that those who opposed the government would be crushed. His audience became threatening and the police opened fire. Two days later, Odinga and other leading members of the KPU – including members of parliament – were arrested, and on 30 October the KPU was banned.[8] This meant that the parliamentary elections held in December 1969 were contested by KANU candidates only. Order had been restored, but only by using force. The Luo had been rendered leaderless and the momentum of their campaign against the government was lost.

Kanu's election success did not mean that the party had won universal popularity. Candidates had relied heavily upon the influence of the provincial administration to ensure their election. At the first session of the new parliament, in February 1970, Kenyatta still found it necessary to emphasize the need for a national outlook, and he urged members not to harass the government but instead to act as a bridge between the government and the people. However, six months later, he felt confident enough to order the release of twelve of the detained members of the KPU. Odinga himself was not released until March 1971, when Kenyatta made a further attempt at reconciliation. In October of the same year Odinga was readmitted to membership of KANU, and said he hoped to run for political office when the next elections took place. The Luo were not wholly appeased. Their charge that the Kikuyu were trying to dominate the government remained as firm as before. Again, Kenyatta promoted a number of non-Kikuyu to posts of no great significance, and he took it upon himself to demonstrate that the members of his cabinet were drawn from all parts of the country. It was clear that there was a general desire to share in the benefits to be derived from having a united country, but it was equally clear that no national identity had as yet emerged.

In 1971 there was a momentary threat from another quarter when the government claimed to have thwarted an attempted *coup d'état*. Thirteen men were tried and convicted, and Major-General Joe Ngolo, the army chief of staff since 1967, a Kamba, and the chief justice, Maluki Kitili Mwenda, resigned when their loyalty was openly questioned. To avert any further threat of a military takeover, Kenyatta took steps to improve the pay and working conditions of the armed services while ensuring that their numbers remained small.

The transfer of 1.6 million acres of large farms intact to wealthy members of the community – mainly Kikuyu closely associated with the president – aroused hostile criticism, though there were sound economic reasons to justify any attempt to prevent the breakup of the large farms. Small farmers were doing well, but the need to increase productivity of staple crops – for consumption as well as for export – suggested that a number of larger farms should be retained. In practice, the benefits expected from this arrangement were not realized, often because of bad management, and there was some justification for the claim that the land might have served a better purpose if it had been distributed to the thousands of landless people clamouring for an opportunity to farm. The protest availed nothing. The beneficiaries of the large gifts of land were men in positions of power, against whom it would be impossible to mount an effective challenge, and the voice of the poor scarcely impinged upon the satisfaction of the hundreds of thousands of smallholders who were busily at work on their recently acquired farms.

The presence of another disgruntled group served to draw the country together rather than to divide it. Kenyatta had shown great magnanimity towards the foreigners who had chosen to stay in Kenya after independence, but he became worried lest Africans with the appropiate education and aptitude were being excluded from jobs of a clerical nature and in business because of the dominant role played by Asians in both those areas. During 1973, 1,418 notices were given to Asians who had not taken Kenyan nationality to leave the country. The government also stated that all secretarial posts must be given to Africans before the end of the year, except where the retention of non-Africans was in the national interest. Although the measure was implemented without apparent malice, it aroused previously dormant feelings of suspicion against Asians, and those feelings could later be manipulated so as to divert hostile criticism from the government to a more vulnerable target. When oil prices rose in 1974, Kenyatta was consequently able to distract public attention from the adverse effects this was having on the economy by raising the issue of Asians in Kenya, and by insisting that all non-citizen traders who had received warning notices should leave the country as soon as their businesses had been handed over.

The announcement in March 1974 that elections to parliament would take place in October again focused the spotlight on Odinga. In June, Kenyatta stated that he would crush anyone who tried to launch a new political party. At the same time, former detainees were informed that they might only stand for election if they had been members of KANU for the previous three years and had been accepted by the party as candidates. Under these new regulations, neither Odinga nor any other of the nine KPU members was allowed to stand. But if they were unable to raise their voices in parliament there was another who was prepared to do so. J.M. Kariuki, a Kikuyu MP and a former Mau Mau detainee, had initially been a close associate of the president, but unlike the majority of the former Mau Mau members he did not remain under Kenyatta's spell. Witnessing the operation of government from the inside he became increasingly critical of the growing corruption in which those in power indulged, not least the members of Kenyatta's own family. As the effects of world-wide inflation began to be felt more severely, he challenged the government to guarantee a fairer distribution of the country's resources. For some time, his criticisms failed to find support in the country at large, partly because a lot of people were enjoying greater prosperity than they had ever previously encountered, or hoped to do so by judiciously wooing those who were in a position to offer patronage. As the economic situation became more serious, however, Kenyatta feared that Kariuki might make a greater impression upon public opinion.

Kariuki's arrest in March 1975 and his subsequent murder, which was followed by a cover-up by government officials, proved a greater threat to stability than he had ever been able to offer while be was alive. There were riots among university students, and in parliament there was a highly charged debate until Kenyatta agreed to appoint an independent commission of inquiry. The report of the commission, which was highly critical of the police and the GSU, created further turbulence in parliament, but once again, in a moment of crisis, the powers of the president saved the day for the government. The deputy speaker and two other MPs were arrested during the parliamentary session and holders of official positions who criticized the government were dismissed or told to resign. Resistance collapsed at once. Loss of office was too great a disaster to contemplate, for it would have meant an end to every opportunity to dispense benefits to family and to a host of supporters and dependents. The unease in the country at large subsided more slowly, but the boom in coffee prices, following upon a disastrous frost in Brazil, meant prosperity for farmers as the demand for Kenyan coffee grew. Although a high proportion of the profits found its way into the pockets of wealthy entrepreneurs, enough reached a sufficiently wide cross section of the population to dilute dissatisfaction.

Behind these varied issues, the question of the succession still lurked disturbingly. A number of prominent Kikuyu in Kiambu continued to work steadily to ensure that their interests, which had been so assiduously cultivated under Kenyatta's rule, should not be adversely affected by the appointment of an unsympathetic successor. Their leading candidate for the succession was Dr Njeroge Mungai, who had been foreign minister until he was defeated in the 1974 elections. But the constitutional amendment of 1974 stood in their way, because it laid down that the vice-president should automatically take over in the event of the president's stepping down in mid term. That provision, they decided, must be changed. Though himself a Kikuyu from Kiambu District, Charles Njonjo, as attorney-general, refused to have any part in such sectional schemes, preferring the option of exercising almost unlimited power in the shadow of Kenyatta rather than plotting against him in the hope of gaining future benefits. When the campaign to amend the constitution was launched in September 1976, Njonjo responded with a forceful denunciation of any attempt to 'compass, imagine, or intend the death or the deposition of the president', and Kenyatta lent his support. Defeated on that front, the plotters switched their campaign to the party conference, because it was the party that would name the candidate to stand for what, in the absence of an opposition party, would be an uncontested election after the three-month interim period required by the constitution had elapsed. Again Kenyatta intervened, calling off the conference. The ageing president had no wish to promote the interests of a potential rival. In May 1977, George Anyona, a leading member of the campaign to amend the constitution, was detained, and in April of the following year an MP who spoke in favour of the campaign's presidential candidate, Mungai, was imprisoned on a criminal charge.[9]

Behind the scenes, more sinister developments were taking place. In the Rift Valley province, the anti-Moi movement had created a private, para-military force within the police force itself. Nominally described as the Anti-Stock Theft Unit, the group had been equipped and trained as parachutists and given uniforms identical with those of the GSU save for the colour of their berets. Kenyatta was known to be very ill and the plan was that, on his death – which they hoped would take place on his farm in the Rift Valley where he now spent a lot of time – the para-military forces would seize Moi and any of his supporters who might be at the president's deathbed. The plan failed because Kenyatta died in Mombasa, after he had insisted upon going to the coast in spite of his illness, and because Moi and Njonjo were too well prepared. As soon as he received the news of Kenyatta's death, Moi hurried to Nairobi, avoiding the ambush waiting for him *en route*. An emergency meeting of the cabinet was called, and Moi was sworn in as interim president. From that moment his position was secure. Using the powers of his office, there was little doubt that he could make sure of his election in three months' time. Even his opponents recognized that they were beaten and hastened to proclaim their loyalty, knowing that, outside the president's circle, their influence – and with it their guarantee of wealth – would soon be lost. On 6 October 1978 Moi was unanimously elected president of KANU and the party's candidate for president of Kenya, an office into which he entered four days later.[10]

The anti-Moi movement had clearly been a sub-tribal bid for power, but not with a view to setting up a separate tribal state. The aim of this influential group was to maintain their status within the country so as to perpetuate and even to strengthen their privileged position as beneficiaries of the economy and as bestowers of patronage. That they were all Kikuyu shows a characteristic reliance upon ethnic links to reinforce mutual trust. They were confident, too, that they could rely on the support of the people of Kiambu district, whose pride in their association with the country's leaders would be buttressed by their hope of material benefits as a reward for their demonstration of loyalty. Not all the Kikuyu supported the movement. Njonjo, of course, opposed it, but so, too, did the brilliant Kikuyu minister of finance, Mwai Kibaki. Kibaki, from Nyeri in northern Kikuyuland, had the strong support of the people of that district, who disliked the dominant role in the state and in the economy which the Kiambu Kikuyu had arrogated to themselves. Kibaki's nomination as vice-president was not a step towards the restoration of Kikuyu hegemony but a further blow against the old guard of Kiambu Kikuyu, who had tried – though with only partial success – to become the dominant force in the country's affairs. Such triumphs as they had previously enjoyed were due to Kenyatta's own desire to have a reliable clique of supporters, and, like most of his fellow-countrymen, he sought them among the people among whom he had grown up. Now, for the time being, it was the Moi/Njonjo/Kibaki triumvirate which wielded power.

Initially all went well. The transfer of power which many had anticipated with grave misgivings took place smoothly because Njonjo and Kibaki had been the organizing force behind Kenyatta for several years. In the aftermath of the coffee boom there was still money available both for the government and for individuals, and the political situation was made easier for the new leaders because seven out of twenty cabinet ministers had been defeated in the elections to parliament, among them some of Moi's known opponents.[11] The president, hitherto a somewhat muted personality, seized the opportunity to win wider support by increasing the size of his cabinet in order to make it representative of as many parts of the country as possible, though without significantly weakening the Kikuyu presence which had been a feature of all Kenyatta's governments.[12] In a special bid to woo the Luo, he appointed Odinga as chairman of the Lint and Seed Marketing Board and restored his life membership of KANU.

The honeymoon period was short. Moi's policy of trying to appease Odinga was shattered when that still ebullient figure denounced the late president as a land grabber. However true the allegation, it did not endear Odinga to the KANU faithful. His application for approval as a candidate for parliament was rejected. This led to further protests by university students from all parts of the country who, with characteristic idealism, looked upon Odinga as the spokesman for greater social justice. Nairobi University had already been closed in 1980 after riots in protest against the poor quality of the food provided for students. The new outburst appeared to have a much more serious political content and the government did not hesitate to send troops who fired over the heads of the demonstrators to disperse them. Again the university was closed.

The ideological and idealistic character of the students' opposition was to become a growing concern for Moi, who saw in their campaign for socialism and social justice a more serious threat to stability than the ethnic discontent which he was gradually getting under control. In a preliminary attempt to answer the students' criticisms, he announced that he proposed to campaign against corruption wherever it might occur. It was an empty promise, for corruption was only the extreme aspect of patronage, which was deeply rooted in Kenyan society and provided a system of outdoor relief which the government was powerless to supply by other means. The government itself survived through the operation of patronage, without which it could never retain the allegiance of many of its supporters. The steep fall in coffee prices after the boom year of 1977, together with the fall in the price offered for maize because of over-production, also provided a foretaste of the sort of economic instability which might lead to grass-roots discontent and lend muscle to student ideological protest.

Any threatening alliance between the masses and the intellectuals was not, however, an immediate issue. More pressing in Moi's estimation was the possibility of a threat to his leadership from his long-time ally, Njonjo – for the president was not unaware that, as yet, he himself was the least significant member of the ruling triumvirate. Having reached the age of 60, the attorney-general announced his resignation. He did not contemplate retirement from the public scene, for he was immediately returned to parliament, unopposed, after a by-election resulting from the timely resignation of one of his supporters. In June 1980 he was appointed minister for home and constitutional affairs, and from that moment his troubles began. In March 1981, a businessman cousin of Njonjo was tried for treason and attempted to implicate the minister. Njonjo denied any involvement, and in due course his cousin was acquitted and he himself was wholly cleared. But he certainly seemed to be making some sort of a bid for power by trying to undermine the popularity of Kibaki, claiming that the latter, as minister of finance, was responsible for the country's grave economic problems. Kibaki countered by seeking to win the support of the Kiambu Kikuyu – the people of Njonjo's home district – in order to deprive his rival of a campaign base. It was not a difficult task, because Njonjo's record as attorney-general had not endeared him to his kinsmen, particularly those involved in the abortive campaign to change the constitution. However, by uniting the Kikuyu behind him, Kibaki unwittingly emerged as a stronger force than the president wished to see. The overriding power which the president could exercise, even though the office-holder was not an outstanding personality, was at once revealed. Moi deprived Njonjo of the home-affairs element of his portfolio, giving it to Kibaki who, in turn, had to surrender the ministry of finance. In a brief moment, a man who had come to office with relatively little support and with no outstanding record was able to demote the two men who had done most to ensure his succession to the presidency, both of whom were members of the most powerful ethnic group in the country. Moi had demonstrated beyond doubt that neither tribal patriotism nor ethnic loyalty could challenge the president, unless there was a profound and widespread conviction that the people's prosperity was in the gravest danger – or unless the army intervened.

As if to underline the strength of his position, Moi expelled Odinga from KANU in May 1982, accusing him of engaging in divisive and destructive propaganda against the government. Another to be expelled from the party was George Anyona, a member of the smaller Kisii group in western Kenya, who compounded his previous error of opposing Moi's succession to the presidency by advocating the formation of an alternative party. He was later arrested – after, it was said, having phoned the *Daily Nation* newspaper to say he had a 'very big story'.[13] Mwangi Stephen Muriithi was also arrested, after unsuccessfully challenging his dismissal from the post of deputy director of the CID. So, too, was John Khaminwa, a lawyer, who had undertaken to act for both men, and who had brought writs of habeas corpus on their behalf. Subsequently all three were detained under the Preservation of Public Security Act, the first political prisoners of Moi's regime. In June 1982 Moi took a further step to outlaw opposition, when parliament approved a bill converting Kenya into a one-party state. It was a situation which had existed *de facto* since 1969, but to establish it as part of the constitution was an indication of Moi's increasing fear of criticism.

It is not easy to estimate the extent to which the president's fear was justified. In retrospect, it appears that the critics lacked any coordination and, though the criticisms came from many quarters, the weight of support for the government – both inside and from external donors of aid – was overwhelming. The arrest of two university lecturers, Maina wa Kinyatti and David Mukara Nganga, the latter having advocated the formation of a second party, may have suggested that Moi was wary of the ideological opposition to the government's policies which was current in university circles. However, when George Githii, editor of *The Standard*, published an article criticizing the detention of the two men, there was an outcry in Parliament – an outcry which resulted in Githii's dismissal. This showed clearly that a parliamentary majority could be mustered without difficulty to support the president.

The powerful position occupied by Moi was further underlined at the beginning of August 1982, when the army easily suppressed a mutiny of airforce ground troops. In an early announcement over the 'Voice of Kenya' radio, the rebels claimed that their action had been provoked by the corruption of government officials, by restrictions upon freedom – particularly by the use of preventative attention – by the economic problems which the government had failed to resolve, and by the poverty of leadership in the country generally. It was a cause which attracted the support of a fair number of university students, while many of the poorer people of Nairobi were quick to join the mutineers in a surge of looting – mainly of Asian-owned shops, offices, and private houses. But the whole operation lacked organization. The better educated and better paid aircrews took no part in it, the army remained loyal to the government, and there was no widespread response to the mutineers. It was a disturbing experience, but one which should have reassured the authorities that there was no grave threat to their position.

The two leaders of the mutiny, both low-ranking airmen, were Luo, as was a high proportion of the others involved. It is reasonable, therefore, to assume that a number of unsophisticated servicemen, discontented with their terms of employment, had succumbed to the argument that the Luo were being unfairly discriminated against. The withdrawal of Odinga's passport only three days before the attempted coup may have appeared to corroborate the view, while the dismissal of two Luo men – Peter Oloo-Aringo, a cabinet minister, and Achieng Oneka, the chairman of the Kenya film company, less than two weeks after the revolt, could also be regarded as evidence of the Luo's fall from favour. Moi, however, rejected any ethnic bias, maintaining that the dismissals were due solely to dissatisfaction with individuals. He also claimed that the unsuccessful coup attempt had helped to unite the peoples of Kenya, rather than dividing them, and he could well have been right. There was little sympathy expressed in Nairobi for the students who had been involved. The latter, still motivated by a youthful mixture of idealism and ideology, were widely regarded as a privileged minority who were never content with their good fortune. When Moi ordered the closure of the university and insisted that before it was reopened it must be reformed – with a view to its making a relevant contribution to Kenya's nation-building programme – his statement won general approval.[14] But the president remained on the alert to prevent the students from providing the leadership needed by any mass movement of dissatisfaction.

It was, however, two more notable figures who attracted Moi's attention in the immediate future. His campaign against Odinga was unabated, for even out of office the latter remained a potent campaigner for universal justice. On 23 September 1982, Odinga's son was accused of treason, and another Luo, Professor Alfred Vincent Otieno of Nairobi University, was charged with failing to report treason. The charges against both men were dropped but they were detained nevertheless. Odinga himself was ordered to remain in his home district in western Kenya and in November was placed under house arrest in Kisumu. Attention then switched to Njonjo, against whom the president launched his campaign in May 1983 with cryptic references to a person who was being primed by a foreign country to take over the presidency and to a plot to undermine the position of Kibaki. Njonjo strongly affirmed his loyalty to the president but Moi seems to have been unconvinced. In a further effort to reinforce his position, the president then announced that there would be elections for parliament in September, more than a year before they were due, and that he was dissatisfied with the performance of some of his ministers and of the civil service. In view of the president's powers in respect of all these offices, his statement amounted to a warning to all who might contemplate opposing him that to do so would jeopardize their prospects.

Njonjo, who as attorney-general had been able to make use of the presidential powers to suit his own ends, was powerless as a minister to challenge Moi. In parliament he was vigorously attacked both by those whose enmity he had incurred as attorney-general and by others who sought to gain advantage from the president's obvious displeasure with his former aide. The displeasure took an active form in June 1983 when Njonjo was suspended from his post as minister of constitutional affairs. Shortly afterwards he resigned his seat in parliament. This latter move was a risky one because to be re-elected he would require the approval of KANU, which was dominated by the president. The issue did not arise, however, because in July he was suspended from the party, and a judicial commission was appointed to hear charges against him. Deprived of the possibility of reviving his position by standing for parliament, Njonjo could only watch while Moi consolidated his position still further. In August, the latter was again nominated as candidate for the presidency, which meant his automatic selection.

Although there was considerable apathy among the electorate, of whom less than half registered as voters, more than forty former MPs were unseated, among them five ministers. Moi then both reduced the size of the cabinet and severely cut Kikuyu representation in it. The distribution of portfolios, for the first time since independence, bore a reasonably close relation to the ethnic distribution of the population, the only exception being that, in addition to himself, Moi appointed three others from his own small Kalenjin group. Moi, like other Kenyans, preferred men about him whom he knew well enough to trust.

The inquiry into the allegations against Njonjo dragged on for more than seven months. The evidence brought against him with regard to issues of real substance was too flimsy to hold up in court. Yet, although there was no proof of his having been involved in either treason or subversion, he was expelled from the party. In December 1984, the president announced that Njonjo had been pardoned in view of his faithful service to the country 'before he started to entertain misguided political ambitions'.[15] The nature of the 'serious offences', of which the president said Njonjo had been found guilty, was not revealed. Moi had made his point. Even the strongest could not stand against him.

After the fall of Njonjo, Moi's behaviour, far from demonstrating greater confidence, seemed to suggest an even deeper sense of insecurity. His response to criticism became increasingly severe. Perhaps his gravest concern was with the behaviour of the members, both senior and junior, of Nairobi University. When students boycotted lectures in February 1985 in protest against the expulsion of three of their number and the withdrawal of the scholarships of five more – which was tantamount to expulsion – police were ordered to fire tear-gas to disperse large numbers of protesters who were attending an outdoor meeting on the campus. One student was killed and 2,500 were sent home after they had refused a government order to return to their lectures. The Press, too, met with the president's disapproval, and was warned that it must not portray 'undesirable weaknesses' in the country, though Moi went on to insist that the constitutional guarantee of a free Press remained 'firm and unshakable'. It was not the action of a confident man, any more than was his decision in June to reshuffle his cabinet so as to ensure that no one could construct too strong a power base in any one sphere of activity. Similarly, the secret execution in July of ten men found guilty of leading the mutiny of 1982 would have been waived by a stronger ruler, or carried out openly. On the other hand, by September all but two of the country's political detainees had been released, one of the two remaining in detention being the younger Odinga.

The same uneasy pattern emerged in 1986. Rumours spread of a secret movement aiming to overthrow the government. Moi treated them with the utmost gravity. Several people were jailed for allegedly being involved in the movement, which was said to be called *Mwakenya*. Most of those concerned were recent university graduates, and Moi's warning to the people in April to beware of educated men with beards once again underlined his fears of what members of the university might do to destabilize the country. Kenyatta University, Kenya's second university institution, had been closed in March, but was permitted to reopen in May. Most of the students, with the exception of 100 of them, were allowed to return after contributing to the cost of the damage done by rioters. In the same mood, Moi attributed the failure of two banks in August to economic sabotage when, in all probability, it was due to the inexperience of the bank managers. Next, he turned on a group of Protestant churches which had criticized his proposal to replace the secret ballot, used in the preliminary stages of the elections for parliament, by a new system which required voters to line up behind their candidates. The churches disapproved of the idea that their pastors should be required to announce their political allegiance publicly because their doing so might unfairly influence the voting pattern of their congregations. Moi chose to regard their criticism as a serious attack upon the government. He was angry, too, when leading churchmen aligned themselves with members of the legal profession in opposing a bill designed to remove security of tenure from holders of the offices of attorney-general and controller and auditor-general, two officials who might be in a position to call the government to account.

The shadow of an entirely novel threat to Kenyan unity fell on the coast towards the end of 1987. For centuries, Islam had been a significant force among the coastal peoples, but apart from some difficulties at the time the country became independent – when the long tradition of a close association between the coast and Zanzibar had created an uneasy relationship between the coastal people and the central government in Nairobi – the Islamic leaders had established a working association with the government which had appeared satisfactory to both sides. It was, therefore, only when foreign countries – notably Iran and Libya – began to invest in the coastal region with a view to winning support among the Muslim community there for their political objectives, or for their version of Islam, that Moi began to show concern. Though Islam was not widespread in Kenya, a fundamentalist movement would not be welcome to a government which was particularly anxious to make sure that the coastal strip should not develop any separatist sentiments. The arrival of three Islamic teachers from Tanzania, preaching a revivalist version of Islam, did nothing to calm the situation. Moi intervened at once and expelled the three, to the satisfaction, it should be said, of the established Muslim leaders along the coast.

The arrest of nine Christian missionaries – eight Americans and one Canadian – after allegations of their involvement in a plot to overthrow the government, won less support. The missionaries were later freed without any explanation being given, but the incident aroused unease among many of the white population of Kenya who were increasingly conscious that Moi suspected them of working against him. Perhaps even more surprising was the demotion of Mwai Kibaki who, in March 1988, was removed from the office of vice-president and transferred to the ministry of health. Kibaki had been one of the most effective ministers under both Kenyatta and Moi. Of a retiring disposition, he had not sought the limelight dear to many politicians. But his considerable ability and his strong support among the Kikuyu troubled a president whose own talents were not so obvious and who belonged to a very small ethnic group. Too powerful a subordinate, however loyal, could be a source of danger.

It was, however, the fear of foreign involvement in university politics which was to become the chief concern of the president. Nairobi University was closed again in November 1987 after riot police had broken up violent demonstrations over the arrest of three student leaders who had criticized Moi and his government. Yet, although Moi rightly saw that a potentially hostile leadership might emerge from the universities, it could never be effective without an adequate following. If *Mwakenya* really does exist, and if it is, as Moi fears, a Kikuyu movement aiming to seize power, there could be a serious problem. But there is little evidence to suggest that the majority of the Kikuyu are disloyal to the government, and the student idealists are unlikely to want to put themselves at the head of a separate tribal movement, even if they would be welcomed in such a role by a group of people who, by Moi's reckoning, are experienced politicians.

If the students are seeking a following, they would be far more likely to find it as a result of the frightening population explosion which is affecting the whole continent, but Kenya most of all. It is this which, more than anything else, could make it difficult, if not impossible, for the government to satisfy the aspirations of a sufficiently large proportion of the population to guarantee continuing support and hence stability. Hitherto, though the repressive methods employed by Kenyatta and Moi have helped to contain dissident elements, it has been the government's success – with the assistance of the western countries to whose economic ideology the two presidents have steadily subscribed – in satisfying the needs of the people which has ensured continuing unity. So long as that success continues, tribal or ethnic separatist movements are unlikely to occur, and movements proclaiming an alternative ideology cannot prosper. If the economic situation were to get seriously worse, it is probable that experienced leaders of powerful ethnic groups – such as the Kikuyu or Luo – would take the lead in an attempt to protect local interests, rather than that a challenge to the government would emerge which would be based on ideological differences and led by an unful-filled intelligentsia. In times of stress, conservatism rather than revolution seems likely to prevail, and Kenya, like Nigeria, could just possibly see ethnicity developing into neo-tribalism in order to play a serious political role. In such circumstances, the loyalty of the army would become a key issue.

6   Senegal: unity in diversity

It is the conventional wisdom, accepted by the country's political leaders and by most foreign observers, that traditional loyalties, whether of a tribal or an ethnic character, play little part in Senegalese politics. The explanation for this is to be found in the country's history. The peoples of Senegal, it is said, have little reason to revere their former rulers. The Wolof speakers who inhabit the heartland of the country, unlike the Ganda of eastern Africa, have no tradition of political unity. They were united in the thirteenth century but split up again in the latter part of the sixteenth century. Their rulers became increasingly committed to the slave trade as their main source of wealth and as a result the people suffered the devastation wrought by internecine warfare. Many were even enslaved by their own overlords. Insecure and frequently threatened by their own masters, the Wolof, it is said, welcomed the overthrow of their native oppressors and the substitution of French administration and Islamic culture in the late nineteenth and early twentieth centuries. The adoption of Islam, virtually an indigenous way of life, compensated for the imposition of an alien government.

In the north, along the Senegal River, the argument continues, the Toucoulor of Futa Toro had also been exploited by their former rulers. In the late seventeenth century Moorish expansion southwards had been followed by the establishment of a Moorish protectorate over Futa Toro. The Fulbe rulers of that region were pasturalists, but hitherto they had controlled a reasonably contented population of agriculturalists, fishermen, and artisans. Now they became wholly subservient to their Moorish overlords and their people were treated like slaves. In the eighteenth century, Futa Toro enjoyed a preview of what was to take place almost throughout Senegal a hundred years later. It was at that time that a local man, Sileymann Baal, who had become a devout Muslim scholar, returned to Futa Toro after studying

in Kayor and later in Futa Jallon in the south-east, where Muslim
leaders had overthrown their pagan rulers and set up an Islamic
regime. He found the country in an unstable condition, which soon
culminated in civil war arising from a disputed succession. Under
Sileymann's leadership, the monarchy was overthrown and a list of
new and more equitable principles of government was drawn up.
Sileymann himself was killed in a struggle to beat off Moorish overrule, but his Muslim followers called upon another devoutly religious
man, Abdul Qadir, better known as Abdul Hammadi, to be their
leader. They insisted, however, that his authority should not be
hereditary. Abdul imposed upon Futa Toro the code drafted by
Sileymann, and reorganized the country's administration and
finances. He also built up a powerful military force and set out to
convert all the neighbouring states to Islam. From 1786 to 1797 he met
with considerable success, but a reaction built up against him. In 1807
he was overthrown by the individual and concerted resistance of those
he had conquered and a group of Frenchmen trading along the
Senegal River who feared his growing power. Even his own people
became jealous of his triumph, and the country reverted to a struggle
for supremacy between conflicting influences.[1] Nevertheless, the
tradition of Islamic theocracy lingered on, and Toucoulor Muslim
clerics from Futa Toro were to play a prominent role in leading the
holy wars which later overthrew the pagan rulers of Senegal and contributed to the creation of a unified nation.

Full-scale French and Islamic expansion in Senegal began only in
the nineteenth century. The ending of the slave trade compelled the
French to seek other forms of commercial enterprise. New types of
trade called for a revision of the relations between the traders and the
indigenous peoples. In 1854, Louis Faidherbe, the governor of the
exiguous French territorial possessions in the area, became convinced
of the need to extend French control along the Senegal River and to
subdue all opposition in order to develop the trade in gum. Such a
move appeared more urgent in the light of the threat to French
interests from Al Haj Umar Tall, a Muslim religious leader. Tall, after
being initiated into the *Tijaniyya* brotherhood in Mecca in 1820 and
having been appointed *Tijaniyya khalifa* for the western Sudan, had
built up an army in Futa Toro in 1852 with the intention of establishing an Islamic empire. To achieve that objective, he was prepared to
fight against the French as well as to wage a holy war against pagan
African rulers and the teachings of the Muslim *Qadiriyya* leaders of
Futa Toro who, he said, were too tolerant towards paganism. Failing
to dislodge the French from their forts along the Senegal River, Tall

eventually turned eastwards in 1859, and built a considerable empire before being killed in battle in 1864.

Tall's work was carried on by his disciples in the *Tijaniyya* brotherhood and also by another revivalist leader, Ahmadou Bamba. Initially the French, who were steadily imposing their administration over the country, co-operated with Bamba because he seemed more attracted by the reflective aspects of Islam than by the idea of waging a holy war. But as his influence over the people grew stronger, the French became nervous, and twice sent him into exile. It was as a result of these experiences that Bamba concluded that, if his work was to prosper, it must cease to be dependent upon his own continuing presence. He therefore founded the *Mouride* brotherhood. Recognizing that not everyone had the gift of reflection, he encouraged others to pursue another of the virtues extolled by the prophet Muhammad – manual labour. In the *Mouride* communities which Bamba established, the *marabout*, or spiritual leader, reflected and taught his followers who, in their turn, worked on his behalf.

Like the *Tijaniyya* brotherhood, the *Mourides* spread rapidly because, for many of the people, Islam appeared as a useful antidote to the pressures of an alien, French culture.[2] Confronted by such firm yet peaceful opposition, the French concluded that their best policy was to seek co-operation with the Muslim leaders if the latter would accept their overlordship. This was the beginning of an important partnership which was later to contribute significantly to Leopold Senghor's successful takeover of the whole country when Senegal became independent. The foundations of the partnership rested upon the decision of the French authorities to allow the *marabouts* to acquire land provided they encouraged their followers to grow groundnuts. The *marabouts* responded willingly, and the *Mouride* doctrine of manual labour for their followers cemented the coalition. Over the years, the *marabouts* extended their ownership over more and more land, while the French strengthened the relationship they had established with these Muslim leaders by offering them a variety of concessions and by giving financial help for building mosques. In their turn, the *marabouts* guaranteed the loyal support of their followers to government policy without claiming any political role for themselves. At the same time, the ground-nut industry enabled the French, and in their turn the Senegalese, to build an adequate if not a rich economy for the whole country.

If the working agreement with the Islamic leaders ensured a satisfactory relationship between the government and the governed, it was the government's association with the Wolof speakers that ensured an effective, unified administration for Senegal. Initially, in the outlying areas, the French made use of members of leading families who were prepared to collaborate with them in administering the country, very much as the British had done in northern Nigeria. It was not easy to follow the same policy in the central, Wolof-speaking region, where resistance to French authority had led to the overthrow of most of the indigenous rulers. There, the French began to educate men of their own choosing to act as their agents. Gradually they extended this method to the whole country, though not always with the instant approval of those whom the agents supplanted. It was, nevertheless, a move which was to prove invaluable in effecting a successful transfer of power to an indigenous central government at independence. Virtually all the post-independence political leaders had been through the same sort of education and training in administrative methods and most knew each other through their school-days or from their subsequent civil service or teaching careers. Former prime minister Mamadou Dia has described vividly the impression made upon him and his fellow students by the teachers at the *Ecole Régionale*, in Diourbel, and the *Ecole Normale William Ponty*, at that time on the island of Gorée, and the lifelong friendships he made there. The important political consequences of those friendships became clear when, together with his friend, Senghor, Dia sought to build up a nation-wide political party in the late 1940s.[3]

Although the official language of the government remained French, the fact that many of the African agents of the government were Wolof speakers meant that the Wolof language spread easily and without compulsion through the country, rather as the Swahili agents of the Germans spread the use of KiSwahili throughout German East Africa – now Tanzania. As has already been suggested, the Wolof, unlike the Ganda, had no strong sense of national identity to divide them instinctively from the rest of the country. Equally important was the role of the *marabouts* who, in most instances, helped to overcome the people's wariness of officials sent from outside the district. Today, although other languages still flourish, it is claimed that 80 per cent of the population can speak Wolof.

One further contribution to the future unity of Senegal was made by the French when they introduced a political system based on their own metropolitan model. From 1920, Senegal had two councils: a General Council which dealt only with the affairs of the four communes of St Louis, Dakar, Gorée, and Rufisque; and a Colonial Council which dealt with the rest of the country. The right to elect members of these councils was limited to the residents of the communes and to people upon whom the rights of French citizenship had been conferred, but it meant that a tradition of political thought which transcended ethnic or cultural boundaries had become firmly established among the future African political leaders long before independence.

The involvement of the rest of the peoples of Senegal in the political arena was primarily the work of Leopold Senghor and, in the earlier years, of his colleague, Mamadou Dia. Although citizens of the four communes had been entitled to elect a deputy to sit in the French Assembly in Paris since the middle of the nineteenth century, and since 1914 the deputy had always been a black African, it was not until 1946 that the electorate was extended to include non-citizens. In 1946, Lamine Guèye, who was himself a deputy from 1945 to 1951, joined with the deputies of other African countries to persuade France to abolish the distinction between citizens and subjects. The former Sengalese subjects then acquired the right to elect a second deputy while the citizens of the communes continued to elect the first deputy.

Leopold Senghor, Senegal's leading academic, had abandoned his teaching career for a life in politics and first stood for office in 1945. Having been born outside the privileged communes he was able to appeal to the electorate – not only because of the great prestige his intellectual achievements gave him, but also because he understood the needs and aspirations of those who were only subjects. Hitherto he had worked in close collaboration with Guèye, but the latter, who, in the late 1930s, had pioneered the involvement of educated non-citizens in Senegalese politics, came to be looked upon by the rural population as the champion of the privileged electorates of the communes. For the rural voters, who greatly outnumbered the inhabitants of the communes, Senghor was the obvious spokesman. Although opposed by Guèye, who had become jealous of his popularity, Senghor was elected second deputy in 1947.[4] He then broke with Guèye's socialist party to set up his own *Bloc Démocratique Sénégalais* (BDS). He still maintained his belief in socialism, but in an African version of it, which drew its strength from traditional African customs and communal responsibilities, and which seemed to him more relevant to the African context than did the European socialism of Guèye. Such an ideology would also contribute to the political implementation of the doctrine of *négritude* which Senghor had helped to formulate and which proclaimed the importance of traditional African culture.

Senghor's socialism was not a divisive movement, because it emphasized qualities believed to be shared by all Africans rather than drawing attention to the wide range of differing cultures which existed in Africa. It was an approach which greatly appealed to the former subjects of Senegal; and Senghor, with Dia, toured the country to persuade teachers, trade union leaders and other educated Africans to take the lead in building up local units of the BDS in areas where they were working. Senghor also paid particular attention to relations with Muslim leaders. Though himself a Roman Catholic, he was unable to convince the *marabouts* that their interests and those of their followers would be better served by the BDS than by the town-based socialism of Guèye. The BDS also turned its attention to rousing the young people who had previously been indifferent to politics.[5] In 1949 the party won its first electoral victory in a contest for a seat on the General Council.

In the 1950s, the BDS rapidly gained an ascendancy over Guèye's party because of its appeal to former subjects. In 1957 it scored a triumphant victory in the territorial elections, the first to be held under the *loi-cadre* of 1956 which authorized the setting up of an African-controlled government. In the following year the rival parties merged to form the *Union Progressiste Sénégalaise* (UPS). Then, in May 1958, Senghor was faced by the choice offered by President de Gaulle of independence for Senegal, total integration with France, or self-government within a new French community. His decision to choose the third option, in the face of strong opposition from trade unionists and the more radical elements of his own party, was a clear indication that he knew where his most influential supporters were to be found. In the countryside, the Muslim leaders feared the challenge to their authority which could arise if the radicals were to triumph, and Senghor knew he must retain their loyalty if he wished to keep the mass of the population on his side. The majority of the people, too, favoured a transfer of power to African hands by whatever means would prove least disruptive to their way of life while at the same time offering the greatest hope of prosperity in the future. To them, Senghor seemed the natural heir to French authority, and his policies appeared to offer the surest prospect of retaining French assistance.

Though the more left-wing members of the party then quitted the UPS, they did so on ideological rather than on regional or ethnic grounds – being of the opinion that Senegal should try to become self-sufficient. A year later, however, when the complete independence of Senegal was negotiated, Senghor achieved a double triumph. In the first place, he strengthened his hold upon the allegiance of the *marabouts* still further by retaining close economic and political ties with France. The *marabouts'* income from ground-nuts was assured and they were content that they were not to be governed by men committed to violent change. At the same time, the radicals' demand for independence had been satisfied. Thus was Senghor able to become president of a united country.

To retain that unity, he was prepared even to act against his prime minister and friend, Mamadou Dia, when the latter decided in 1962 to introduce measures to socialize the economy and to reduce Senegal's economic dependence upon France.[6] Two conclusions could be drawn from this brief contest. First, it was clear that the position of Senghor was virtually unassailable. Once again he had proved that although he was a Roman Catholic his more conservative policies had a greater attraction for the Muslim leaders, who controlled a large proportion of the electorate, than had the more radical economic programme proposed even by as devout a Muslim as Dia. Second, the important role which the army could play was clearly demonstrated, because Senghor's triumph had, without question, owed a great deal to the army's support. Most of the senior officers had been trained in France and had served in the French army. In the event of a dispute, their sympathies clearly lay with the person who sought closer links with France.

This attitude among the army officers was reaffirmed on later occasions when Senghor's authority was challenged, notably in 1968 when the trade unions organized strikes to persuade the government to speed up the Africanization of the economy. Senghor did not hesitate to use force to end the strikes, but, as was to be his wont, having asserted his authority he took steps to meet his critics' demands. He showed his strength in similar fashion when students called for increased grants and the introduction of a higher proportion of African lecturers into the university. Again he made concessions after he had secured his position. Students were constantly among the main critics of the government, and university professors often became leaders of opposition parties. In 1968 a student strike which started as a protest against inadequate grants, proved, in reality, to be an expression of general discontent voiced in the only way possible in the absence of official opposition parties, all of which had either been banned by that time or else incorporated into the UPS. Once more, Senghor did not hesitate to call upon the army to arrest the ringleaders and to expel the students from the campus.

The disappearance of opposition parties meant that the UPS was in an unchallenged position to exercise patronage of every kind throughout the whole country. Every hope of advancement or preferment rested with the government, and in a land where economic opportunities were so severely restricted a bureaucratic appointment offered comparative riches to the recipient. As in other African countries, this proved to be a unifying factor of paramount importance. It was, therefore, an indication of Senghor's complete confidence in the support he commanded that in 1974 he was prepared to give recognition to the *Parti Démocratique Sénégalais* (PDS), led by the experienced politician Abdoulaye Wade. It was a sign, too, of Senghor's academic delight in organized argument that in 1976 he decided to amend the constitution in order to admit a third party to the political arena. The character of the opposition he was prepared to countenance was also academic, but in the more pejorative sense of the word, for he insisted that the new party should profess a Marxist–Leninist ideology while Wade's party must adopt a liberal programme. His own party then changed its name to *Parti Socialist* (PS) to emphasize its role as the upholder of a democratic socialist philosophy. Senghor also retained the right to determine whether or not the parties were pursuing their predetermined ideologies correctly and to impose sanctions if they failed to do so. Bound by such restrictions, the opposition parties could scarcely hope to mount a serious attack on the PS.

Various suggestions have been made to explain why Senghor should have gone to such lengths to recreate an opposition movement, and particularly one with such palpably false credentials.[7] The reason almost certainly was that the president felt the need for the intellectual stimulus of criticism, but it must not pose a serious threat to the unity of the country. It was essential, too, that behind the contrived façade of political dialectic he should still be able to rely upon those elements in the population which had supported him so loyally – the army, the civil service, the French and Senegalese business communities, and the religious leaders.

Senghor's decision to retire at the end of 1980 came as a shock to the whole country. The constitution stated that he should be succeeded by the prime minister, who would hold office as president until the next elections were held. But the prime minister in 1980, Abdou Diouf, seemed scarcely the man to aspire to the charismatic role played by Senghor – a role which had seemed vital to the country's continuing stability. The retiring president had projected himself as a liberal intellectual, the spokesman for black culture and for the struggling Third World. Though few of his people had been uncomfortably conscious of it, he had, in fact, pursued a rather different policy in practice. He had been punctilious in his behaviour towards the French, and in particular in his dealings with French capital upon which he acknowledged that Senegal relied heavily. Towards his own people his manner had been autocratic. The country's economy, its culture, and its institutions had all been moulded by him to his own pattern. Intellectuals, religious leaders, and politicians had all become accustomed to serving him.

Diouf, a very able young technocrat – one of the many upon whom Senghor had come increasingly to rely – had been greatly over-shadowed by his mentor. He had loyally carried out the president's policies while giving no indication of possessing any marked leader-ship qualities. His performance as interim president from 1981 to 1983 only seemed to confirm the greyness of his personality, to the extent that there were some who were bold enough to challenge his automatic right to succeed Senghor. But Diouf, undaunted, placed heavy reliance on the old leaders of the party, the men who had built up the almost unassailable authority of the PS in the regions. They, for their part, were content to exercise the influence which Senghor, through main-taining a strict control, had allowed them to enjoy. With their backing, Diouf was able to handle further student unrest in 1981 in the approved Senghor fashion. He used force to put an end to the demon-strations, then instituted an investigation into the reasons for the protest after which he made important concessions to the students' demands. He then took a more positive step towards winning public favour when he attended an Islamic conference in Saudia Arabia and established himself as the spokesman for the small, French-speaking West African states. He also obtained financial aid from both Saudia Arabia and Iraq to develop the Senegal River basin. In 1982 he paid a second visit to Saudia Arabia, and in so doing consolidated the support he had won among the religious leaders in Senegal.[8]

The presidential and parliamentary elections of 1983 brought a marked change in Diouf's behaviour. Although there were complaints of vote rigging there can be no doubt about the strength of the support the president could command in the country and that his victory cannot be questioned on grounds of electoral malpractice. The *marabouts* had given him their unanimous support and that meant that the whole of the Muslim population was on his side. Encouraged by his victory, Diouf at once set about shedding those members of the old guard who might threaten his supremacy. He was able to do this by carefully constructing his government so as to include representa-tives of every other significant interest.[9] He also abolished the office of prime minister, lest it should become a rival centre of authority, even though, at the time, it was held by a lifelong friend. In addition, the powerful foreign minister, Mustapha Niasse, was replaced, and he quitted politics for a lucrative post in the financial world. For the rest, the president made a point of choosing ministers of ability, but he also weighted the balance slightly to the political Left, so that the main challenge from outside the government, which also came from the Left, was more than adequately matched within his cabinet – where its protagonists received better rewards but were kept under closer surveillance. Diouf also gave full representation to the trade unions and to the various regions into which the country was divided. Once again official patronage was skilfully deployed to maintain unity.

Yet Diouf was fully aware of the fragile nature of democracy in Senegal and that it could easily crack under the pressure of the economic difficulties which the country had to face. Those difficulties arose mainly from Senegal's acute lack of resources, amplified in recent years by long periods of drought which have contributed to the southward advance of the desert. But dedicated socialist opposition groups were not averse from attempting to persuade the people that they were caused by the mixed economy which the government had espoused and which had made too many concessions to French and American capitalists instead of holding firm to the socialism which the governing party professed. In his New Year message to the country in 1985, Diouf deemed it necessary to warn the people of the hardship and austerity which faced them. In order to obtain an eighteen-month loan agreement at the end of the previous year, his government had had to give in to pressure from the IMF to increase the price of rice. Diouf hoped that the increase would encourage people to grow more rice and other cereals in Senegal, but he knew that his action would stir up discontent which the opposition parties would use to their advantage. Indeed, two of those parties at once denounced the measure, but, fortunately for Diouf, they were only very small, and the absence of Wade in Paris left the more dangerous PDS unable to pounce at the crucial moment. Two attempts by students to organize protest meetings on the university campus in Dakar were stopped by the authorities, and it is some indication of the ineffectiveness of the opposition groups that this was the only serious demonstration against the price increase. It was with some relief that the president was able to announce a reduction in prices three years later.

Diouf was also reassured by the confidence shown in his policies by the principal aid donors, who were impressed by the determination with which he appeared to be tackling the country's problems. His reward came when 1985 proved to be a year of relative plenty. After ten years of drought there was an excellent harvest. Food became available in abundance, partly because of an improved rainfall but also as a result of the efforts made by the growers themselves and because of the government's New Agricultural Policy which had made possible the widespread distribution of seed and fertilizers to farmers. Simultaneously, and again spurred on by the IMF and the World Bank, Diouf launched a campaign to encourage the growers to organize themselves in order to market their crops, rather than waiting for the state to act on their behalf. He was conscious that the maintenance of an inflated bureaucracy was proving too heavy a burden for the country to bear and, if he could encourage more private initiatives, he felt he could reduce that burden. Adopting President Mitterrand's slogan 'less of the state, but the best of the state' he closed a number of para-statal bodies in the agricultural sector.

In parallel with these reforms in the rural areas, Diouf introduced his New Industrial Policy — which envisaged that Senegalese businesses should become more competitive in the home market and more vigorous in producing goods for export. It was a programme which, he hoped, would win the support of the population in general because, if it was successful, they would have to pay less for both home-produced and imported goods. It was also intended to give encouragement to foreign investors without penalizing Senegalese businessmen. But, inevitably, it provided an opportunity for the opposition parties to denounce the government's increasing reliance upon external aid. Abdoulaye Bathily, secretary-general of one of the smaller opposition parties, claimed that the policy was even bad for the governing party itself because it involved the country in such heavy external debt payments that nothing was left to oil the wheels of patronage.[10] Yet he had to admit that Senegalese traders were getting favourable treatment in New York because of the government's support for US policies.

Bathily came closer to his target when he pointed to the crisis in the educational world. His accusation that Diouf had shelved the reform programme which had been agreed in 1981 because the USA and IMF had decided that the cost of education must be cut was not, however, a wholly accurate diagnosis of the reason for the malaise. More serious was the sharp reduction in the opportunities for employment open to that very sector of the population which was, traditionally, most critical of official policies. Initially, independence had widened the scope of educated young people seeking stimulating and gainful employment. The higher reaches of the civil service had become accessible to a degree never previously experienced. Particularly after Diouf's 1981 educational reforms, there had been many new openings in the teaching profession as Frenchmen were replaced by Senegalese nationals. There were opportunities, too, for employment with international agencies and with both foreign and internal business enterprises as a result of extensive Africanization programmes. But these opportunities were not limitless, and, as the vacancies became filled, newer generations of graduates found it increasingly difficult to find satisfactory employment. Recent efforts by the government to cut back the civil service for the sake of economy exacerbated the problem and aroused both discontent and understandable fear. It is not surprising that these disgruntled elements among the better-educated sections of the population should be tempted to join the opposition parties. But, although those parties became ever more vocal in their criticisms of the government, their challenge did not become more effective.

Another outlet for the discontent of students was to be found in religion. Men who were denied the opportunity to achieve distinction in the public service or in the commercial world might seek fulfilment in devotion to religion. Herein might be found the seeds of an Islamic fundamentalist movement like those that had occurred in a number of countries in other parts of Africa and the Middle East. Against such a possibility were ranged the vested interests of the brotherhoods, themselves revolutionary bodies in their time but now anxious to preserve the privileged status acquired under French rule and maintained by Senghor after independence. It was as vital for them to support stable government as it was for Diouf to guarantee them their security. This explains the president's tireless endeavours to demonstrate publicly his devotion to Islam and to establish himself as the political leader of West African Muslims.

It was from the position of relative strength which Diouf had both inherited and developed – through contacts with a wide range of influential bodies inside and outside Senegal – that he was able to handle with such firmness the student demonstrations which took place early in 1987. It was with equal firmness, too, that he dealt with the police strike which followed shortly afterwards in April. He was helped in that instance by the fact that the immediate cause of the strike – the disciplining of a number of police officers found guilty of torturing an arrested criminal – could scarcely be expected to arouse public sympathy for the police. Nevertheless, although the gendarmes moved in efficiently to carry out the duties of more than 6,000 police officers dimissed by Diouf, it was a difficult moment for the government.

In that critical instant another important figure emerged from the place he had previously occupied in the president's shadow. Jean Collin, a French-born, naturalized Senegalese who was secretary-general in the president's office, proved himself to be the power that many had for long believed him to be. Collin had held many offices in his time, but none more important than the one he held in 1987. Generally acknowledged to be wholly incorruptible in a society where corruption was far from rare, wholly devoted to the well-being of his adopted country and totally committed to upholding the government, he was a man of towering influence in a post from which he could control virtually every aspect of government activity. Every communication with the president was channelled through Collin's office. Little was done by any official without his knowledge. The police force was believed to be his own creation during his years as interior minister under Senghor. Now, in the moment of crisis, he returned to the same ministry and reorganized the force while reducing it in size, after which he handed over the task of overseeing the changes to one of his own protégés, André Sonko.[11]

With the presidential and parliamentary elections in the offing, no prospective support could be ignored — least of all that of the Muslim leaders. Diouf's visit to Egypt, Kuwait, and Saudi Arabia to discuss arrangements for an Islamic summit meeting — to which Senegal hoped to act as host in 1990 — was a well-timed move, guaranteed to arouse enthusiasm among Senegal's Muslims. His reward for this, and for the support he had constantly given to the commercial activities of the Muslim leaders, was a call from the khalif-general of the *Mourides* during his annual pilgrimage to the holy city of Touba, urging all his followers to support Diouf's candidature for the presidency. Although the leader of the *Tijaniyya* brotherhood did not make such an overt appeal, it was generally believed that he, too, requested his people to vote in the same way. In spite of the structural divisions between the brotherhoods, Islam represented a shared communal identity of the greatest importance for 90 per cent of Senegal's population. It was noteworthy that the leaders and members of the *Tijaniyyas* and *Mourides* were invited to attend the annual celebrations organized by the *Qadriyya* brotherhood in Dakar on 7 March 1987.[12] Against such solidarity among the established Muslim authorities, the young, would-be fundamentalists could not hope to make any significant advance.[13] The one factor which might operate in their favour was the tightness of the economic situation which, if it were to become more serious, might undermine the people's confidence in the government. But even in that area the position of the government was eased in November 1987, when the Paris Club showed its confidence in Diouf's leadership by agreeing to reschedule part of Senegal's debt.

In the light of all these developments, Diouf was able to contemplate the presidential and parliamentary elections of February 1988 with confidence, knowing that the incumbency factor weighed heavily in his favour. He knew that the religious establishment was on his side, and that the foreign countries, particularly France and the USA, which had a significant stake in the country wanted him to succeed – in order to ensure stability and to guarantee the protection of their interests. The bureaucracy, too, that privileged elite which administered the country's affairs and controlled an important section of its patronage, was working for him to defend its own position. Such unity of purpose was difficult to challenge. Why, then, did the president embark upon an extensive tour of the country in 1987, paying particular attention to the more remote districts, and stressing wherever he went the importance of unity in diversity?

The explanation is not far to seek. Diouf recognized that along the country's borders there still persisted feelings of ethnic difference which, if manipulated by his political opponents, might prove to be the one immediately effective focus of dissatisfaction. Casamance, for example, in the extreme south and separated from the rest of Senegal by the Gambia River, was in every way an exception to the rule of unity which the government was striving to maintain. The Diola who lived there had never wholly accepted the authority of the central government, and Islam had made little progress among them. In the eastern part of the region, the majority of the population was animist. Nearer the coast, the Portuguese, centuries earlier, had made numerous conversions to Christianity and that tradition lived on. The Diola also resented Wolof domination of the senior posts in the local bureaucracy, a relic of the French system of training Senegalese administrators. As dessication spread in the northern parts of the country, causing people to go in search of more fertile land elsewhere, they feared Wolof expansion into their territory. For them, as for most Africans, land was not only a source of wealth. It was part of their cultural heritage, inherited from their ancestors and held in trust for their descendants. They consequently opposed the declaration that all land belonged to the state and were incensed by Diouf's proposal to create state farms in their region.

In an attempt to establish a closer accord with these distrustful people, the Senegalese government tried to create a confederal relationship with the intervening state of Gambia. The move met with limited success, and the Casamance remained sullenly aloof. Diouf had also made a point of ensuring full representation for the region in his cabinet after the reforms of 1983, but the Diola still believed they were being subjected to unfavourable discrimination. If the central government had, indeed, neglected Casamance, any such default was due to the remoteness of the district and the physical difficulties involved in meeting the people's needs. Nevertheless, in the prevailing atmosphere of suspicion, the separatist movement which was growing up in the Casamance quickly took upon itself an ethnic character even though its fundamental motivation was economic.

Not every inhabitant of the region, whether Diola or a member of another ethnic group, supported the movement, but so strong did it become that the government was compelled to take action to control it. In January 1984 a peaceful march was organized in the town of Ziguinchor where there was a large Christian minority. When the marchers refused to halt on the orders of officials, government forces opened fire and many of the demonstrators were killed. This led to reprisals from both sides. As a result, a powerful sense of cultural identity developed in lower Casamance – spontaneously and with little organized leadership as befitted a people who had never relished centralized control. Nevertheless, a form of tribalism began to emerge and manifested itself in a move to break the links with Senegal and to join forces with other Diola in neighbouring Equatorial Guinea. It was an unpromising solution to an intractable problem, though it was hoped that, by demonstrating tribal solidarity, help which Senegal had been unable to provide would be attracted to the region from other quarters. Needless to say, the Senegalese government did not take kindly to the idea, and it became especially wary when Wade returned from a lengthy stay in Paris towards the end of 1987 and visited Casamance in the hope of using local feelings of neglect to win support for his own campaign. Diouf immediately countered by carrying out a similar tour.

It was to prevent the development of similar separatist movements in other outlying areas, and their exploitation by his political opponents, that the president took such pains to woo the border regions. It was fortunate for him that in Senegal any latent tribalism was, in the geographical sense, peripheral, and therefore less likely to affect the rest of the country. Nevertheless, he had no desire to take unnecessary risks. So he visisted the Toucoulor who, like the Diola, had been arbitrarily separated from their ethnic fellows by the boundaries laid down by Europeans. Those living in Senegal still had strong feelings of affinity with the Toucoulor living north of the Senegal River in Mauritania. Like the Diola, too, they felt excluded from the mainstream of Senegalese life, because communications with the rest of the country were poor and their main link with the outside world was the river itself rather than any man-made system.

Diouf developed his campaign along two lines. First he praised the

Toucoulor for the richness of their Islamic heritage, from which, he said, had sprung many of the country's most notable religious leaders. This distinctive tradition, if correctly channelled under the direction of his government, could continue as a source of strength to the whole of Senegal. Second, and in return, he promised that the government would provide valuable benefits for the Fleuve region. The Toucoulor had, the president acknowledged, suffered a measure of neglect in the past, but by united effort all this could be changed. There would be new channels of communication to put an end to the district's isolation. The telephonic system would be improved. Better radio and television reception would be provided. New roads would link the region with the country's main arterial system. There was an emergency plan to drill more boreholes and to dig more wells to increase the water supply. Most important of all, the new dam under construction at Diama on the Senegal River would provide sufficient irrigation to bring 240,000 hectares of land into production. It was a reassuring statement, but the Toucoulor were not wholly convinced by it. They were particularly worried by the president's enthusiastic reference to the new approach to cultivation which the construction of the barrage would make possible. Essentially conservative, the Toucoulor relied upon traditional farming methods to guarantee their security. In advocating novelty, Diouf had miscalculated badly, for the Toucoulor were also afraid that with the introduction of new methods would come an influx of speculators, anxious to exploit traditionally owned land for their own, alien purposes.

Yet the president's visit to the Fleuve region was not wholly wasted, for he had impressed the people there by insisting that whatever neglect they had suffered in the past was due to their remoteness and had no origin in ethnic differences. He therefore pursued a similar line with the Malinke of the south-east, in the department of Kedougou, to whom he also spoke of the manner in which their unique traditional culture had made a distinctive contribution to the communal well-being of the country, and again he stressed the mutual benefits which would accrue to all those participating in their particular fashion in the building of a nation.

Diouf's concern to win the support of these outlying districts did not arise entirely from his fear of his rivals' political opportunism. No part of Senegal, however distant from the capital, was as isolated as might appear from the perusal of a map. Muslim communities in particular had a long tradition of itinerant scholarship which involved students in travelling considerable distances in search of teachers. As a result, in every district there was an influential element whose horizons extended far beyond the limits of their own region. Artisans, too, had travelled from town to town to pursue their crafts more profitably, often returning to their homes speaking Wolof and thinking of themselves as part of a wider community of craftsmen. Such people could be both a source of strength to the central government or, if dissatisfied, could become the leaders of dissident movements which, though based in the outlying districts, might well impinge seriously upon the country's heartland. Even in Casamance, where Islam had made little headway and where geography made the development of a separatist movement more feasible than among the Toucoulor, links with Dakar were strong.

Diouf's appeal to the inhabitants of St Louis and to the people of Kayor, near the capital, was based upon different premises. Though to the former he spoke of the leading role their forefathers had played in establishing Senegal's administrative system in the days when their city had been the country's capital, and to the latter he referred to the fight of their former ruler, Lat Dior, against French aggression, he did not do this from any fear of tribal separatism. There was no likelihood that either of these regions would feel too remote from the centre to attract attention. Diouf's concern arose from his anxiety lest his party should not be alert to the challenge which the opposition could offer in urban areas where educated, and potentially disillusioned, people were more numerous. Though the PS had its share of intellectuals, the fiercest opposition to the government was usually to be found among the better-educated section of the community.

It is, to some extent, a relic of Senghor's own academic approach to politics that opposition in Senegal tends to take the form of ideological disputation instead of producing an effective organization capable of challenging the government. This is reflected in the proliferation of political parties since 1981, which Diouf had done nothing to discourage. Indeed, the more numerous they are the less likelihood is there that they can mount an alternative government. All the parties are of the Left and differ only in the emphasis they put upon socialist or Marxist−Leninist principles. Most reflect the intellectual idiosyncracies of their leaders, and on that account, if no other, are unlikely to coalesce into an effective opposition party − even if that were permitted by law, which it is not. None of the parties has any ethnic or even regional affiliation, though any one of them would be ready to take advantage of local disaffection. All are small, and only Abdoulaye Wade's PDS can lay any claim to being a nation-wide party.

Despite the serious manner in which Diouf prepared for the 1988 elections, his confidence in the prospects of success seemed justified, and was reflected not only in his rejection of Wade's call for electoral reform but also in his readiness to hand over the conduct and supervision of the elections to the supreme court – a more patently neutral body than the ministry of the interior which had previously performed those functions. Wade, for his part, and the whole PDS – although clearly the only opposition group likely to attract any notable following – were beginning to suffer from the symptoms of depression commonly felt by those who are constantly seen as outsiders. The rhetoric in which Wade increasingly indulged was largely the product of despair. There was little substance in his accusations of corrupt dealings by the government in the run-up to the elections, because Diouf felt too secure to need to resort to such practices.

Wade might have been on stronger ground if he had drawn attention to the difficulty which the president experienced in controlling the local branches of the PS – which were not averse to using violent or dishonest methods against their opponents. His declaration in November 1987 that, if there were any election-rigging or violation of the popular will, his party would physically oppose the formation of the government and that he himself would be prepared to form his own government, caused a dangerous heightening in the tension which was already manifesting itself as the elections drew near. When he denounced the polls as a masquerade and declared as ridiculous the unofficial announcement that 'Diouf had won an easy victory', he fuelled the rivalry which had already produced violence between supporters of the contending parties. Diouf's declaration of a state of emergency in Dakar, and the arrest of Wade and several other members of the opposition – which in other circumstances might have aroused widespread resentment – was now received with some degree of resignation. Only the ever-volatile students, many of whom had already declared their allegiance to Wade simply because he opposed the government, were active in his support. They, however, were very firmly dealt with, although Diouf admitted that there had been a regrettable breakdown in communication between the government and the young people of the country.

The 1988 elections confirmed the solidity of the ground on which the government stood, in spite of a high proportion of abstentions among the potential voters. According to official sources, Wade polled only 26 per cent of the votes cast in the presidential election to Diouf's 73 per cent. The PDS and PS had similar results in the elections to the national assembly. Both these results were challenged by Wade who claimed that it was he, not Diouf, who had been elected, and there is little doubt that he had picked up some support in disaffected rural areas. That support, because of its geographical location, was likely to have been of an ethnic nature, but the disaffection which lay behind it was the result of regional problems rather than arising from ethnic loyalty, and it counted for little against the strength of feeling which carried the PS to victory. Some candidates from every party were successful in their own ethnic areas, but in Senegal more than in virtually any other African country it was possible for a person to build a career in a region other than the one in which he was born and had grown up, and to create a political opening for himself in so doing. Neither Wade nor Diouf could hope to play the ethnic card to a degree which might seriously affect the result unless the two sides were very closely balanced. The main area in which opposition candidates might hope for support was, in fact, in the towns – where ethnic loyalties were less important, but where poverty and riches were to be found more blatantly side by side and discontent might be more easily aroused. Yet, even in urban areas, the power of the government made a strong breakaway movement improbable. The government still controlled the road to preferment, and against those who had little hope of advancing along that road it controlled the forces of law and order to suppress disruption.

One question mark hangs delicately over the government's head. Can it continue indefinitely to rely upon the loyalty of the army? While the senior officers unhesitatingly support the government, there is always the possibility that the national pride of the younger officers might make them resent the country's overt dependence upon outside support. The presence, unobtrusive though it may be, of French troops strategically located near Dakar airport might appear to these young men as a threat to their own position. That both the USA and France look upon Senegal as a centre of political and economic stability in the fluctuating sea of West African affairs, and mean to keep it so in defence of their own interests, could be a source of unity or of disruption. It could help to unite Senegal so long as outside help is clearly seen to benefit the country. On the other hand, it could encourage disruption if the economic situation were to become so bad that opposition parties were able to convince the people that their sufferings were due to foreign intervention.

It is to the government's advantage that, while independence from foreign control is a proud slogan wherewith to win popular support and to challenge the party in power, the sheer need to survive is likely to dissuade more hard-headed people from casually rejecting proffered assistance. So many interests are vested in the protection of the status quo that only a total breakdown in the economy is likely to disrupt it. The demand for *sopi* – the Wolof word for 'change' – is the sort of cry which stirs the blood of the young but only arouses wariness among those who are benefiting from the existing system. Certainly there is little evidence that tribalism is likely to create any serious difficulties. Opposition parties might, in desperation, look to regional problems as a source of support, but neither tribalism nor ethnic loyalties are likely to provide them with any real hope of seizing power. Senegal's history has shown that a European educational system has been able to form a working alliance with both a semi-indigenous religion and a variety of genuine indigenous cultures to create a unity of purpose which will not easily be destroyed, though it may well be shaken in such a way as to ensure that it does not become fossilized. That is as Senghor would have wished. Casamance remains the exception to this generalization. There, tribalism offers no satisfactory solution to the problems of the Diola, but it remains a problem, if no more, for the government of Senegal.

7 Guinea: united against the world

Probably more than any other African country, the former French dependency of Guinea owes its present form to the influence of one man. Four years after his death, and in spite of a military coup which overthrew those of his supporters who sought to perpetuate his ideals, Ahmed Sékou-Touré's shadow still hangs over the country. For many, this means that a nation has come into being and will triumph over the obstacles put in its way by enemies both at home and abroad. For others, it is a threat to every effort to utilize freely the natural resources with which Guinea is generously endowed in order to create a prosperous society.

From the beginning of his career – initially as a trade-union leader – Sékou-Touré's principal objective was to restore the dignity of the African people which, he believed, had been gravely distorted by the influence of Europe. His aim was not restricted to his own ethnic group, the Malinke, or even to the French dependency of Guinea. It embraced the whole of French West Africa, and he was convinced that the African peoples must unite to present their case effectively to their French overlords if they were ever to achieve that aim. He himself co-operated closely with the *Rassemblement Démocratique Africain* (RDA), founded by Félix Houphouët-Boigny of the Ivory Coast, to translate the pious rhetoric of the French *loi-cadre* of 1946 into genuine African participation in the control of West African affairs. To that end, too, he became the driving force behind the formation of the *Confédération Générale des Travailleurs Africains* in 1956 which, in the following January, joined with a number of other unions to form the *Union Générale des Travailleurs d'Afrique Noir*.

That Sékou-Touré became associated with the attempt to create a national identity for Guinea alone was due to a quirk of fortune, and he did not accept that task wholeheartedly until compelled to do so by force of circumstances. Two years after the second *loi-cadre* of 1956

135

abolished the French West African Federation, General de Gaulle decided to create a new French community which individual dependencies would be invited to join. Sékou-Touré was in favour of joining the new community, but only if it could be done in three stages. First, the territories must be given their independence. Next, they should be given the opportunity to form a West African federation if they wished to do so. Only then, at the third stage, should the federation, as a single unit, consider whether it wished to join a community in partnership with France. Under this plan, the initiative would come from both sides, and the African peoples would not simply be required to accept terms laid down by France. By forming a West African federation before joining the community, the Africans would have a better opportunity of dealing on equal terms with France. When these preconditions were rejected, Sékou-Touré turned down de Gaulle's offer, though not with the intention of isolating Guinea from the other West African territories. That that was in fact the outcome was largely due to a clash of personalities. Sékou-Touré's pride could not accept a future in which Guinea remained subservient to France – which he believed would be the case if his country joined the proposed community on de Gaulle's terms. Given that response, the equally proud French president immediately severed all links with France's former dependency. It was a petulant reaction, unworthy of the leader of a great nation.

Sékou-Touré had made a brave if naïve gesture on behalf of the African peoples, and Guinea was confronted with grave problems. For what were primarily economic reasons, the other West African dependencies decided that they could not support him. Suddenly and unexpectedly, Guinea became both independent and isolated from its neighbours. It was a disturbing setback, although for a time Sékou-Touré did not believe it to be irreversible. But de Gaulle's implacable hostility to any *rapprochement*, and the coolness of other western powers, forced him to recognize that Guinea must work out its own destiny. Thus, fortuitously, was Sékou-Touré faced with the task of creating a nation from what was widely acknowledged to be one of the least united of all the countries arbitrarily created by the imperial powers. Here, if anywhere, would be put to the test the viability of a country which had never been planned to stand alone. It was a challenge which he took up courageously, but with neither the expertise nor the generous external help needed to make his undertaking a success.

Geographically, ethnically, historically, and politically, the peoples of Guinea differed widely. During nearly 80 years of conquest, collaboration, and domination, the French had tried to impose at least a uniform system of administration. Their aim had been to promote the interests of a handful of French traders and settlers who were seeking, somewhat peripherally, to exploit the country's resources. But they had shown little interest in, and had made no attempt to understand, the differing cultural traditions of the peoples they incorporated in their Guinean dependency. The successive policies of assimilation and association, so seriously bruited in the metropolis, made little impact upon the practice of French administrators in Guinea, save where expediency and the lack of European manpower made it necessary to make use of them. Those same administrators did all in their power to destroy traditional institutions, but the lack of European supervisors, and the hostility aroused by the oppressive methods of French officials and their African collaborators, served ultimately to strengthen the people's attachment to their traditional loyalties.

The pastoral Fulani, for example, had created an Islamic empire on the plateau of Futa Jallon on the foundations of an existing hierarchical society in the early eighteenth century. In many instances, the religious leaders of the empire had deemed it wise to co-operate with the French in the early days of French expansion in Guinea. But co-operation turned to hostility and hatred when the French changed their approach and tried to wipe out every vestige of traditional authority. The Malinke of the north-eastern savannah – traditionally the region's foremost traders and farmers – had been more recently united under the leadership of the able military adventurer, Samory, but their pride in the new empire and their loyalty to its leader were strong and they deeply resented their conquest by the French in 1898. Their hostility became more marked when their imperial achievements were rejected by their new rulers and French administration was arbitrarily introduced. The less united peoples of the forests and mountains of the south-east, some of whom had successfully resisted the attacks of Samory, also mounted a stout opposition to the French. But they, like their stronger neighbours, were crushed into truculent submission, though sometimes they were able to seek sanctuary over the largely notional, but in this instance extremely useful, boundary with Liberia. The Sousou had been the first to come under French rule, not because of any failure to oppose their conquerors, but because, on the coast – where the Sousou were located – the French were operating from bases easily supplied by their navy and their trading ships, and their power was consequently irresistable.

Until the end of the Second World War, opposition to French

administration, though subdued, remained strong. Generally it was uncoordinated, operating on a local basis which, in the south-east, might with some justification be described as tribal. Elsewhere, local loyalties of a wider nature – based upon more recent political alignments and underlined by common ethnic and linguistic traditions – could well be thought of as national patriotism. Yet even in these larger polities, more ancient and more circumscribed loyalties still played an important role in the everyday life of the people.

The promise of a brighter future for Africans in the French dependencies, which was given during the Brazzaville Conference of 1944 under pressure from America, resulted in two new types of political development among the people of Guinea. In 1946 the *loi-cadre* gave the franchise to all adults, together with the right to elect deputies to the assembly in Paris and to a representative assembly in Guinea. This led some people to conclude that, if they co-operated with the French, a new era of prosperity would develop. The members of this group were drawn mainly from the relatively small, but now increasing, number of those who had received a measure of European-style education, and also from the much larger number of Fulani pastoralists and Malinke traders who hoped for the restoration of their former freedom to exploit opportunities for their own economic benefit. By contrast, the leaders of the potentially less prosperous peoples of the forest region, and those who had felt themselves to be exploited as poorly-paid labourers on French-owned plantations or in the towns, decided that their only hope lay in ridding the country of French rule, though not necessarily in dissolving all links with France. In response to these conflicting ideas, two types of political organization developed: one primarily of an ethnic character – at least among the Fulani; the other seeking initially to promote within Guinea the broader political objectives of the RDA.

Not surprisingly, the French administrators were better disposed towards the first of these two groups, represented most strikingly by the Fulani-dominated *Bloc Africain de Guinée* (BAG). The second, from which sprang the *Parti Démocratique de Guinée* (PDG), benefited from the leadership of Sékou-Touré, who was appointed secretary-general in 1952. Sékou-Touré had boundless energy, admirable powers of organization, and a deeply-rooted faith in himself and in the African people. Though the BAG was successful in the elections to the Guinean assembly in 1954, the pendulum thereafter began to swing in favour of the PDG. Support for the party grew rapidly, mainly as a result of tireless travelling and campaigning by Sékou-Touré, who planted party organizers in every village with the task of building up cells of supporters and of propagating party ideology. Spurning the divisive forces of ethnicity, Sékou-Touré himself stood for election as mayor of the Sousou-dominated town of Conakry, while four other members of his party were successful in local elections outside their own ethnic areas. In the same year, Sékou-Touré and another member of the PDG were elected as deputies to sit in the French assembly, after a fierce struggle with the BAG. In 1957 those initial successes were followed by the overwhelming victory of the PDG in the elections to the national assembly – of which, under the new *loi-cadre* of 1956, Sékou-Touré became vice-president. Under the new constitution, the president was still a Frenchman.

The popular appeal of the PDG lay primarily in its insistence upon the dignity of the African people, to which scant attention was paid by the French in spite of their assertions to the contrary. To ensure recognition of that dignity, the PDG maintained, called for a united endeavour by all Africans. Sectional interests, whether racial or economic, must be rejected. As a first step in that direction, the new PDG government abolished the office of chief which, it declared, was not an African title but one that had been introduced by the French, who had used it mainly as an instrument for the subjugation of the African people. In fact, at the lowest levels, the title had usually been bestowed upon traditional leaders, though it is true that they then became a part of the French administrative system. The new measure, therefore, not only struck a blow at alien domination but was also intended to eliminate what the PDG regarded as the divisive influence of local loyalties. The chiefs were to be replaced by the party organization which, it was claimed, would make known the wishes of all the people to the higher echelons of the party. In practice it acted mainly as the channel through which the party made known its ideology to the people, the ideology having been formulated in the first place by Sékou-Touré himself. In 1958 all party committees of an ethnic character were also forbidden, and a single youth movement, the *Jeunesse de la Révolution Démocratique Africaine* (JRDA), was created to embody all locally-based youth associations.

These changes were not received with universal enthusiasm, and the national elections held in March 1958 were accompanied by local acts of violence stimulated by ethnic loyalties. Nevertheless, hostility to French rule was so widely felt that Sékou-Touré was able to orchestrate it skilfully to overcome local differences and to win an overwhelming vote in favour of rejecting de Gaulle's offer of membership of the French community. By that time party membership had risen to 800,000, and after independence every adult automatically became a party member by payment of a subscription as part of his state tax.

Though anti-French feeling was dominant in 1958, Sékou-Touré was faced with a difficult task in maintaining the same high level of unity after independence, more particularly when France peremptorily severed all its links with its former dependency. If he were to be successful in spite of the divisions which had existed almost to the day of independence, he had to demonstrate that the interests of every section of the population would be fully promoted. But instead of looking first at the economy – upon which the satisfaction of those interests depended – he tried to achieve his objective by instilling into the population the doctrine of party supremacy. In the meantime, he hoped that any immediate economic strain might be dealt with by looking to Europe's eastern-bloc countries for assistance. It was a forlorn hope but, in the absence of qualified Guineans to carry out the task, he had at least the good sense to use French experts to draft a three-year economic plan to take effect from 1960.

Not everyone was convinced by PDG propaganda, and Sékou-Touré's ideology proved unacceptable to some sections of the population. Opposition took the form of an attempt in 1960 to overthrow the government and to re-establish links with France. Those involved were the people who had contrived to make a satisfactory living under French rule and who were afraid that their economic prospects would be endangered by the radical egalitarianism professed by the ruling party. They were assisted by French soldiers from Senegal and the Ivory Coast, but the attempt was defeated – largely because Sékou-Touré still retained the loyalty of an appreciable majority of the Guinean people. These latter the president was able to rally enthusiastically with the call to resist all threats to the country's independence from traitors within and from foreign neo-imperialists.

He was less able to deal with the flight of refugees seeking sanctuary in Senegal, in the Ivory Coast, or in France, which followed upon the failure of the coup. The exodus became a flood as the years went by and from the beginning the refugees were mainly drawn from those sections of the population possessing the qualifications, initiatives or experience which might have made a vital contribution to the country's future. This was made particularly clear by the outcome of what came to be described as the 'teachers' plot' of December 1961 This second attempted coup was attributed by the government to the machinations of some of the country's more left-wing teachers prompted by Soviet diplomats. Whether or not the charge was just the steps taken against both elements greatly increased the outward flow of educated Guineans and alienated the Eastern Bloc countries upon which the government had hoped to rely for assistance. Perhaps worst of all, it reduced the possibility that any informed internal criticism of Sékou-Touré's ideology might ever be heard. To emphasize still further the internal solidarity upon which he insisted, Sékou-Touré wrote in 1962:

> There is no room in the Republic of Guinea for the Malinke race, the Sousou race, the Foulah race, the Landouma or Kissi. . . . Thus, every youth of Guinea, every adult of Guinea asked about his race will reply that he is African.[1]

African not Guinean, it should be noted, and it is interesting that, even at this early stage, he was beginning to suspect that excessive local self-interest was acting as a source of discontent and disunity.

In fact, it was economic rather than ethnic problems which had so quickly intruded upon the euphoria engendered by apparent solidarity. The French economic planners employed by Sékou-Touré had wisely concentrated upon schemes for rural development, because of the fertility of the soil and the variety of climatic conditions which Guinea enjoyed. But because of the tardy introduction of education under French rule, and because many of those who had benefited from it had gone into exile, the country lacked the trained personnel to implement the plans proposed. Aid from the Soviet Union – upon which Sékou-Touré had hoped to rely as an interim measure – proved inadequate and often inappropriate. Emergency efforts to improve the situation only made things worse. Incompetent interference by the government in the activities of the farmers, and an attempt to impose a form of collectivism which was unacceptable to the farming community, aroused strong opposition. Once again it was some of the Fulani pastoralists who led the flight over the border into Senegal. An attempt to control prices in turn led to the sale of black-market produce across the frontier. Sadly, and not wholly accurately, Sékou-Touré deplored the persistence of regionalism and racialism. He would have been wiser to look more closely at the economic rather than at the ethnic preoccupations of the disgruntled sections of the population.

If there was discontent among the rural population, the people of the towns were no happier. Neglected by the government, traders and prospective small-scale industrialists had pursued their own ends as they saw fit. But in 1964 Sékou-Touré rounded on them, denouncing them as exploiters of the masses. In the following year, a 'traders' plot' was said to have been uncovered, and Sékou-Touré accused the commercial classes of intriguing with France to promote their own interests at the expense of the people of Guinea. Henceforward, he said, no trader or industrialist might hold office within the party. Once again he had rejected men of ability in favour of those who accepted his ideology without question. And once again many of those he had attacked fled the country.

Until 1967 Sékou-Touré never clearly formulated his political philosophy, and even after that date his policies were inclined to be idiosyncratic. In that year, however, he claimed to have adopted a policy of scientific socialism, distinct from the African socialism extolled by a number of African leaders which he himself dismissed as romantic idealism. He did not, in fact, pursue a consistently Marxist–Leninist line, but his public support for that doctrine aroused suspicion and hostility among important sections of the population and increased the enmity of the, by then, considerable contingent of influential Guinean exiles in other African countries and in Europe. Nor did it win support among the disapproving leaders of the western powers. On the other hand, it helped considerably to bind together more strongly those who supported Sékou-Touré and who were not only impressed by PDG propaganda but had also been disturbed by the overthrow of President Nkrumah of Ghana in 1966 – an act they attributed to collusion between traitors and external capitalist interests.

With events in Ghana very much in the forefront of their minds, the fear of external threat from exiles and foreign forces hostile to the government was a matter of daily concern to the Guinean people who remained in the country. Internal forces, too, presented problems. In 1969 it was claimed that there had been an unsuccessful coup attempt by dissident elements in the army. This was a matter of double significance. Potentially the army, as in other African states, was the most powerful agency within the country. Hitherto, however, it had pursued its professional role, showing no interest in politics. But while membership of the government and of the senior offices within the party had, by no deliberate design, fallen to members of the different ethnic groups roughly in proportion to the size of those groups within the population as a whole, the officer corps of the army contained a disproportionately large number of Sousou, with the Malinke in second place, and the others poorly represented. By his heavy-handed intrusion into farming methods, Sékou-Touré had already caused discontent among the Fulani – from which group a high proportion of the disaffected intellectuals had also been drawn – and he had disturbed the Malinke by his condemnation of traders and industrialists. Now he set about alienating leading figures among another ethnic group – the Sousou. Rather than appeasing the disgruntled officers by trying to discover the grounds for their discontent, Sékou-Touré decided that a new force was needed to counterbalance that of the professional army. He therefore created a militia from within the party's youth movement which, he felt confident, would be ideologically committed to the government.

In spite of these measures, and the president's suspicions which had prompted them, opposition to the government was still, essentially, neither tribal nor ethnic in origin. But Sékou-Touré's behaviour caused traditional loyalties to become more significant as the government's critics were forced to conclude that the president was wholly insensitive to regional interests and to deeply ingrained social customs. To add to the discontent, a second three-year economic plan, which had been intended to take effect from 1964, was proving to be a failure. Anxious to avoid any reliance upon external assistance, with its potential for interference, Sékou-Touré had left the formulation of the plan to party members. They, however, had lacked the expertise to carry out the task and had taken little account of the realities of the situation in Guinea. The result was not even a list of objectives but only of aspirations. Yet the attempt to control the economy, ineffective though it was, still contrived to stir up discontent among those who resented its implications, and disappointment among the party's faithful because it failed to produce the results they had expected.

One factor which did initially help to unite the people of Guinea was Sékou-Touré's education policy. Education, though gravely neglected by the French administrators until after the Second World War, was, for the president, one of the keys to successful nation building. Educational provision was widened at all levels in the first decade of his rule, and at all levels the aim was to tie education to the achievement of the party's objectives. In 1961 it was announced that scholarships enabling students to advance to higher levels of education would be awarded on the basis of loyalty to the party and to Guinea. Students in secondary schools were required to follow a compulsory course in political education which introduced them to the history and aims of the PDG. Students at the higher levels were prepared for service in the upper echelon of the party and the state and, more particularly – after the disturbances of the late 1960s – emphasis was placed on teaching about the threat of neo-colonialism and the need to fight to preserve the country's independence. Research by students of history in the polytechnics – later to become universities – was almost uniformly devoted to questions of local resistance to French conquest and administration and to the struggle for independence.[2] As a result of this type of education, the younger generation of Guineans not unnaturally became less critical of the government than were some of their elders. The ease with which the new graduates found positions of responsibility within the party and the state also meant that there were few disgruntled young intellectuals to reinforce the older intellectual critics of Sékou-Touré's ideology.

Surprisingly, then, though the president might have believed that he was acting pragmatically to defuse an acknowledged threat, he introduced a parallel programme which seemed to run counter to the aims already fixed by his educational system. Addressing the first graduates of Conakry Polytechnic in 1968 he acknowledged that tribal and ethnic groups were historical facts and that those groups were deeply conscious of their geographical and linguistic unity. This situation, he said, must be accepted and account must be taken of those differences when national policies were being formulated. Nevertheless, he still intended that the development of the different groups should take place within the national community, for, if the nation collapsed, ethnic groups could not survive.[3] His recipe for promoting these apparently conflicting objectives sounded equally unconvincing. Developing his theme shortly afterwards, he announced his decision to encourage the teaching of eight of the country's traditional languages. Initially the idea sprang from the laudable desire to promote adult literacy, but it was soon extended to become an integral part of the country's educational system at primary level. The object was to ensure that indigenous languages were the normal means of communication for the first eight years of instruction, though French was to be taught from the third year onwards.

It was a programme beset with problems. Particularly at the higher levels of education, the use of a range of languages created confusion. For the mass of the population, however, it merely served to emphasize the divisions which already existed within the community. To the casual observer such an apparent concession to regionalism amounted to a complete reversal of policy. Not surprisingly, after the muddle that ensued, a return to teaching in French was one of the earliest proposals of the military government which took office in 1984.[4]

In 1970 there was an attempted invasion by Guinean exiles acting in co-operation with the Portuguese – who were anxious to release some prisoners of the Guinea–Bissau liberation movement who were being held in Guinea. The effort needed to suppress the invasion demonstrated all too clearly the strength of the exile opposition to Sékou

Touré's government. The invasion was not, however, the product of any tribal or ethnic movement, though it doubtless drew sustenance from communal feelings of dissatisfaction. It was primarily an attempt to rid the country of an ideology which those who took part in the invasion believed to be detrimental to their own interests if not to the whole people. Nevertheless, Sékou-Touré reacted as if he believed that ethnic opposition lay at the root of the troubles. The violent purges which he carried out after the invasion had been repulsed were directly mainly against people of Fulani origin, including some of those who had seemed to be most consistently loyal to the regime and who were among the president's closest advisors.

It was this suspicion, even of his nearest colleagues, which caused Sékou-Touré to rely increasingly upon younger men who had been educated since he came to power and who were uncritically devoted to the concept of a united Guinea. One by one, the older men were removed from office. First went those who had formerly led opposition groups but who had later joined the PDG – men like Ibrahima Barry and Diawandu Barry, both Fulani. Then followed those who, although they had supported Sékou-Touré's efforts to assert the dignity of the Guinean people, had never felt at ease within his ideological system. Again they were mainly Fulani. However, one of them, Saifoulaye Diallo, though relieved of office, was allowed to remain in honourable retirement, and his death in 1981 was marked by three days of national mourning. In place of these senior statesmen came Sékou-Touré's younger men, eager to seek within the party hierarchy the only sort of remunerative and purposeful occupation open to educated people in a country where the economy had stagnated rapidly during the years since independence.

That money was available to pay the salaries of the rapidly expanding party bureaucracy was due entirely to the income from the country's bauxite mines. With a view to developing those resources, the richest of their kind in the world, the French had handed over the working of the first of the mines to an international consortium just before Guinea became unexpectedly independent. After lengthy negotiation, Sékou-Touré succeeded in 1973 in recovering part of the ownership and two-thirds of the taxable profits for Guinea. Five years earlier he had made a similar arrangement with a mixed enterprise company to develop other bauxite deposits. By the mid-1970s, almost the whole country's foreign-currency earnings came from bauxite and allied products. All other forms of industrial enterprise, including transport, were under direct government control and had become virtually derelict because of the inexperience and incompetence of those responsible for operating them.

Another attempt to promote collectivization in the farming sector in the mid-1970s produced further opposition and again led to accusations that the opposition was the result of an ethnic plot. Not surprisingly, it had been the Fulani, with their traditionally hierarchical system of government and their deep personal attachment to their cattle, who had reacted most strongly against the unproductive egalitarianism and collectivism proclaimed by Sékou-Touré's government. The plot, which was said to have had the support of France, Senegal, and the Ivory Coast, produced a violent response from the government.[5] The Fulani, it was claimed, were pursuing racist aims, and demands were made for the extradition of a number of Guineans in exile. They met with no success, but again Sékou-Touré resorted to purges at home and seized the opportunity to rid himself of two leading figures who, for differing reasons, he feared might constitute a threat to the government. Telli Diallo had returned to Guinea after serving as secretary-general of the OAU and had been given a ministerial appointment. Sékou-Touré quickly came to the conclusion that, for those who opposed his regime, Telli Diallo must appear as his natural successor. Though Diallo himself was embarassed to be cast in such a role, it was a situation which the president felt he could not ignore, and Diallo was dismissed. The other prominent person who was similarly involved was Alioune Dramée, who had served the government loyally for eighteen years but was now suspect because of the President's intense feeling against the Fulani. From this time, it became obvious that Sékou-Touré was finding it increasingly necessary to fill the important offices of state – not just with members of his own ethnic group but more especially with people who were closely related to him and who might, for that reason, be committed to supporting him. Yet even his influential half-brother, Ismael Touré, was briefly dismissed from office because he was suspected of wanting to abandon the president's Marxist policy.[6]

Suspicion of everyone, save of his closest associates, had by now replaced Sékou-Touré's boast of a united people. In 1977 his punitive measures against those he deemed to be his opponents led to a call to the United Nations from the International League for Human Rights for an enquiry into a 'reign of terror and massive violation of human rights' in Guinea. But again, in November, another unsuccessful attempt to invade the country and to seize Conakry led to the arrest of many more presumed collaborators. Sékou-Touré was not unaware of the unfavourable impression his actions were making upon external observers, and he was becoming increasingly conscious that he must moderate his former contempt for external criticism if Guinea was to get the outside aid which his regime needed for its survival, a fact which he was now coming to recognize if not publicly to acknowledge. At the time of independence the proud claim to 'prefer freedom in poverty to riches in slavery' rallied without difficulty those whose experience had only been of poverty under French rule. It had not impressed those who had begun to enjoy a measure of prosperity before independence. Now the reality behind the slogan seemed distinctly less attractive to those of Sékou-Touré's supporters who did not belong to the party heirarchy, and who looked out upon an apparently endless vista of poverty and increasingly limited freedom. Though foreign rule was a thing of the past, freedom under the new regime seemed less than complete, and Sékou-Touré himself was beginning to realize that the inheritance of the political kingdom had not, of itself, led to the creation of a nation. What his people wanted, irrespective of tribal or ethnic origins, was stability and economic prosperity. The government's failure to produce results was the chief cause of internal discord. Unfortunately for Sékou-Touré's hopes, the western powers had not relented, in spite of Guinea's new insistence upon its non-aligned role in world affairs, and no help was forthcoming.

It was against this background that, in the late 1970s, Sékou-Touré began to woo France once again. In a paradoxical way he still trusted France more than any other country. Bowing to external pressure, he released 300 political prisoners in December 1977, and early in 1978 diplomatic links were restored with the Ivory Coast and Senegal. In December of that year, President Giscard d'Estaing of France paid a visit of reconciliation to Guinea, but it was some years before Sékou-Touré was able to return the compliment. Guinea's relations with France continued to be ambiguous, even after Sékou-Touré, in February 1979, ended the agreement granting the USSR airforce and naval-base facilities in Conakry. Commercial discussions took place with representatives of Ivory Coast trading interests, however, and from 1 July 1979 small-scale private commerce was permitted within Guinea itself.

In spite of these modest improvements in Guinea's relations with the outside world, Sékou-Touré still did not feel secure, and he railed against 'corrupt cadres and disguised counter-revolutionaries' even within his own party.[7] His fears were not without foundation. In May 1980 and again in February 1981 he escaped assassination attempts. On each occasion he responded by ordering numerous arrests and by purging the army and the PDG. A year later, in February 1982, he claimed to have foiled yet another plot against his regime and in May he was re-elected, as his party's only candidate, to a further seven-year term as president. In September he paid his long-delayed official visit to a France which, now that its pride had been satisfied by Sékou-Touré's years of strain, was anxious to share in Guinea's rich mineral deposits. Nevertheless, the visit had its drawbacks. Sékou-Touré was greeted by hostile demonstrations from Guinean refugees who condemned the record of his treatment of political opponents.

France was not the only non-African country to which Sékou-Touré turned for assistance. Economic nationalism, for all its fine independent façade, had still failed to fill the vacuum created by the flight of French capital in 1958. The subsequent loss of its own men of experience had meant that Guinea's industries, its commerce, and even its output of export and food crops, had fallen far below the people's expectations and had even fallen short of their day-to-day requirements. During a visit to the USA in 1982, Sékou-Touré attended a Guinea Investment Forum in New York at which he said:

> We are eager to cooperate, because what we particularly lack today is capital. God has given us immense natural wealth, but we don't have the capital or the technology or the know-how to develop it.[8]

Times, and attitudes, were clearly changing. Arab countries in the Middle East also offered help, and a nominal attempt was made to encourage private-sector activities in Guinea itself. But Sékou-Touré was reluctant to abandon the idea of economic nationalism completely. He still could not rid himself of the belief that communal solidarity must triumph in the long run and, in any case, was the only sure bulwark against the exploitation of the weak by the strong. It was this conviction that led him to persist in trying to introduce collectivism into the farming sector. It was to prove a triumph of ideology over experience.

Sékou-Touré's death after an operation carried out in the USA in April 1984 put his achievements to the test while challenging his fears of ethnic opposition to his government. Lansana Beavogui, prime minister since 1972, who was believed to have been a pliant supporter of Sékou-Touré, temporarily took the reins of government into his hands. Three days after the president's funeral, however, there took place a military coup such as Sékou-Touré had feared for some time. The objective of the coup, it was said, was to put an end to an alleged power struggle which had broken out among the associates of the former president and to rid the country of twenty-six years of repression, poverty, and corruption. This was a remarkable statement, because it challenged the vested interests of a whole generation of bureaucrats who, in spite of the growing disillusionment with the performance of the economy, still recognized that their own positions depended upon the survival of the old regime, and who were still prepared to lay the blame for the shortcomings of the Sékou-Touré era at the door of malign foreign powers.

The first public announcement on behalf of the coup was made by Colonel Lansana Conté. He spoke, not in French but in Sousou, though the immediate assumption that this had ethnic implications was balanced by the fact that Conté's closest associate was Colonel Diara Traore — a Malinke as Sékou-Touré had been. Conté also announced that, although the leaders of the former government had been arrested, there would be no executions, but some might be called upon to answer administrative or economic charges. The PDG was dissolved and an eighteen-member Military Committee of National Redress (CMRN) was installed. Conté became president and Traore was appointed prime minister. The CMRN announced that its members would remain in office until racialism, regionalism, and sectarianism had been eliminated. This was a reference not to the exiles, whom Sékou-Touré had frequently castigated for their ethnic loyalties, but rather to the former president's own increasing reliance upon his close relations to fill the high offices of state.

Messages of support for the new government poured in from exiles of all ethnic groups, and many former refugees immediately began to contemplate a return to Guinea. The western powers also looked with approval on the change of government, but, after years of detachment and even of suspicion, they were slow to convert their approbation into active assistance, although the new regime quickly made it clear that it was prepared to give unconditional support to private enterprise. A limited amount of aid was provided, but it was expected that the main help would come from the IMF — with all that might involve by way of strict economic controls.

The task of regenerating the country's economy was retarded by the new regime's immediate concern with establishing its legitimacy. There may have been unanimity among the coup leaders about the desirability of ridding the country of Sékou-Touré's ideology, but there was a lack of unanimity about who should rule in his place. As early as December 1984, Conté announced that state corruption had forced him to take over the offices of prime minister and minister of defence in addition to the presidency. The former prime minister, Colonel Traore, was demoted to the ministry of education but remained in the cabinet. Nine other members left the government and five new members were added to it. Conté stated ominously that other members might be removed if they did not put the interests of the state above all others.

Traore's demotion may have resulted from his weakness in high office, but it was more probably a cunning test of his loyalty, for a strange occurrence took place in July 1985. President Conté left the country to attend a conference, but before his departure he took the precaution of disposing some of his troops in strategic positions to check any uprising. His prescience was rewarded when an attempted military coup, led by Colonel Traore, was successfully suppressed because of the precautions he had taken. The fate of Traore is not known, though it is rumoured that he was killed in fighting for control of the radio station. It is also widely believed that, during the struggle, troops supporting Conté stormed the prison at Kindia and shot some of the members and officials of Sékou-Touré's government who were detained there. Credence was given to this latter claim in May 1987 when the government unexpectedly announced that secret trials had recently taken place at which members of Sékou-Touré's government, as well as some of those involved in the attempted coup, had been found guilty of capital offences and had been executed. Others had been found guilty in their absence and still more had been sentenced to terms of imprisonment with hard labour. Among those condemned to death were seven relatives of Sékou-Touré, all of whom had held ministerial office! One general, two colonels, eleven majors and six captains of the Guinean army, whose names were not published, were sentenced to death in their absence.[9]

Immediately after the coup there had also been a purge of the army directed particularly against the Malinke, and many of the officers who had fled the country were from that same ethnic group. Reprisals were subsequently taken against civilians of Malinke origin also, which may suggest that the government had serious doubts about the loyalty of that group. The Malinke were certainly under-represented in the cabinet, and it was also noted that Conté had been in no hurry to increase the number of Fulani members, although the Fulani had been particular sufferers under the regime of Sékou-Touré.

For all his claims to be above internal divisions, it seemed that Conté was beginning to follow in the footsteps of Sékou-Touré in relying increasingly upon a close circle of colleagues who belonged to his own ethnic group. The problem was that the influence of Sékou-Touré's years in office could not easily be dispelled. It was not simply that the former government had led the country into total disarray.

The new regime was handicapped by the fact that it lacked the means, and the people lacked the will, to change the situation. By 1987, representatives of a number of countries – meeting under the chairmanship of the World Bank – had accepted that Guinea must have assistance, and the Guinean government, for its part, had offered incentives to encourage private-sector activity. The main obstacle, however, was the absence of appropriate manpower to put this programme into effect. Whatever Conté's plans, their implementation depended upon the co-operation of such educated people as remained in the country. As in Sékou-Touré's time, these were mainly young men who had filled the party bureaucracy in numbers far exceeding the requirements of the system, and they were still wholeheartedly committed to Sékou-Touré's ideology. Conté's willingness to acknowledge Guinea's dependence upon outside aid was anathema to them – Sékou-Touré having, by his rhetoric, carefully concealed his own partial acknowledgement of that position. Even more strongly resented was Conte's proposal to reduce the number of state employees from 90,000 to 60,000. Not even the promise of higher salaries for those who were retained could win acceptance for the plan. The suggestion that those who retired might profitably engage in the much needed expansion of the country's agricultural sector met with little enthusiasm.

The opposition to Conté was in no sense ethnic in composition. The men who filled the state bureaucracy still indulged in the pan-Africanist rhetoric with which Sékou-Touré had rallied the country in 1958. They remained an influential group because, for twenty-six years, they had borne the responsibility for organizing support for the party and for disseminating their leader's ideology. There were few who dared challenge their authority, particulary in the towns. Few, too, ventured to utter criticisms of Sékou-Touré, even four years after his death. It was this continuing loyalty to the old order which had such a depressing effect upon the exiles who returned to Guinea with high hopes after Conté's coup. Many of them, having reviewed the scene, left again in despair. The insistence upon self-reliance, which the bureaucracy had imbibed under Sékou-Touré's influence, and which they still embraced unquestioningly, seemed to the returning exiles a recipe for continuing economic ruin.

If President Conté is to have any prospect of surmounting this enormous obstacle, he will need the co-operation of the Fulani and Malinke, as well as of his own Sousou and the people of the forest region. Above all, he will need the help of the refugee elite – who alone have the experience to see the situation in Guinea in a wider context, and the flexibility to adapt Guinea's resources to meet its need. It would be disastrous if Conté were thought to be too suspicious of the Malinke and too wary of the Fulani to make use of their talents. Sékou-Touré's fears of ethnic opposition had, it could be argued, been responsible for creating such opposition out of what were essentially disagreements over economic policies. The Fulani pastoralists had been led by his attack upon them to believe that collectivism was deliberately directed against them as an ethnic group. The Malinke, too, had felt themselves singled out for victimization by the exclusion of traders and industrialists from office in the PDG. Suspicion had bred suspicion and Sékou-Touré had increasingly persecuted the Fulani leaders. By stages the conflict between the government and its opponents had taken on an increasingly ethnic character, though ultimately Sékou-Touré had become isolated even from his own Malinke people.

So far as the Fulani were concerned, the fault did not lie wholly on the government's side. They, after all, had created a largely self-contained state which had survived for more than two centuries. Their relations with their neighbours, whether Malinke or Sousou, had been essentially those of a nation with foreign states. Their links with the Muslim peoples of Senegal were probably stronger than with the people with whom they had been associated in one administrative unit by the coincidence of imperial expansion in Africa. The Malinke, too, had not been wholly committed to Sékou-Touré's objective of uniting the country. They still retained feelings of pride in the achievements of their former leader, Samory, and they, too, were disinclined to be associated unreservedly with the Fulani to the west, or with the forest people to the south. It was those feelings of local pride which had reinforced economic uncertainty and had led so many Guineans to flee the country rather than submit to the all-embracing party control which Sékou-Touré had sought to impose. Conté's prospects of success depend heavily upon restoring their confidence in their country, and it is the survival of Sékou-Touré's unifying ideology among the younger, better educated section of society which, ironically, presents the biggest obstacle to Conté's hopes of persuading the people to work together.

That ideology, while perpetuating the concept of a pan-African culture, paradoxically bred suspicion of everyone, even of Africans, but especially of Europeans. It also created a fierce pride in the ability of the Guinean people to rely upon their own resources which restricted, and still restricts, their ability to learn from others. The support of France, now wholehearted, has to be given with discretion lest it should arouse the hostility of the ideologically opposed middle-aged *'jeunesse'* of the Sékou-Touré era. The IMF had been particularly lenient in offering a standby loan in spite of Guinea's failure to fulfil the conditions laid down when aid was inaugurated. But there is increasing internal hostility to the restrictions upon which the IMF has insisted, and Conté is faced with the problem of convincing his people that short-term suffering and inconvenience will lead to long-term prosperity. The cuts he has imposed upon the civil service have produced a sharp outcry from the more vocal element in the population. At the same time, the government's offer of help to private enterprise in the agricultural sector has not resulted in the benefits for which people had hoped. The press and radio have uniformly supported the military regime, but this could have the effect of stifling dissent rather than of extending toleration.

Conté's call on 1 October 1988 to the 'new Guineans' to respond to the challenge of the future in a responsible manner was accompanied by the admission that 'generalized corruption, incessant embezzlement, laxity in implementing budget estimates and malfunctioning of our administrative systems' had, so far, paralysed all the recovery programmes that had been launched. All these shortcomings he attributed, in part at least, to the 'Guinean mentality',[10] a claim which in itself was an indictment of Sékou-Touré's legacy to his country. The self-reliance which, though initially forced upon Guinea by adverse circumstances, the former president had converted into a slogan to be proudly cherished, has produced in his supporters an uncritical arrogance which has justified any action, no matter how inefficient or corrupt, provided it was of their own doing. As a result, internal initiatives which might have benefited the country as a whole were rare. With most of the ablest people in exile, US aid alone had saved the country from food shortages. Even in the bauxite industry, the one reliable source of revenue, the Guinean people had played only a menial role. While boasting of its independence, the country had lived on foreign industry and aid. It is this legacy, now reinforced by ethnic suspicion, with which the government of Conté has to contend, while denied the help of the exiles whose return is effectively discouraged by the hostility and incomprehension of the leaders of Sékou-Touré's generation.

8 Zaire: the authentic Africa?

If President Diouf has accepted Senegal's dependence on western aid with a calm dignity, President Mobutu Sese Seko has played Zaire's dependence to the limit. Though his country is heavily in debt, and he himself is unpopular with both a large section of his own people and most of Zaire's creditors, he continues to function with an apparent insouciance which belies his political cunning. For nearly a quarter of a century, and thanks largely to foreign support but not forgetting his own ruthless pursuit of power, he has held together an enormous country which, for the previous five years, had been torn by internal strife until it seemed in danger of breaking apart. From the standpoint of its economy, Zaire's record under Mobutu's rule can scarcely be seen as a success story, though market forces have contributed as much to that situation as have either corruption or incompetence. Nor is democratic government strongly in evidence, opposition being treated as sedition rather than as an intellectual stimulant. Few Zaireans cherish feelings of nationhood, and unity owes more to the difficulty of breaking away than from any strong desire to belong. Yet Mobutu survives, and appears to flourish, and Zaire is still one country, though no one is more aware than the president of the fissiparous tendencies that exist, and must be taken into account, even if not too openly acknowledged.

It was in 1971 that Joseph-Désiré Mobutu, then president of the Democratic Republic of the Congo, began his search for authenticity. He was not seeking to reintroduce a state of multi-tribalism, as some western observers thought. But the country's name was indeed changed to Zaire, Christian names were rejected in favour of African names – the president himself becoming Sese Seko instead of Joseph-Désiré[1] – and a commission was appointed to codify traditional law.[2] Mobutu was fully aware that such changes were superficial things. He recognized that French was the only acceptable official language in multi-lingual Zaire. He knew that traditional law, with all its variations from one part of the country to another, could not apply to commercial dealings with foreign companies. He was conscious, too, of his country's dependence on outside expertise and foreign investment for the successful exploitation of its copper, cobalt, and other mineral deposits which were the main source of foreign exchange. But he knew that if he appeared to accept all these things submissively Zaire would never become a nation. Conflicting loyalties, enhanced by vast geographical distances and poor communications, would triumph. The country would fall apart as it had so nearly done in the years immediately after it became independent in 1960, not because of any positive longing for a return to tribalism, but from fear that the central government was not sufficiently concerned to protect local interests. So he undertook his authenticity campaign as an important propaganda exercise to demonstrate that he was not insensitive to traditional ideas. His real object was to strengthen the centralizing policy which he had introduced on taking office in 1965 to counter the destructive centrifugal forces of regionalism.

Nor had size alone, or even the rich variety of cultures which existed in the Congo, been the only obstacles to centralized control. To a greater degree even than in British and French dependencies, Belgian rule in the Congo had been a question of foreign administration rather than of the development of indigenous capabilities. A bureaucratic machine had functioned in a realm as detached from the Congo people as possible, commensurate with the need to maintain order and to ensure the effective operation of the mining industry. The scandals of Leopold II's misrule had acted as a constant reminder of what might happen if efficiency and the disinterested exercise of authority were neglected. As a result, any consideration of the ultimate transfer of power to an African majority was ignored almost to the day of independence. Education for Africans, above the primary level, was almost non-existent, for how could it be necessary when they were not expected to play any role within the framework of a European-ordered society which might require further education? At the same time, Belgium's inability to provide the large number of officials needed to fulfil its aims had meant that, at the lower levels of bureaucracy, reliance had had to be placed upon indigenous, traditional authorities. Though there had been every intention that those authorities would be closely supervised, and their character and powers modified if necessary to meet the needs of the government, the result had been to encourage people to rely, as they had done in the past, upon local leaders who controlled their daily lives, rather than upon an alien, remote, central government.

In such circumstances, it was highly improbable that any African would conceive of an identity stretching beyond the boundaries of his own locality. The most significant anti-Belgian movement to emerge in the 1950s, the Bakongo Alliance (ABAKO), for example, was initially no more than a cultural movement aimed at preserving the Kongo language. Its leader, Joseph Kasavubu, soon outstripped this limitation, but only to advocate the reunion of the Kongo people who lived near the mouth of the Congo River. As a more remote possibility he might also have considered attempting to revive the Kongo kingdom – which had been divided between the French, the Belgians, and the Portuguese at the time of the European imperial advance into Africa. Even these ideas were, at first, little more than pipe-dreams, because the Kongo kingdom had broken up into scores of minor socio-political groups long before the European scramble for Africa had taken place, and those groups had become more central to the lives of their members than any residual loyalty to a bygone kingdom. It was only at times of uncertainty, such as occurred in the late 1950s, that there was a tendency to look for stronger local loyalties of the kind contemplated by Kasavubu to protect regional interests against the threat of insecurity and external rivalry. When other, similar movements developed it is noticeable that they, too, tended to look to the real or imagined past for their inspiration, each one seeking what appeared to be a more powerful and reliable focus of local loyalty upon which to place its trust.

One person contrived to escape the bonds of locality and ethnicity. Patrice Lumumba drew upon a limited education at both Catholic and Protestant missionary schools and upon wide reading and varied experience in minor official posts, leading to membership and sub-quently to the presidency of an African staff association in Stanleyville (later Kisangani), to enable him to look at the Belgian Congo as a whole. Perhaps the fact that he belonged to a small tribal group, the Tetela in Kasai Province, saved him from any desire to restore some traditional kingdom or empire, real or imagined. It was not, however, until General de Gaulle offered the neighbouring French Congo a choice between membership of a new French community or of complete independence in 1958 that Lumumba began to think of African participation in planning the future of the Belgian Congo and of eventual independence for the whole country. Shortly afterwards, in December, he represented the *Mouvement National Congolais* (MNC), which he and a number of like-minded colleagues had founded to promote their aims, at the inspirational All African Peoples' Conference held in Accra. He returned from that conference to Leopoldville (later Kinshasa) in a spirit of exultation to address a mass meeting at which he called for immediate independence.

Lumumba had no means of knowing how an independent country the size of the Belgian Congo could be organized. The problem of creating an alternative to imperial rule in the Congo was, in fact, more immediately acute than in any other tropical African dependency. There was no widely accepted African leader and there was no political party which could command general support. There were no ready-made senior African civil servants and no one to manage the economy. Even among the country's tiny educated elite there was a dearth of political interest. Lumumba himself had an ecstatic vision of liberty but no experience of building or maintaining the administrative infrastructure needed to support it. When, in 1960, the Belgian government took an ill-judged risk and offered independence, without any preparation for it, scores of political parties were quickly formed to contest the precipitately organized elections. Inevitably they consisted for the most part of local groups which, in so far as they had thought about it, preferred a federal to a unitary system of government. They hoped that the retention of as much as possible of traditional forms would guarantee security and stability in a new, uncharted, political future. In the prevailing conditions this could only be a recipe for anarchy.

It was remarkable, therefore, that the party so hurriedly organized by Lumumba on what he hoped would prove to be a nationwide basis was the most successful competitor in the elections, for Lumumba was in no sense a widely acknowledged political leader. The MNC even gained a few seats in the first independent house of representatives in constituencies outside Lumumba's own province. It was less remarkable that, after prolonged negotiations which enabled Lumumba to form a coalition and take office as prime minister, violence broke out in Kasai Province. Kasai was the home of Albert Kalonji, a former member of the MNC, who had led a splinter group which refused to join the coalition. Kalonji was inspired primarily by personal jealousy of Lumumba, but he gained local support because his fellow-Luba feared that control of the diamond mines in their province might be lost to a central government indifferent to their interests. On the other hand, he lost the support of the Lulua inhabitants of Kasai. They, for their part, had no wish to be dominated by the Luba, who would have little concern for the Lulua if Kasai were to become independent.

Such divisions were not surprising. The six provinces into which the Belgian Congo had been divided, and which were retained for a time after independence, were the product of administrative convenience and lacked every vestige of internal cohesion. Kasai itself was sharply divided between two main ethnic groups with no common tradition to bind them together. Katanga Province, to the east, probably had a more culturally homogeneous population, but traditional authorities, even within one ethnicity, were jealous of their local power and watched each other warily. The other provinces were made up of peoples possessing widely disparate cultures. There, loyalty to any would-be political leader was most likely to depend upon the prospect he offered of security and prosperity. In the absence of any widespread political awareness there was no deep attachment to any political ideology. Tribalism or ethnicity could, therefore, create considerable problems for anything but the most powerful and economically successful central government.

The mutiny of the *Force Publique*, which followed hard on the heels of independence, had no tribal or ethnic motivation, however. It was, essentially, due to the unrequited aspirations of African soldiers, hoping to take the place of the Belgian officers who controlled the corps. But the panic which the mutiny inspired among Belgian expatriates, especially the civil servants, followed by their confused abandonment of the country, took the Belgian government by surprise. It had been confidently expected that the African politicians would retain both the European civil service and European army officers for the foreseeable future. Now, in its anxiety for the safety of its citizens, the Belgian government immediately dispatched troops to the Congo for their protection, an alien intrusion which proved to be a severe blow to Lumumba's fragile authority. Moise Tshombe, a member of a wealthy commercial family related to the ruling family of the Lunda, seized upon it as justification for announcing the secession of Katanga Province from a country which appeared to be dissolving into anarchy.

The Lunda had little desire to be subsumed within the new, independent Congo, but in giving their support to Tshombe they were motivated more by the desire to prevent control of the mineral wealth of their province falling into the hands of Lumumba's government than by any uniform local loyalty. Faced with such a critical situation, however, they were prepared to set aside internal differences. It was an attitude that was strongly reinforced by the support of powerful European financial interests, anxious to hold on to the benefits they derived from working the rich copper and cobalt deposits.[3] But the loss of that wealth would be crippling to Lumumba's government. Kalonji, quick to follow Tshombe's example, declared the mining state of Kasai independent. Once again, the combination of economic forces and local self-interest proved to be of vital importance to the would-be leaders of the people. Lumumba's successful appeal to the UN for military help made it possible for Belgium to withdraw its troops, but Tshombe retained the services of a number of former Belgian officers and technicians in Katanga, and it was largely due to their help that the secessionist state was able to withstand the military onslaughts levelled against it.

Kasavubu who, with American approval, had been elected president at the time of independence, dismissed Lumumba on 5 September 1960. It was the first step towards the rejection of Lumumba's hopes of a united Congo and the acceptance of a federal or confederal solution in a situation where the central government seemed incapable of controlling all the constituent parts of the country. The movement was temporarily frustrated, however, when, only a week later, the army seized power under the leadership of Colonel Joseph-Désiré Mobutu with the aim of retaining a strong central government. Mobutu, from Equateur Province, dismissed Kasavabu and his nominee prime minister, Joseph Ileo, and also Lumumba, who still claimed to be the rightful office holder. At that stage Mobutu did not feel ready to take ultimate responsibility for governing the country so, as a temporary measure, the army handed over administration to a committee of students. But the new government lacked experience and, after a time, Mobutu came to a working agreement with Kasavubu who resumed his duties as president. Although brief, the army's intervention had provided a foretaste of the important role which it alone seemed capable of playing in enforcing unity in an otherwise deeply divided country.

The murder of Lumumba, early in 1961, divided the country still further, and the supporters of the late prime minister set up their own government in Orientale Province under the leadership of Lumumba's former deputy, Antoine Gizenga. Further disintegration was again temporarily halted by the intervention of the UN, which strengthened its military forces in the Congo. Against this background a conference of the country's various leaders, excluding Gizenga, met in Tananarive and agreed to form a confederation. The national parliament was re-convened in July 1961 but Katanga failed to send representatives. Kasavubu at once took steps to put an end to what seemed like the threat of another secessionist movement. He obtained the agreement of the government to send Congolese forces, together with

UN troops, to restore law and order in Katanga and to arrest the foreign mercenaries upon whom Tshombe relied heavily in challenging the authority of the central government.

In November 1961 the UN security council passed a resolution demanding the reunification of Katanga with the rest of the republic. Tshombe's response was to prepare for war. Meanwhile, Gizenga's breakaway government was brought to an end in January 1962 with help from UN troops. There was a brief flurry of fighting in Katanga also, but the rest of the year was taken up with a series of attempts, mainly by the UN, to bring about a *rapprochement* between the central authorities and the secessionist state. Confident that he had the tacit approval, if not the active support, of Belgium, France, and Britain, as well as of some of Europe's most powerful financial interests, Tshombe was unwilling to co-operate wholeheartedly with Kasavubu's new prime minister, Cyrille Adoula. In the eyes of those Europeans who had a financial stake in Katanga's mineral wealth, Tshombe himself seemed to be the leader most likely to protect their interests. Adoula, however, had the support of President Kennedy's administration in America, and it was with US approval that UN forces launched a vigorous military operation against Katanga in December 1962. After some stubborn resistance, Tshombe agreed to give up his secessionist claims in January 1963 and shortly afterwards he left for Europe. The breakaway movement in Kasai also collapsed some months later and Kalonji, its leader, was jailed.

Briefly it seemed as if the central government, with UN support, had asserted its authority. But criticism of Adoula persisted, particularly among supporters of the late Patrice Lumumba. The division of the six provinces into twenty-one would, it was hoped, break down large power bases, such as existed in Katanga, which threatened the central government. At the same time, it would give greater recognition to the ethnic and regional needs of the various groups within the population. The plan was not as successful as had been anticipated, however, because even the new, smaller provinces were not inhabited by homogeneous ethnic groups, nor were the interests of the people within each province so clear-cut as to be readily identifiable or easily dealt with. Divisions remained as stark as ever, encouraging reliance upon tribalism or upon larger ethnic groupings to protect what were seen as local interests. Even the introduction of a new constitution, which gave more power to the head of state at the expense of the legislature, and the continuing presence until June 1964 of UN troops, could not contain the disorders. Pierre Mulele led a rebellion which broke out in the Kwilu region in January 1964.

Further south, in southern Kivu and northern Katanga, another rebellion erupted in April. Both lacked any effective organization or clear-cut objectives. Those who took part did so mainly because they were disillusioned by the constant turmoil and disruption which had followed independence.

Distrustful of distant leaders whom they did not know and about whom they had no opportunity of learning, and dismayed by the destruction of the economy, the vast majority of the people were too unsophisticated politically to think of secession as anything more than an escape mechanism. For the most part they were content to support anyone who, in trying to seize control of the central government, held out the promise of satisfying their local demands. In so far as tribal or ethnic considerations played any part in the rebellion they did so in a purely defensive role.

Unable to suppress these outbreaks of military opposition, Kasavubu took the surprising step of inviting Tshombe to return from exile and to become prime minister in July 1964. In doing so he had the approval of Mobutu and the army and, in the background, of Belgium and France. But his action produced a contrary response from the rebels who stepped up their military opposition to the government. Arms and equipment were sent by the USA to help Kasavubu's forces while UN and Belgian troops were flown in to rescue European hostages held by the rebels and to recapture Stanley-ville. The final defeat of the rebels was accomplished by the army, assisted by Tshombe's Katangese gendarmes and by European mercenaries whom he had also introduced into the country. By this time, however, the devastation to crops and homes, especially in Kivu province, was so serious that there were desperate shortages of food and the return to normality was a slow process.

New elections in March and April 1965 were contested by Tshombe's supporters on the one hand and by the alliance of nationalist Congolese Lumumbist movements on the other. Each of the groups – they lacked the unity to deserve the designation of political parties – was seeking to control the feeble machinery of central government to protect its own interests. Ideologically they have been described as Right and Left-wing movements, but in practice ideology was less important than support for, or opposition to, Tshombe himself, and the interpretation each side put upon the probable impact his government would have on the lives of their members.

Though Tshombe and his supporters were manifestly victorious in the elections, Kasavubu decided that, in view of the strength of the opposition, there should be a coalition government. Tshombe objected and was dismissed on 13 October 1965. The following month General Mobutu, as he had now become, grew tired of the endless bickering between the politicians, and with the covert support of the American CIA he again intervened, with the army, to make himself head of state. Kasavubu retired from politics until his death in 1969 and Tshombe took refuge in Europe. To test public reaction to a proposed new constitution which provided for presidential rule with a centralized administration and a single legislature, Mobutu organized a referendum in June 1967. The widespread desire for the restoration of order was reflected in the 90 per cent vote of approval, a result which could scarcely have been imposed upon the people by *force majeure*. It was clear that security and stability were, by now, the main preoccupations of people all over the Congo, and only the army seemed capable of offering either. Local interests were subsumed in this one prime concern.

For a short period the hope of peace and unity was rekindled and the army seemed both confident and powerful. The world demand for copper was heavy, prices were good, and the balance of trade improved. The government therefore decided to increase the export tax on copper from 17 to 30 per cent and, in an attempt to wrest control of the economy from foreign hands, announced that all companies legally constituted in the Congo must have their headquarters there. This did not please the powerful *Union Minière* which controlled Katanga's copper, but it tried in vain to modify the proposal, only to have its assets confiscated on 31 December 1966 when a new company was set up in its place. It was a brave gesture on the part of the government, but it quickly became obvious that the Congo lacked the indigenous experts to operate the plant and it was necessary to accept a compomise whereby a Belgian company took charge on the government's behalf.

This was a setback, but it was of less significance than the continuing threat of violence from a small number of inveterate opponents of the regime. First, the Katangese gendarmes loyal to Tshombe, who had been only too ready to assist in the suppression of the Lumumbist rebellion in 1965, now turned against Mobutu and mutinied in Stanleyville. Tshombe's other supporters, the European mercenaries, co-operated with the government in putting down the mutiny, but their loyalty to Mobutu was short-lived. In March 1967 Tshombe was sentenced to death in his absence by a military court on a charge of organizing the gendarmes' mutiny. In the meantime, he had been kidnapped while flying over the Mediterranean and was held in Algeria. Almost at once the European mercenaries mutinied, claiming that their pay was in arrears, but in reality hoping to be able to rescue Tshombe and restore him to power. Mobutu was ready for them. After some early successes the mercenaries were forced by the army to withdraw into neighbouring Rwanda, from whence Mobutu agreed in 1968 that they should be repatriated to Europe on the understanding that they should never be permitted to return to Africa.

Though disaffection remained among those who had aspired to leadership in the event of Mobutu's overthrow, peace was gradually restored, greatly to the relief of most of the country's inhabitants who, whatever their views about Mobutu − and he was not widely popular − were weary of civil war. The Katangese gendarmes, who had joined the mercenaries in their revolt, were either repatriated to the Congo or else took refuge in neighbouring Angola, and the death of Tshombe in captivity in June 1969 removed another potential source of danger to the government. Others remained, but Mobutu now felt strong enough to adopt a more clement approach to his former critics. Nevertheless, his execution of Pierre Mulele, who had taken part in the 1965 rebellion, made it clear that criticism might eventually be forgiven but levying war against the government would not.

To strengthen his grip on the governmental machine, Mobutu employed a tactic which was to become his main method of undermining potential opposition throughout his career − he reorganized the cabinet and the administration. In October 1966 he abolished the office of prime minister to rid himself of a possible rival, and in December he reduced the number of ministries by four, displacing eight ministers and transferring five others. Such was the power of patronage which could be exercised by officers of government that Mobutu was determined that no one should remain long enough in one post to build up a base of support sufficiently powerful to challenge the president. By moving even his closest supporters from one position to another, or even by dismissing them if only temporarily, he made sure that they were unable to wield continuous authority in one area of government. Out of office they could ponder on the loss they had sustained and learn to appreciate the advantage of remaining loyal to their leader.

If, by these various means, Mobutu was able to keep control of the upper echelons of the state, he had a more difficult task in unifying and controlling the country as a whole. In 1967 he had created the *Mouvement Populaire de la Révolution* (MPR), and all other political parties had been banned. Everyone had to be a member of the MPR, including young people who were recruited into a youth wing. In this way a veneer of unity was created, but in practice the party never gained a strong hold in the rural areas where people remained loyal to traditional authorities. In the same year, Mobutu also introduced the first of a series of measures intended to provide the infrastructure of a united state. The number of provinces was reduced from twenty-one to eight, provincial governments and provincial assemblies were abolished, and provincial governors became state officials appointed by the central government.

In August 1969 Mobutu removed from office the powerful foreign minister, Justin Bomboko, transferring him to Washington as ambassador to the USA. The president's growing confidence was shared by the US government which had supported his economic reforms in 1967 and was now impressed by the reduction he had achieved in government spending. Belgium, too, was beginning to show its approval of the Mobutu regime, and the continuing support of these two countries, the leading importers of the country's mineral products, was to provide the all-important foundation upon which Mobutu's power would rest. With copper prices high, the powerful Lonrho company, too, became interested in winning the contract for managing Katanga's copper mines. In 1970 Mobutu visited the USA and assured anyone who cared to listen that the nationalization of foreign assets formed no part of his economic programme. When asked how he could reconcile that statement with the fate of the *Union Minière* he replied that the company had refused to obey the laws of the country but had since acknowledged its error and was about to resume operations in the Congo. The news came as a blow to Lonrho's hopes.

As a result of the elections held in October 1970, Mobutu was returned by an overwhelming majority for another seven-year term as president. He marked his success characteristically by dismissing eight ministers and reshuffling his cabinet once more. More significantly, he announced an amnesty for all rebels who returned to the country by 31 January 1971. This was an important advance upon his action in executing Mulele, and it suggested that Mobutu was now convinced there was no serious military opposition to his government. But he was still on his guard. As in other countries where political opposition parties were non-existent, it was the universities which provided the liveliest criticism of the government's policies. After demonstrations at the University of Lovanium in June, almost the whole student body was conscripted into the army for two years. The university was temporarily closed and renamed as the University of Kinshasa. Students at the University of Lubumbashi (formerly Elizabethville),

who had the temerity to volunteer to undergo the same military training as a gesture of sympathy with their fellow-students in Kinshasa,
were drafted into the army for seven years. Thus, summarily, did
Mobutu silence another area of disaffection. It was at this point that
he decided to launch his authenticity campaign which changed the
country's name to Zaire.

In 1972 a new shadow dimmed the euphoria which had begun to
develop both at home and abroad. The price of copper, which had
recently been so buoyant, fell suddenly. It was never to recover,
though that posibility was not yet foreseen. In the short term it was a
serious blow to the economy because copper accounted for more than
half the country's export earnings. The proposal to make good the
shortfall by increasing output was frustrated by transport difficulties.
The two main outlets for Zaire's copper, the Benguela Railway and
the railway running through Zambia and Southern Rhodesia, were
both threatened, the latter by possible reprisals against Zambia by
Southern Rhodesia while the former was shortly to be closed altogether
by civil war in Angola. At last Zaire was face to face with the sort of
problem which had bedevilled so many other African countries. From
this time it was the weakness of the economy which offered the
greatest threat to the survival of Mobutu, or of any other central
government in Zaire. If the country were to be forced to revert to a
subsistence economy, clearly that could best be organized on a local
basis. Local interests, which had already played a prominent role in
determining the people's allegiance, could now constitute an ever
greater danger to national unity. But Zaire and its products were too
important to too many people for such a contingency to be allowed to
occur, a state of affairs from which Mobutu was to profit with
growing confidence.

A number of western countries, together with Japan and communist China which Mobutu visited in 1973, were quick to offer aid,
but while this was valuable in dealing with the immediate budget
deficit, it also contributed to the worrying growth in the national debt.
At the time this did not, it is true, seem unduly important because it
was thought there would soon be a notable increase in agricultural and
industrial output. But this proved to be an optimistic prognosis.
Ignoring his earlier assurances, in November 1973 Mobutu felt compelled to nationalize foreign-owned land and to call upon foreign-
owned mining companies to surrender 50 per cent of their equity to
the government.[4] Though it was not until more than a year later that
he took the further step of controlling the essential sectors of the
country's economy in an attempt to check inflation, these preliminary

measures nevertheless aroused opposition both inside and outside Zaire. In June 1975 there was an unsuccessful attempt to assassinate the president. Seven army officers were condemned to death and twenty-six others were sentenced to imprisonment. The US ambassador was expelled because there was a suspicion that the Central Intelligence Agency (CIA) had been involved in the plot,[5] and relations with Belgium were strained until Mobutu offered compensation for any losses resulting from his nationalization policy. As a further conciliatory measure the government also decided to restore more than half the foreign-owned companies which had been nationalized. Although he still proudly rejected arbitrary foreign interference, Mobutu knew full well that Zaire could no longer survive without external aid.

That aid became even more necessary in 1977 and Mobutu's pride had to be swallowed rapidly. For some time the president had been assisting his brother-in-law, Holden Roberto, in his struggle to seize power in Angola after the withdrawal of the Portuguese government. In 1976 Roberto's efforts had been thwarted when the Russian-backed Popular Movement for the Liberation of Angola, led by Agostinho Neto, had declared itself to be the government. Roberto continued to wage a guerrilla struggle from bases in Zaire and the new Angolan government took reprisals by encouraging refugee Katangese gendarmes to launch an attack into Shaba (formerly Katanga) Province. The remarkable degree of success achieved by the small invading force, and the friendly reception given it by the inhabitants of Shaba Province, highlighted the ineffectiveness of the Zairean army and Mobutu's unpopularity in the region. An appeal to the USA for assistance in expelling the invaders brought a cautious response – not surprisingly, in view of recent events. America was prepared to make an airlift of medical and military supplies but would send no arms. France reacted more positively by supplying planes to transport a contingent of Moroccan troops who were responsible for driving the invaders back into Angola.

This brief contretemps focused world attention upon Zaire because its cobalt and uranian, as well as its copper, were of vital importance to the defence industries of the western powers. The reaction of those powers to local circumstances gave a clear indication both of the strategic importance of Zaire and the fallibility of its internal structure. Though they had ceased to view Mobutu with much enthusiasm, they had come to accept that his presence was vital to his country's survival. At all levels there appeared to be no alternative to Mobutu's government. Neither tribalism nor regionalism offered a viable substitute for unitary government. There was a total lack of any effective focus of loyalty save that imposed by Mobuto and the army. The leaders among those who sought his overthrow were, for the most part, in exile overseas and quite incapable of mustering local support. Nor were they united among themselves. Within Zaire there were some who, while recognizing the importance of the regime as a unifying force, believed that Mobutu himself should go. It was a view which only served to emphasize the lack of political understanding among the president's critics, for the regime clearly existed only by virtue of Mobutu's presence. The strength of his position was fully demonstrated in August 1977 when he arrested the one man whom some thought capable of succeeding him, Nguza Karl-I-Bond, the foreign minister, who was a Lunda and a nephew of Moise Tshombe. Nguza was charged with concealing prior knowledge of the invasion of Shaba,[6] found guilty and sentenced to death. Under pressure from foreign diplomats, Mobutu reprieved him and commuted the sentence to one of life imprisonment,[7] then once again he took the opportunity to reshuffle his cabinet.

Though he was able to demonstrate his ability to deal with internal opposition, Mobutu had been seriously perturbed by the near success of the invasion. He had never wholly relied upon the loyalty of the inhabitants of Shaba province, but their willingness to support those who took up arms against his government could clearly act as an example to others whose dissatisfaction sprang from economic rather than ethnic motives. Still worse, the failure of the army to deal with the invaders had undermined one of the most widely accepted justifications for Mobutu's rule – his ability to maintain order. To strengthen his position further, therefore, he visited France to thank the president for the help he had received and to build up goodwill in that quarter. In so far as the western powers were concerned, he was in a more favourable position than perhaps he deserved, because Zaire's financial debt to the west had become so great that the powers were anxious to guarantee the country's stability in order to protect the economy from total collapse.

The importance of that external support and the fragility of the country's internal cohesion were to be fully tested in 1978. The output of the agricultural sector remained depressingly low. Exports of coffee, rubber, and palm oil showed no sign of recovery, while the corn surplus of 1960 had been transformed by civil war and by administrative incompetence into a large shortfall which made it necessary to import corn even to meet the country's own needs. Dislike of Mobutu, too, was becoming more widespread but remained uncoordinated.

Mutiny among a section of the army and an attempt to encourage an armed revolt were successfully crushed and the leaders were executed or imprisoned.[8] But this left the ill-disciplined and badly equipped armed forces in no condition to resist another invasion of Shaba Province by Katangese refugees from Angola in May. The only well-trained force in Zaire was a presidential guard recruited mainly from Mobutu's own province, Equateur, but that was permanently based in Kinshasa.

The hard core of the invading force again consisted of former Katangese gendarmes, erstwhile supporters of Tshombe, whose objective was to re-establish a Lunda homeland in Shaba because they believed they could manage their own affairs better than a government based in Kinshasa could ever hope to do. That was the extent to which tribalism played any part in the military operations. The vast majority of the invaders were much younger men aiming simply to overthrow Mobutu's government because they thought it was tyrannical, but having little clear idea about what should replace it. Again the guerrillas were welcomed by those Lunda who had remained in Shaba but had never shown any disposition to accept Mobutu as ruler. Fortunately for the president, the rest of the country remained unimpressed by the invasion.[9] This was due in part to the widespread hostility to any suggestion that the Tshombe era should be revived and in part to the remoteness of the armed struggle which seemed to have little relevance for most of the population. The swift response of France to Mobutu's call for assistance resulted in the ejection of the rebels by French paratroops. Belgium responded more tardily but also supplied military forces to assist in the re-establishment of Mobutu's control. Nevertheless, the invasion had caused the temporary closure of the mines in Kolwezi which, in 1977, had supplied 47 per cent of the world's cobalt, and this led to flooding and a serious drop in output.

The predicament which had previously faced the western powers was now even more acute. Reluctant though they might be to continue to support a state which appeared so unstable, they could not stand by while Zaire lapsed into a chaos which would threaten their investments and possibly provide an opportunity for Russian involvement in the region. Support for Mobutu's regime remained essential. The arrival of an African security force consisting of troops from Morocco, Senegal, and other African countries, flown in by the US airforce in June, promised to provide an element of stability. An accord reached between Zaire and the government of Angola in October 1978 would, it was hoped, bring to an end the danger from that quarter. These moves were followed by the reinstatement of Nguza Karl-I-Bond as foreign minister, which Mobutu hoped would win the approval of the western powers. In these circumstances, the IMF, though still doubtful about Mobutu's government, agreed in August 1979 to make a further loan. President Carter, equally convinced of Zaire's strategic importance in his campaign against the spread of communism in Africa, persuaded the US government to increase its assistance. The belief that members of the Zairean government and the armed forces were deeply involved in corruption and embezzlement continued to worry external creditors, however, and gave rise to grave discontent inside the country.

By 1980 the inflation rate was running at 100 per cent and the government was having to act firmly against dissidents. Promises of further aid from the IMF and other donors were made strictly dependent upon the introduction of more effective measures to control the economy and to restore public order. But there was little immediate prospect of improvement on either front, in spite of Mobutu's efforts to reform the army with the help of French, Belgian, and Chinese instructors. Yet, thanks to the assistance of the IMF,[10] by 1981 the situation was beginning to improve. The deficit had been reduced and inflation had dropped to 50 per cent, though little impression had been made on the size of the external debt and there was still an acute shortage of foreign exchange. The IMF, therefore, granted a further loan aimed at reducing the inflation rate still further and at helping to improve the balance of payments. The USA, too, promised further help in the course of a visit which Mobutu paid to that country in 1981. These arrangements were made in the reluctant knowledge that, whatever his shortcomings, Mobutu was still the only man capable of holding Zaire together.

Once again, the president had been shuffling his cabinet. Justin Bomboko made a brief reappearance, first as state commissioner for foreign affairs, then as deputy prime minister, before again being consigned to the political wilderness. As a surprising alternative to this pattern, Nguza Karl-I-Bond, who had been promoted to the office of prime minister, took the initiative out of the hands of the president and resigned during a visit to Belgium in April 1981. From that haven he called upon the people of Zaire to overthrow the government and, in an attempt to enlist US support for his campaign, he published a document prepared by the Zairean parliament which alleged that Mobutu had misappropriated sums amounting to $150 million. The US government responded warily, reaffirming its support for Mobutu, the bird in the hand, rather than pursuing the less tangible prospect of acceptable government offered by Nguza. The American fear that Zaire might fall under Russo-Cuban influence was more pressing than any constitutional preference. Belgium, too, while urging greater freedom in Zaire, insisted that it wished to retain good relations with the existing government, being not unaware of its dependence upon the country's mineral exports. Within Zaire itself, the most vocal criticism at this stage came from the Roman Catholic Church, which denounced widespread corruption among the country's officials and pointed to the misery this brought upon the population. Here, too, however, the demand was for reform rather than for the overthrow of the government.

In spite of its concern to maintain stability, the patience of the IMF was severely tested in 1982. Because of administrative incompetence, receipts from all Zaire's main exports – copper, cobalt, coffee, industrial diamonds – fell below their expected levels and once again the inflation rate soared.[11] The loan agreement of 1981 was withdrawn and relations with the USA were strained when Mobutu renounced all aid from that quarter on learning of accusations in Congress that he had embezzled some of the funds already paid to Zaire. It is a clear indication of Mobutu's confidence in the western powers' dependence upon him that he could act so wilfully. The president's critics at home were active, however – some of them the self-same members of parliament who, according to Nguza, had accused the government of corruption. To promote their opinions they had founded a new political party, *L'union pour la démocratie et le progrès social* (UDPS), contrary to the terms of the reformed constitution of 1978 which had converted Zaire into a one-party state. For their temerity they were sentenced to fifteen years' imprisonment. Zairean exiles in Belgium were also becoming increasingly critical of the government and in October 1982 they showed a greater measure of unity than had previously been noted when they formed themselves into a popular front, claiming to have as their objective the restoration of democracy in Zaire. The following year Nguza formed a shadow cabinet in exile pledged to bring an end to Mobutu's government, if necessary by force. In May he firmly rejected the president's offer of a political amnesty on the ground that it would be contrary to his principles and to those of his associates to return to Zaire – a hollow claim, as events were to prove.

For his part, Mobutu introduced a number of measures aimed at running the country more economically. He reduced the number of ministries by ten, and in March 1983 a vigorous effort was made to impose greater central control on the country's finances, and in particular to restrain the power of administrators to alter the appropriation of funds without reference to the government. New people were also appointed to the finance and planning ministries with a view to creating a more effective team.

It is interesting that, in spite of the multitudinous difficulties which beset him, Mobutu never seemed at a loss to find financial aid. The reopening of relations with Israel in 1982 was balanced by the hostility shown by some Arab states which previously had been well-disposed to Zaire, but the loss of their help was made good by assistance from South Korea and the African Development Fund. The World Bank's International Development Association similarly offered to fund a rural development scheme in the north-east, intended to benefit more than 100,000 farming and stock-raising families in a region which had not previously been noted for its enthusiastic support for the government. Portugal was another country prepared to offer technical aid, while a visit to Paris by Mobutu in 1984 resulted in a promise of further French assistance. In July the president was in Belgium, Zaire's most important trading partner, where he was able to get further help in spite of the disruptive presence in Brussels of a considerable number of refugees from Zaire. Meanwhile, the International Development Association had made a grant of $26 million to improve the railway system which was essential for the transportation of minerals and agricultural produce. Even the USA relented to the extent of rescheduling much of Zaire's debt.

With all this support, and by adhering as carefully as possible to the IMF's recommendations, the economy once again began to show signs of improvement. Prices began to stabilize, and the currency was depreciating less rapidly. Inflation, too, took a down turn. Satisfied with this progress, the IMF made further funds available in 1985 and confidence in the government's efforts brought a loan from Italy for agricultural improvement in lower Zaire. The USA offered a further loan for road building and medical and water projects in Shaba province, where America had a strategic interest as part of its campaign to support Jonas Savimbi's struggle against the government of Angola. In 1986 Yugoslavia and Britain demonstrated their interest in investing in Zaire, while the International Development Association provided a loan to expand electricity supplies in Kivu province.

This assistance, and particularly the high cost of servicing the national debt which followed in its wake, had adverse effects as well as benefits for Zaire, and Mobutu sensed that too much external aid might, paradoxically, cause problems for his people. In October 1986, therefore, he challenged all his creditors by stating that the rate of servicing foreign debts would be reduced to 10 per cent of export earnings and 20 per cent of the government's operating income. This represented a reduction of 60 per cent from the previous level of payment. At the same time he transferred Kengo wa Dondo from the office of prime minister to that of foreign secretary. Kengo had been known to be a supporter of the view that Zaire should subscribe wholeheartedly to the IMF's policies. His removal from office and his replacement by Mabi Mulumba, a known critic of those policies, was intended to demonstrate to the people that the president was responsive to their complaints and concerned about their sufferings.

Once again Mobutu escaped what might have been expected to be the adverse consequences of his actions. Within less than two months he had received new offers of loans from the African Development Fund and the African Development Bank to assist in reactivating the Kilo-Moto Gold Mining Corporation. The USA, too, anxious to retain its military base at Kamina in the Shaba province, urged the IMF to help Zaire. US troops had already been permitted to train in Shaba, near the Angolan border. This was a mutually beneficial arrangement because, from the Zairean government's point of view, the presence of US military forces in that area was a warning to potential dissidents to proceed with caution in their opposition to Mobutu. At the same time, the president made it clear to his people that he was not the servant of the USA by opening diplomatic relations with Nicaragua, by signing a technical-assistance agreement with Romania, and by discussing the possibility of strengthening bilateral co-operation with the USSR. With an equal and compensatory measure of independence he then expelled three Russians accused of spying. Faced with such a display of buoyancy the IMF gave way, and in return the government agreed to improve its financial and budgeting discipline, starting with increases in petrol prices, but with corresponding increases in public-sector wages to attract better qualified people and in the hope of reducing dishonesty. The Paris Club followed the IMF's example by agreeing to a rescheduling of debt repayments as, too, did a meeting of private creditors.

Inside and outside Zaire, Mobutu's opponents continued to be active, though their efforts proved only mildly disruptive to the government. In Kinshasa, a bomb explosion in March 1984 killed five people and injured others. In June, supporters of the late Patrice Lumumba, calling themselves *Le mouvement national Congolais Lumumba* (MNCL), were arrested in connection with the explosion. At the other end of the country, a rising in Shaba province in November was quelled with the help of French troops. The government attributed the problem to rebels based in Tanzania, but the

Tanzanian government denied harbouring Mobutu's opponents. Zairean exiles in Belgium suggested that there had, in fact, been an army mutiny, and although Mobutu did not openly accept that view he did demand the retirement of a number of senior army officers shortly afterwards. In spite of this there was another attack in Shaba in June, and again Mobutu laid the blame on hostile elements based in Tanzania. About the same time, several members of the banned UDPS, who had been under arrest since 1982, were released. But a UDPS meeting in Kinshasa in October 1985 was broken up by government troops and some of the participants were arrested.

In 1986 the government renewed its campaign against the UDPS, which had now become the main focus of opposition to Mobutu. In January the minister of public affairs tried unsuccessfully to have two leading members imprisoned. They were Etienne Tshisekedi wa Mulumba and Kanana Tshongo, former members of the legislature. In June, however, they were restricted to their places of origin for allegedly writing and publishing seditious leaflets and encouraging university students to revolt. In March, Amnesty International had already claimed that, towards the end of the previous year, more than 100 supporters of the UDPS had been arrested in Kinshasa and in eastern Kasai, and that some of them had been tortured and executed. It also accused the government of similar offences in putting down the disturbances in Shaba province earlier in 1985. Mobutu publicly admitted on 24 June 1986 that he had embarked upon a policy of greater firmness against dissidents supported by foreign countries, and he deplored the proliferation of religious sects and the resurgeance of tribalism. On the latter count he was undoubtedly thinking primarily of events in Shaba, where the Lunda had persisted in their hostility to the government, though by that time the majority of them were motivated as much by a simple dislike of Mobutu as by any tribal or secessionist aim.

Elsewhere, the temptations of office which Mobutu could hold out to anyone prepared to support him vied with the hope of benefiting from his overthrow. In June 1987, Tshisekedi was one of two members of the UDPS – the other being Kibasa Maliba – to be welcomed back to membership of the MPR by Mobutu who spoke of them as long-lost sons.[12] Then, in October, the president accepted an oath of loyalty from seventeen new members of the central committee (cabinet), among them Kibasa Maliba. Yet in January 1988, Tshisekedi and Kibasa were the organizers of the demonstration in Kinshasa at which was sung the former national anthem of the Democratic Republic of the Congo, a demonstration which was broken up by the police who arrested hundreds of participants, including Tshisekedi himself. In response to the government's action, fifty-eight US congressmen warned Mobutu of the possibility that American aid to Zaire might be jeopardized if his country's human-rights record did not improve. Amnesty International, too, called for the release of Tshisekedi from detention – where he was said to be suffering from severe ill treatment.[13] Mobutu agreed to Tshisekedi's release, but a crowd of 5,000 UDPS supporters who turned out to greet him was set upon and many were injured.

A new challenge to the government came from the MNCL. More inclined to violence than the UDPS, members of the rebel movement attacked two eastern towns in July 1987. Then, in September, representatives of eleven opposition movements attended a meeting in Switzerland at which they agreed to set up a government in exile under the presidency of Paul-Roger Mokede with Albert-Jerry Mahele as prime minister. Their aim was to overthrow Mobutu's government, but their credibility, never very great, received a sharp setback when Mokede denied being involved and called upon the exiles to return to Zaire. They had, in any case, lost one of their key figures some years earlier. In June 1985, Nguza Karl-I-Bond had again renounced his opposition to Mobutu and had returned to Zaire in response to an appeal by the president himself. This action amounted to a clear admission by Mobutu's leading opponent that, without external assistance – and that would not be forthcoming – any attempt to overthrow Mobutu was doomed to failure. Nguza was at once appointed ambassador to Washington, from which post he was recalled to become foreign minister. Mobutu's ability to manipulate potential opponents still rendered opposition innocuous.

To make the administration more effective and more capable of controlling local disaffection, Mobutu next decided to increase the number of provinces. The experiment had already been tried in Kasai and Leopoldville and was now to be extended to Equateur, Kivu, Haut Zaire, and Shaba. At the same time it was decided to increase the number of members of the legislature representing Kinshasa from twelve to twenty-four. Mobutu was concerned, he said, by the ethnic and regionalistic trend in the voting, particularly in Kinshasa, in the elections to the legislature held in September 1987. Only three of Kinshasa's eight regions were directly represented in parliament; to restore the balance, by-elections were to be held in which only people resident in the five unrepresented regions would be allowed to take part. That such political engineering was necessary was almost certainly due to the unwillingness of people to vote for anyone they did not know well and suggested that ethnic bonds remained strong in such circumstances.

Indeed, after more than 20 years of Mobutu's rule, the majority of the population still feels confident only in its local affiliations. Yet they have come to accept that a strong central government, even one which is in so many ways distasteful, is the only guarantee of peace. Nevertheless, Mobutu's centralized regime has failed to win genuine popular support. His strength lies in a comprehensive intelligence and security network which provides him with information about his political opponents. He is indebted, too, to the loyalty of the army, which he preserves by generous treatment, particularly of the junior officers, who in some other countries have been a focus of discontent. Above all, the patronage which Mobutu has at his diposal makes it virtually impossible for any opponent to muster sufficient support to threaten his government. As in so many African countries, economic necessity drives many people to protect their interests by adherence to the man in power. At the same time, a breakdown in the country's economy would pose a serious threat to the government, but too many foreign powers are interested in Zaire's survival to make such a contingency probable. The USA may be beginning to feel less apprehensive about Russo-Cuban involvement in Central Africa, now that an accord over Angola has been reached, and may then lead the other western powers in showing less tolerance for Mobutu's more flamboyant expressions of his country's independence. But for some time to come the western powers will still be anxious to protect their interests in Zaire by guaranteeing a stable government. Against such an array of vested interest and governmental power, neither tribalism nor regionalism is likely to triumph, least of all in Shaba where the mineral deposits are so vital to so many people.

Mobutu himself remains an enigma. His motivation is difficult to fathom. He delights in wielding power and he is believed to be inordinately wealthy. He is widely unpopular both at home and abroad, yet there is no question-mark over his ability to survive. He is shrewd enough to realize that he can take risks because of the general fear of anarchy if his government were to collapse. Yet, in flouting the IMF he may not only have been concerned about the reaction of his people to the burden imposed by too close an adherence to IMF guidelines. It is possible that he has a genuine pride in his country and that, by asserting its independence in the face of outside disapproval he is satisfying a profound feeling of patriotism.

9   Angola: no man's land

'Is it not time for the West to show some sense of proportion about
Angola?' asked an editorial writer in *West Africa* on 7 September
1987. By 'the West' he meant, specifically, the United States which, in
his view, has pursued its own ideological and strategic ends in such a
manner as to deprive Angola of every prospect of developing its
potential. Other western countries, too, were not blameless, he said.
Although they had come to terms with the existence of the MPLA
(Popular Movement for the Liberation of Angola) government, they
had made no attempt to persuade their American allies to do the same.
Some of Europe's most prominent politicians were even supporters of
Jonas Savimbi's UNITA (National Union for the Total Independence
of Angola) rebellion. He might with justice have extended his
complaint to include South Africa, the USSR, Cuba, East Germany,
Czechoslovakia, China, Zaire, and several other countries, all of
which have been deeply involved in the affairs of Angola, and not
always to its benefit.

Ever since the Portuguese walked out of the country without being
able to hand over power to any generally accepted indigenous
successor, groups striving to seize control have relied upon external
assistance more than upon popular internal support. This is partly due
to the state of Angola's economy. Though the country is potentially
prosperous by African standards, the Portuguese had made little
effort to involve the indigenous people in the production of wealth
other than as unskilled labourers. The Portuguese withdrawal had
consequently resulted in the immediate loss of almost the whole of
Angola's trained personnel, and had completely destabilized the
country's economy. The more recent development of the petroleum
industry in the Cabinda enclave – again by foreign capital and
expertise – has created a new source of wealth, but much of it has been
spent on waging an internal war which no side seems able to win

but in the course of which each participant has turned increasingly for help to countries willing to provide military assistance and supplies of arms but uniformly reluctant to encourage economic development. The so-called civil war has thus become a struggle between external powers striving to establish a controlling position in Central and Southern Africa to fulfil their own strategic purposes. To that end the affairs of Angola have been wholly subordinated.

To speak of tribal or ethnic issues in such a context is almost an irrelevance. What is important internally is the rivalry between different groups of educated Angolans, each seeking to become the heir to the imperial inheritance. Nevertheless, the fact that the struggle has been particularly acute in Angola is due in part to the destructive and divisive nature of Portuguese conquest, and to the tenacity with which Portugal clung to what it conceived to be a potential source of wealth for the metropolis. First, the Portuguese slave trade had set one group of people against another, contributing to the breakdown of traditional societies. Then, the need to impose at least nominal control over the country in order to meet the demands of the Berlin and Brussels Acts led the Portuguese to use armed force to subdue all indigenous claimants to power. Next followed the disruptive demand for forced labour which resulted in the transportation of thousands of people over vast distances, away from their own societies, to regions where roads and buildings were under construction, where European settlers needed workers to tend their coffee crops or to tap wild rubber trees, or where industrialists were exploiting the country's diamond resources. From 1912, too, a new administrative system was introduced with the aim of destroying the remaining vestiges of indigenous authority and of setting one group against another so as to make it easier for the Portuguese authorities to maintain overall control.

While all these activities undermined the formal existence of traditional societies, they simultaneously enhanced the need for the Angolan peoples to cling to what was familiar in a world dominated by alien practices. In the circumstances of the time, this could only lead to the strengthening of small village communities. Large-scale protest was impossible, but the resentment felt towards Portuguese rule, though muted, was almost universal.

The Second World War saw the beginnings of change. In the early 1940s the formation of the Movement of Young Intellectuals of Angola in Luanda transformed some of the resentment into a positive attempt to emphasize the value of Angolan cultures. About the same time, young Africans from a number of Portuguese African dependencies who were living in Lisbon formed a Centre for African Studies with the objective of promoting the study of African identity. The Portuguese authorities closed the Institute, but in the 1950s a small nationalist movement was founded in Luanda. It called itself the Party for the United Campaign of Angolan Africans (PLUA). In 1956 the new group joined with the Angolan Communist Party to form the MPLA. It retained its base in Luanda because it was there, in the capital, that the handful of educated Angolan Africans congregated. Although paying tribute to Marxist–Leninist ideology, most of the leaders agreed that such a political programme would need adaptation to suit the needs of Africa. This did not mean that they wished to revive traditional polities, or even that they had any strong links with the mass of the population or any understanding of what form of government would appeal to the people. Their primary aim was to rid the country of Portuguese rule, an objective which they knew would attract widespread support, and to seize power themselves, an aim which might not be accorded such universal approval.

Another movement which developed in the 1950s was, initially, of a very different character. The Union of the People of Northern Angola (UPNA) had its base among the Kongo people on both sides of the Angolan/Belgian Congo border. Its leaders were associated with the former ruling families of the Kongo and claimed that the Kongo was still a separate political entity. It is some indication of the unreality of that claim and of the divisions that had long since destroyed that unity, to which reference has already been made in the context of political movements in Zaire, that the UPNA made no common cause with Kasavubu's ABAKO. To such a degree had European intrusion in Africa divided former African polities asunder. The UPNA, at this stage, was clearly a Kongo rather than an Angolan national movement. One of its leaders, Holden Roberto, attended the All-African People's Congress in Accra in 1958, where he realized that such a limitation appeared to be an anachronism in modern Africa. On his return he induced his fellow leaders to drop the 'Northern' epithet and when the name was changed to the Union of the People's of Angola (UPA) he himself became president. Nevertheless, though it recognized the need to look beyond the former Kongo kingdom for support, the UPA continued to draw its strength from the north. This in no way discouraged Roberto from accusing the MPLA of being unrepresentative. It consisted, he said, of intellectuals only, and they were even prepared to admit to their movement people of mixed blood, men who were not even true Africans.

Late in the 1950s the Portuguese authorities clamped down on these embryonic movements and the leaders of the MPLA were either arrested, like Agostinho Neto, or fled the country, like Mario de Andrade (the party's president), Viriato da Cruz, and Lucia Lara, who all three took refuge first in Paris, then in Conakry, and finally in Leopoldville. The UPA, too, set up its base in the capital of the former Belgian Congo when that country became independent in 1960. From there Roberto was able to keep in touch with his Kongo supporters and to establish himself, in the eyes of the outside world, as the most significant figure in the Angolan nationalist movement.

Military action against the Portuguese by the MPLA and the UPA began almost simultaneously. In February 1961 the MPLA engineered a rising in Luanda aimed at releasing political prisoners. The revolt was firmly suppressed and those who were able to make their escape fled north-eastward to the Denbos forest. From that refuge they launched occasional attacks in an attempt to disrupt the administration of the country. It was about that time that the USSR first showed an interest in the MPLA in response to an appeal for solidarity from Mario de Andrade, though its effort amounted to little more than an expression of sympathy. Meanwhile the UPA had launched its first military operation over the Congo border into northern Angola. It resulted in the death of a number of Portuguese nationals, as well as of educated Africans and people of mixed origin, thereby emphasizing the exclusively African objectives of Roberto. Again the Portuguese responded vigorously and the operation was quickly brought to an end. The struggle against a common enemy did not draw the MPLA and UPA together. Instead, their mutual hostility grew stronger because the leaders of each group were seeking power for themselves.

Neto's release from prison and his flight to the Congo in 1962, when he succeeded de Andrade as president of the MPLA, led to a split in the party. Neto was a typical member of the MPLA leadership. He was the mulatto son of a Methodist pastor and had qualified as a doctor under Portuguese rule. Da Cruz, too, was an intellectual, but that did not prevent his expulsion from the party, along with his supporters. Shortly afterwards, Neto and his own followers were driven from the Congo and moved their headquarters to Brazzaville. During this period the reputation of the MPLA sank very low in the estimation of outside observers. By contrast, and in spite of his own difficulties, Roberto kept a firm grip on his party, now renamed the National Front for the Liberation of Angola (FNLA). He set up a government in exile which was officially recognized by the Organization of African Unity in 1963 while the MPLA was in disarray. Although still essentially a movement of the Kongo people, the FNLA had clearly become the most effective group operating against the

Portuguese, and Roberto continued to insist that he was leading an Angolan nationalist movement, not a campaign to revive Kongo traditionalism.

Though cut off geographically and by the opposition of the FNLA from the remnants of his guerrilla movement in Angola, Neto did not give up the struggle. He restructured his party's organization and set out his socialist ideology uncompromisingly. This won for him the sympathy of the USSR, and with Russian approval Cuban military advisers helped to train MPLA troops in Brazzaville. China, too, gave some material aid. This was the starting point of the external involvement which was soon to dominate events in Angola. To the eastern bloc, intervention in Angola was a counterblast to American activities in Zaire. At the same time, other MPLA headquarters were set up in Dar-es-Salaam and in Lusaka. With Zambia's assistance, the movement was able to begin operations in the eastern portion of Angola's Moxico Province in 1966. In this way the obstacle interposed by the presence of the FNLA in the north was bypassed. Supplied with arms from the USSR and China via Tanzania and Zambia, the MPLA took up the challenge for the leadership of the anti-Portuguese campaign. Nevertheless, although its guerrilla operations were now more widely dispersed than those of the FNLA, its popular following remained small. Its support was still derived primarily from the educated elite.

It was at this moment that a new contestant for the Angolan political inheritance entered the lists. Jonas Savimbi had been a prominent member of the FNLA for some time. Flamboyant in style, he had frequently clashed with Roberto over policy matters. When the latter enlisted the aid of da Cruz, the former member of the MPLA, Savimbi quit the party. An attempt to join the MPLA having failed, he set up his own movement with a membership drawn mainly from his own Ovimbundu people. Subsequent observers were inclined to stress the ethnic basis of Savimbi's following, but he certainly never had any intention of establishing an Ovimbundu state. From the outset Savimbi saw himself as a leader of an Angolan nationalist movement even more clearly than Roberto had done. Initially, however, like many other African leaders, he found it necessary to seek support from the people who knew him best. But he quickly ensured that the leadership of his movement was chosen from a wide spectrum of Angolan peoples.

In time the Ovimbundu became the main victims of the war waged by Savimbi, and as a result their support for him became less than enthusiastic. Like the majority of those who suffer the pains of a civil war over which they have no control, the Ovimbundu came to have little sympathy for any of the combatants. Savimbi's followers, meanwhile, having started out to rid the country of Portuguese rule, soon became freebooters, living off the land until the time when they could force their rivals to share power with them. After unsuccessfully attempting to enlist the support of the USSR, Czechoslovakia, Hungary, East Germany, and China, they launched sporadic guerrilla operations in Moxico Province in 1966, claiming to be the only nationalist group to have its base in Angola itself. Soon, Savimbi was able to convince China that his was the most effective anti-colonial movement in Angola and so won support from that quarter.

Another political movement of a different character emerged as a result of the amalgamation of a number of factions in the Cabinda enclave. The Cabindan Liberation Front (FLEC) called for the right of self-determination for the enclave. It was a movement which certainly contained some ethnic elements, but the chief concern of its members was to prevent the profits from the region's oil resources from being controlled by whichever group governed Angola when it became independent. With an eye to winning potential advantages for themselves, several neighbouring countries were prepared to recognize Cabinda's separatist aspirations. Zaire, for example, persuaded Roberto and the FNLA not to intervene, though Neto and the MPLA would accept no such commitment. At the time, the MPLA was torn by internal power struggles between the leaders of the party's different areas of operation. Eventually, in 1974, Daniel Chipenda, who had made a good impression on the Chinese government, abandoned the MPLA and took the party's share of Chinese aid, together with his own local supporters, to the FNLA. To counter this, the MPLA's commitment to a Marxist–Leninist ideology brought still closer ties with the USSR, and a plentiful supply of Soviet arms gave Neto a new lease of life.

The aid was well timed. The Portuguese revolution of 1974 had given a new sense of urgency to the Angolan nationalist movement. But every attempt by the leaders of other African countries to encourage some measure of co-operation between the three main parties contesting the succession resulted only in frustration. Each group agreed separately to a ceasefire with the Portuguese but looked upon the arrangement as an opportunity to build up arms supplies in preparation for an internal power struggle. China and Rumania sent military supplies to the FNLA, which also gained considerable support from President Mobutu of Zaire, to whom Roberto was related by marriage. Help was also secretly provided by the USA on the initiative of the secretary of state, Dr Henry Kissinger, who hoped thereby to score a point in his continuing diplomatic campaign against Russia.[1] Simultaneously, the MPLA was receiving supplies from the USSR, from Cuba, and from a number of eastern European countries. The great-power struggle for a controlling influence in Central Africa – or to prevent any other nation from exercising control – began to build up, with puppet Angolan forces willingly employed to do battle in the hope of triumphing over their rivals in their own struggle for power. One nation which was to become profoundly concerned in the outcome of the struggle had not yet shown its hand, but the Republic of South Africa clearly could not sit back indefinitely and watch the build-up of forces overtly hostile to its very existence.

President Mobutu of Zaire was also watching events in Angola with considerable anxiety. His country was in difficulties and he did not want to see the USSR establish a dominant position in neighbouring Angola by co-operating with a party which was not well disposed towards Zaire. President Kaunda of Zambia was also concerned lest Russia should gain control over the operations of the Benguela Railway, one of his country's main export routes. It was, in fact, on Kaunda's initiative that the OAU put pressure on the three rival groups in Angola in January 1975 to come to an agreement with the Portuguese, as a result of which a transitional coalition government was set up in preparation for independence on 11 November. Hostility between the leaders of the groups was as strong as ever, however, and the committee of the American National Security Council decided to give covert aid to the FNLA. At about the same time, the USSR began to increase its arms supplies to the MPLA and 230 Cuban military advisers arrived to train the MPLA's armed forces in line with the training being provided for the FNLA by China.

The fears of Mobutu and Kaunda were not without foundation. Outside interference was escalating steadily, encouraging the contestants to become more active and less co-operative. In April the FNLA attacked a number of isolated MPLA posts in Luanda and the MPLA responded vigorously, having recruited several thousand Katangese gendarmes, former supporters of Tshombe, who had taken refuge in Angola, and financed, with tragic irony, by royalties from the American company, Gulf Oil, which was operating in Cabinda. Angered by this move, President Mobutu sent more than 1,000 Zairean troops to assist Roberto. President Kaunda, deeply concerned, warned the OAU in April that the fighting was becoming more serious. In June the OAU again summoned the three leaders to a conference where they agreed to renounce force and defined their various responsibilities during the remaining months of transition.

The USA still hesitated to become officially involved, but in June South Africa sent troops over Angola's southern border, though it was not until early August that they moved forward to take up positions protecting the Cunene hydro-electric project in which Pretoria had invested heavily and upon which industrial development in Namibia would depend. In July heavy fighting broke out again between the rival claimants to power despite the agreements reached in the previous month. Generously armed with American weapons the FNLA forces advanced southward, intent upon capturing Luanda before independence. Huge supplies of Russian arms which poured into the country in June and July helped the MPLA to contain the threat, but it was better organization and more determined leadership which proved to be the determining factors in the struggle. Roberto was no commanding general and, as events were soon to show, his Zairean allies were not to be relied upon when resistence against them stiffened. Nevertheless, in August, more CIA money was made available to the FNLA and it is clear the Kissinger at least believed, even if Congress made wary by events in Vietnam did not, that the only way to check Russian influence in central and southern Africa was to demonstrate that America would resist any advance by the USSR.

By this time the MPLA had become the most effective military force operating in Angola, but Savimbi was widely believed to command the largest popular following. Many African countries had been impressed by his efforts to make the coalition government work while his rivals were at each others' throats. Doubtless his own relative military weakness contributed to Savimbi's decision to play the role of mediator, but this weighed little with outside observers compared with the appeal of his exuberant and extrovert personality. At this juncture, the OAU's fear of intervening in the affairs of African countries proved a great disservice to Angola. An OAU commission of enquiry did, indeed, recommend that the Organization should send a peace-keeping force to Angola, but the MPLA, increasingly confident of military success, rejected the idea. Instead of insisting upon implementing the commission's proposal, the OAU wasted valuable time in discussing the situation. As a result, there developed a lively possibility that Angola would split into three parts on an ethnic basis, not because of any strong ethnic feelings but simply because the three rivals dominated different ethnic regions.

While the OAU hesitated, others were not so reticent. In response to further appeals from the MPLA and with Russian encouragement, Cuba sent heavy weapons and hundreds of soldiers who began to arrive in Angola in late September and October. Their task was probably only to act in a supporting role, but in mid-October, when the Cuban troops in Angola already numbered between 1,000 and 1,500, an invading force led by South African officers and backed by Chipenda's followers began a northward advance into the country. The column was joined by South African armoured car units supported by helicopter gunships and supplied by air. Savimbi later claimed that the South Africans acted in response to requests from Zambia, Zaire, and Ivory Coast after he himself had appealed to those countries for support. This seems not unlikely, for although South African troops had already helped UNITA forces to stabilize their position in the Ovimbundu plateau area, the new move constituted a far more serious threat to the MPLA. But is also had an adverse effect upon both the FNLA and UNITA, because the Cubans at once stepped up their military operations while African states which had been inclined to favour Savimbi became wary of a friendship which promised to link them with the hated practitioner of apartheid.

By this stage the Portuguese had ceased to play a military role. Their armed forces, which had been intended to share military responsibility with the nationalist forces of a coalition government, had been largely withdrawn. The transitional government was dissolved by Portugal late in August, but the independence date of 11 November remained. As that day drew closer, fighting between the rival parties grew more intense. Helped by the Cubans, the MPLA turned the FNLA and Zairean forces back from Luanda in December. Exploiting its success, the MPLA went on to destroy the FNLA as a significant fighting force before the end of the year. Henceforward the FNLA was reduced to minor guerrilla skirmishes in the extreme northwest. A half-hearted attempt by Cabindan secessionists to invade the enclave from Zaire in November was also repulsed decisively by the MPLA.

To crown its efforts the MPLA, in co-operation with the Cubans, turned against the UNITA and South African forces to the east and south of the capital. The resistance put up by UNITA was inadequate and Savimbi had to retreat. By February 1976 his campaign was at an end. Like the FNLA, though with South African assistance, UNITA reverted to guerrilla warfare in the east and south-east. Most important of all, the South African column which had come close to threatening Luanda turned back in January 1976 when the USA, disturbed by memories of Vietnam and distrusting Kissinger's arrogant and secretive style of diplomacy, signified its disapproval of South Africa's role in Luanda. In December 1975, the American Senate had inflicted a decisive defeat upon the administration by voting to cut off immediately all covert military aid to Angola, and many American experts on African affairs believed the administration's fears of unlimited Russian intervention in Southern Africa were greatly exaggerated.[2] Kissinger remained convinced that the senate's decision would encourage the Russians to renew their help to the MPLA, although they had previously suspended their airlift of military supplies for three weeks. In his opinion it was the absence of American aid rather than the presence of South African troops which had opened the door to the Cubans, and it could indeed be argued that the Cubans had begun their large-scale reinforcement of the MPLA as early as November 1975.

The MPLA had proclaimed a People's Republic of Angola (PRA) at the time of independence and the self-styled state was immediately accorded diplomatic recognition by the USSR and a number of other Communist countries. African governments were divided equally between those which supported the MPLA's initiative and those who disliked the party's radical policies and Communist friends. But South African intervention on behalf of UNITA had a more powerful impact on African opinion than did the presence of Cuban soldiers and Russian arms. Above all, the MPLA's convincing military victory turned the scales of African opinion in its favour. In February 1976 the PRA was admitted to membership of the OAU.

Beyond doubt the MPLA had a far greater number of educated leaders than did the other two parties, and it was far better equipped to set up a credible government. Roberto's hostility to whites and to people of mixed race, and his need to rely upon the Kongo people for support suggested that he was unfit to lead the country. Savimbi was very popular, but he lacked followers of leadership calibre. Nevertheless, the MPLA unquestionably came to power only with Cuban military aid, and neither it nor any of the other parties had nationwide support. Lord Chalfont, writing in *The Times* on 5 January 1976, insisted that tribalism must be a crucial factor in determining the way in which events were developing and that the MPLA, a detribalized movement with its roots in the urban areas, commanded little respect or support outside the towns. UNITA, by contrast, could rely on the Mbundu and Chokwe of Central and Southern Angola, and Savimbi's oft expressed desire for free elections was an indication of his confidence in popular support. The FNLA, meanwhile, had the backing only of the Kongo people. A leader in *The Times* of the same date made the far more significant point that, in spite of the OAU's insistence that Angola was an African problem, it had clearly become a superpower concern and that the OAU was powerless to do anything about it. In deciding to recognize one side or the other it was a question of choosing between competing outside interests rather than between tribal or ideological factions. This, indeed, has been the story of Angola since before independence.

The leaders of the MPLA, excluding a few who may have had strong pro-Russian sympathies, wanted to introduce some kind of socialism adapted to local needs, rather than importing a wholly alien ideology. But it remained a question as to whether the USSR would be prepared to restrict its intervention in Angola to accommodate such a policy. American attitudes were also important. As early as January 1976 there were indications that many MPLA leaders were aware that, in spite of their reliance upon Russia and Cuba for military aid, the reconstruction of their war-torn country would, in the final analysis, only be possible with assistance from the west, and that it was vital the USA should be induced to look favourably upon the idea.[3] In fact, before the end of January, and in spite of a strong counter-proposal by President Ford, the American House of Representatives confirmed the position taken by the Senate by voting overwhelmingly to ban all military aid to the anti-MPLA forces. It seemed, therefore, that popular opinion in America was prepared for some sort of *rapprochement* with the MPLA government.

One of the obstacles in the way of any such move was the tendency of the western press to insist upon describing the MPLA as Marxist and the FNLA and UNITA as pro-Western. Although some MPLA leaders were prone to emphasize their loyalty to Marxism they did little to put their protestations into practice. Savimbi, on the other hand, was not averse from trying to win support by parading the Russian menace, claiming that the USSR was trying to establish a Russian satellite in Angola and that those who defended Russian and Cuban intervention as a counter to South African involvement were lackeys of socialist imperialism. In a land of opportunists Savimbi was a leading exponent of the art. Ideology was never an important element in the struggle between the three groups. Each was anxious to seize power and each was willing to receive help from any quarter which seemed sympathetic and reliable.[4]

The first western power to recognize the MPLA government on 17 February 1976 was France, to the dismay of its EEC partners, who were prepared to accept the MPLA's military victory but considered that a joint approach should be made to the new government, discreetly rather than precipitately. France, however, though it had hitherto supported President Mobutu and hence the FNLA, was anxious to share in whatever benefits could be derived in Angola and would not wait for its partners. The decision of five other members to follow suit a day later seemed to many African countries an act of betrayal, particularly since Zambia was pressing for further attempts to reconcile the rival parties rather than recognizing the MPLA at once.

By the end of February, however, agreement was reached between the government of Angola and its long-standing opponent, Zaire, that neither would allow military activity to be organized against the other within its territory. This implied that the FNLA would no longer be able to use Zaire as a military base, but it proved to be an agreement which was honoured in the breach rather than in its observance. The American administration's reaction was one of concern lest Cuban troops should now be freer to become involved in Namibia, Mozambique, or Rhodesia. It was a concern that was in no way modified by an announcement from the presidents of Cuba, Guinea, and Guinea Bissau in March that they had pledged help for President Neto in his struggle against imperialism, colonialism, and apartheid in southern Africa.[5] Even the withdrawal of the last of South Africa's invading force across the Angolan border at the end of March brought little assurance of future peace, least of all to those who had taken refuge from the MPLA advance in South African camps inside Angola.

In the meantime, with the minimum permitted support of nine nations, the United Nations Security Council had passed a resolution condemning South African intervention in Angola. China did not take part in the voting. The USA, Britain, France, Italy, and Japan abstained, not because they approved of what South Africa had done but because they considered the motion should also have mentioned Cuban and Russian involvement. Russia and Cuba countered with the argument that they had intervened in Angola to help the Angolans and they could not now withdraw because the country was still threatened by the illegal presence of South African troops in neighbouring Namibia. The supporters of the MPLA government inside Angola firmly believed that the presence of the Cubans was their main protection against a renewal of the civil war. Neto certainly relied heavily upon Cuban and Russian advisors in key ministries. It was probably concern about the activities of UNITA in the south-east which also led him to invite Savimbi to take part in peace talks in June 1976. In the meantime, the MPLA handled its relations with the Ovimbundu of the central plateau – former supporters of Savimbi – with considerable caution and with some success. In June, however, the USA vetoed Angola's application for admission to the United Nations, and in July the government complained that the western imperialist powers were running a violent campaign of defamation against it under the influence of UNITA and FNLA propaganda.[6]

Against this background of conflicting interests, the government's task was enormous. The civil war had severely undermined an already thoroughly disorganized economy, and there was a grave shortage of the skills needed to effect a recovery in the industrial sector. Damage to roads made the problem of distribution acute, and although an attempt was being made to revive agricultural production as rapidly as possible, the lack of transport and skilled personnel reduced the impact of the operation. In the urban areas there was a shortage of food and the main export crops (particularly coffee) were almost non-existent because of neglect, while maize (a staple food crop) was in short supply.[7]

In May 1977, Neto, by prompt action, prevented a serious threat from within his own party. An armed rising led by Nito Akves – who had recently been dismissed from his post as interior minister – and supported by dissident troops, was put down by forces loyal to the president. It was originally thought that the prime motive behind the rising was resentment of the dominant role played in the government by people of mixed descent. Later reflection suggested that Portugal, France, and South Africa had also been involved, though the motives of the first two countries are difficult to comprehend. The role of the Cuban troops was also uncertain, though Basil Davidson claimed that they made their support for Neto clear even if they played no part in suppressing the rising.[8] Another commentator, however, claimed that he had it on high authority that the Cuban army, some 15,000 strong, refrained from taking sides until the rising had clearly failed.[9]

While the government was dealing with its internal problems, UNITA reacted vigorously in the south-east to a campaign launched by MPLA and Cuban troops. In July 1978 Claude Cheysson, EEC commissioner responsible for relations with the Third World, visited Luanda to try to initiate a scheme for economic aid which would enable the west to counterbalance the influential position established by the USSR and Cuba. In its turn, the US administration, having concluded that the UNITA forces could never overthrow Neto's government without the sort of massive aid which Congress was not prepared to give, turned its attention to reducing the guerrilla threat to Neto because that seemed the only way to bring about a Cuban withdrawal from Angola. To this end, the US government put pressure on

President Mobutu to stop assisting the FNLA and UNITA. Both Neto and Mobutu saw advantages in reaching a practical accommodation which would be more effective than their previous agreement. Angola had, in fact, continued to provide the bases from which the National Front for the Liberation of Zaire had launched its attack on Kolwezi early in the year, while Mobutu had supported the FNLA's incursions into Angola. A meeting between the two presidents in August 1978 gave hope of future co-operation.

Soon the threat from South Africa increased, after an agreement between the MPLA government and President Castro committed Cuba to giving still further military support. Neto, now in poor health, had also to beat off another attempt from inside his party to oust him from the leadership and to replace him with someone more committed to Marxist principles. Having repulsed the challenge, and after dismissing several senior ministers, Neto even admitted he favoured a moderate degree of private enterprise so long as it did not clash with the MPLA's socialist policies.[10] He also announced that he was ready to establish diplomatic relations with the USA, and accepted an invitation to open diplomatic relations with China in spite of the hostile reaction with which the USSR would almost certainly greet the news. West Germany, too, established diplomatic relations with Angola in August 1979, while East Germans, bringing sophisticated weaponry, were increasingly employed by the MPLA in supporting roles.

President Neto died of cancer in Moscow on 11 September 1979. He had done nothing to groom a successor and had spent the last year of his life shuffling his cabinet in order to ensure that potential successors could not establish a firm power base. Most of these latter were people of mixed blood – *mesticos* – against whom Nito Alves had launched his abortive coup; in the event, José Edouardo dos Santos, another *mestico*, became president. Within the MPLA, dos Santos appeared to have wide support, and he affirmed his commitment to Neto's policies – particularly in respect of the development of ties with the west. But he still had to deal with the same economic problems. Coffee production, which had averaged 212,000 tonnes in the years 1970 to 1974, had dropped to 54,000 tonnes in 1979.[11] Moreover, the government believed it necessary to maintain some sort of balance between conflicting external interests and, after a visit to Moscow by dos Santos, a strong Russian military mission arrived in Angola early in January 1980. This coincided with the announcement that a purge had begun to eliminate all those who disagreed with the MPLA's Marxist line.

In June, South African troops invaded Angola, occupying part of Cunene Province immediately over the border from Namibia. The aim of the operation was to destroy SWAPO guerrilla bases, and the troops withdrew by the beginning of July only after their mission had been accomplished and not in response to protests from the UN. Almost immediately, too, South Africa carried out another raid over the border, while UNITA forces destroyed harbour installations and fuel tanks in Lobito, the Atlantic end of the Benguela Railway which Savimbi's troops had rendered inoperative since independence. Nevertheless, in spite of UNITA's widely scattered operations and further raids from South Africa, the government held firm control of the central plateau region, the home of the Ovimbundu who, if the Press were to be believed, were the tribal allies of Savimbi.

Abroad, the US administration remained hostile in spite of a change of president. Alexander Haig, Ronald Reagan's nominee for the position of secretary of state, announced that the USA could not recognize Angola as long as Cuban troops remained in the country. If the MPLA government had a change of heart, he said, the situation would be different, but the new American administration was looking for results, not promises. This firm attitude produced the opposite effect to what had been intended. In December 1980, only a month after it had substituted an indirectly elected people's assembly to replace the provisional council of the revolution, the hitherto cautious government took steps towards introducing a fully Marxist state.[12]

Though the government might make its political gestures – provided they had the support of one or other of the major powers – on the economic front it was forced to admit that a more pragmatic approach was needed to deal with the apparently endless crisis. For example, incentives would have to be given to induce small farmers to produce more for sale. The lack of transport which had prevented them from sending their crops to the urban centres, and the absence of manufactured goods for them to buy with their profits, had for some time discouraged them from growing more than they needed for their own subsistence. By putting most of its energy and resources into providing seed and fertiliser for the nationalized farms taken over from the Portuguese, the government had also failed in its attempt to stimulate the production of crops for export. This, too, had to be changed.

Military matters also called for more than statements of principle. South Africa had recently become even more aggressive in response to Robert Mugabe's victory in the pre-independence elections in Rhodesia – now Zimbabwe – in 1980. The South African government had planned to build a constellation of southern African states, consisting of its own homelands together with the former British protectorates and Namibia. It would then be prepared to extend economic and commercial help to its neighbours provided they recognized the new political arrangement. Under Bishop Muzorewa's brief leadership, Zimbabwe had seemed ready to co-operate in this plan. Mugabe's victory, however, had replaced an amenable leader by an actively hostile one. At the same time, the democratic Turnhalle alliance, through which South Africa had hoped to retain friendly relations with Namibia, had also collapsed.[13] In these circumstances, Angola had every cause to look warily over its southern border.

The situation became still worse when the US government asked Congress, early in 1981, to repeal the law passed in 1976 forbidding the supply of aid to insurgents in Angola. Since the USA had not recognized the MPLA government, it was argued, there should be no obstacle put in the way of helping its opponents. Inevitably, the proposals stirred up fears in Africa that the Reagan administration intended to favour South Africa openly. In fact, the underlying aim of the convoluted – and, to African observers, thoroughly confusing – policy of the USA was to try to frighten the Angolan government into putting an end to its dependence on Cuba and the USSR, thereby strengthening America's hand in its efforts to induce South Africa to accept Namibian independence. At the time it seemed unlikely that either Angola or South Africa would respond favourably to such tactics. Angola did not trust South Africa's intentions, while South Africa was opposed to any suggestion that Namibia should achieve independence under UN auspices lest it should pave the way for the victory of SWAPO. Nevertheless, whether or not it was aware of these difficulties, the US Senate voted to repeal the ban on aid to UNITA.

In the event, the election of President Reagan seemed only to boost South Africa's confidence in adopting an aggressive policy. The previous year, the government in Pretoria had been discussing Namibian independence with a five-power western contact group consisting of the USA, Britain, France, West Germany, and Canada. Now it was determined to destroy SWAPO completely, in the belief that Reagan would welcome the creation of an anti-communist alliance with South Africa.[14] This view was reinforced when the USA vetoed a Security Council resolution condemning South African incursions into southern Angola. For its part, the Angolan government concluded that South Africa now intended to set up an independent buffer state along the Namibian border which would be controlled by UNITA, and in despair offered to negotiate with the USA at any time. The economic cost of maintaining the confrontation with South Africa was crippling, and the MPLA was distressed to learn of the warm welcome given to Savimbi when he visited the USA. Perhaps, in an unexpected way, the US plans were already beginning to bear fruit.

Nevertheless, dos Santos felt that he could not honourably withdraw his support from SWAPO, but in the new circumstances – as he saw them – he felt increasingly constrained to work for Namibia's independence by negotiation rather than through military victory. The help Angola had already given to SWAPO's military struggle had resulted in the loss of control of about 50,000 square miles of Angolan territory along its southern border, a loss which the government could scarcely view with equanimity. In an attempt to weaken South Africa's position by peaceful means, therefore, Angola joined eight other African states in signing a preferential trade treaty in December 1981 which, they hoped, would reduce their economic dependence on South Africa. It was a hazardous undertaking in the light of dos Santos's admission that there had been a 26 per cent drop in food production in 1981, which meant that there was likely to be a severe food shortage in 1982. Worse was to follow. Two years of plentiful oil on the world market had seriously reduced Angola's profits from the Cabinda oilfield, and technical problems in the oil sector added to the government's problems by causing a sharp decline in oil production. At the same time, a persistent drought made agricultural recovery virtually impossible.

In March 1982 South Africa recommenced its raids, and, when ground troops were not involved, war planes attacked targets in Angolan territory. Three months later, Prime Minister Botha, believing he would have American support, said that South Africa was ready to accept western terms for a Namibian settlement provided all Cuban troops were withdrawn from Angola. Angola, however, insisted that the presence of Cuban troops was essential for the security of the country and was in no way related to the question of Namibia's future. President Castro added to the confusion by maintaining that Cuban troops would remain in Angola until all South African troops had been withdrawn from Namibia and there had been an end to aggression against Angola and to all external help for rebels.[15] The US government also intervened, claiming that a parallel withdrawal of Cuban forces from Angola and of South African forces from Namibia was the key to a settlement in south-west Africa.[16] While the various participants were busy affirming their principles and intentions, South African troops held on to southern Angola and carried out sporadic raids northwards. UNITA forces, gaining in confidence, surrounded the town of Huamba on the Benguela Railway. Once more the Angolan government was beleaguered on every side, and once again the Ovimbundu suffered most severely as a result of the fighting, and were no more gently handled by UNITA than by the MPLA.

Another power struggle within the MPLA leadership marked the beginning of 1983. This was the culmination of a lengthy period of criticism from those who disliked the 'right-wing' tendencies of dos Santos and his supporters. The president, his opponents claimed, appeared to favour the removal of Cuban troops in order to open negotiations with UNITA. Although dos Santos refused to change his policy to appease his critics, he was under strong pressure from Moscow not to give in to America's call for the withdrawal of Cuban troops.[17] He even took the offensive and strengthened his position by the temporary suspension of some of the more left-wing elements in the party leadership, confident that he had the support of the MPLA's central committee in pursuing a policy of negotiation with South Africa and UNITA. Against a background of intensified fighting between South African troops and SWAPO, Angolan and South African officials met in the Cape Verde islands to discuss a ceasefire, but their efforts were undermined by SWAPO's bellicosity. The irony of the situation lay in the fact that Angola was far more involved economically with the west and with South Africa than with either the communist bloc or her other African neighbours. While 85 per cent of Angola's exports, mainly oil, went to the west, only 8 per cent of its overseas trade was with the USSR. Similarly, 90 per cent of Angola's trade within Africa was with South Africa.[18]

The complicated nature of Angola's foreign relations and the disruptive effect it had upon the country's policies became even more disconcerting when dos Santos visited Moscow in May and made a joint announcement with the Russian leaders claiming that the main sources of tension in Southern Africa were racism, colonialism, and South Africa's policy of apartheid. Not surprisingly, the five members of the contact group – with the possible exception of France – were led to conclude that there was more to be gained from maintaining good relations with South Africa than with Angola. Faced with further South African aggression and continued guerrilla incursions among the Ovimbundu by UNITA, the Angolan government then blamed the USA as much as South Africa for its predicament. African observers believed it not inconceivable that the US government had decided that Savimbi, with South African support, seemed likely to win an outright victory over the MPLA. When, therefore, South Africa proposed in December 1983 that it should withdraw all its forces from Angola if satisfactory conditions could be agreed, most African countries received the offer with scepticism. Both the Angolan government and SWAPO rejected South Africa's offer of a trial cease-fire. In reply, South Africa launched its biggest attack on Angola since 1981. On the sidelines, Britain and West Germany condemned South Africa's action but went no further. Yet another example of the paradoxical situation in which Angola found itself was that the country's diamond mines were almost totally controlled by the South African De Beers Company, yet such profits from the mines as reached the government were largely used to maintain the military struggle against South Africa.

In January 1984, dos Santos wrote to the UN secretary-general to say that Angola was ready to implement a thirty-day truce from the end of the month, provided that South Africa pledged to initiate the seven-month process leading to UN-supervised elections in Namibia within a further fifteen days. He made it clear, however, that this had no bearing on Cuban withdrawal from Angola. It was a vain proposal, because Angola was in no position to insist on its terms while South African forces were making important gains in fighting 125 miles inside the country and powerful groups of UNITA fighters had crossed the Benguela Railway and were marching on the capital, Luanda.

Savimbi, meantime, was proclaiming the nobility of his intentions by stressing that his object was to encompass the withdrawal of all Cuban forces and eastern European advisors with a view to forming an interim coalition government to be followed by a general election. While admitting that he was not himself in a position to set up a government for the whole country, he argued that UNITA was in its strongest military position since 1975. It controlled the whole of the Angolan border with Zambia and 200 miles of the border with Zaire. His propaganda machine, it is true, sometimes exaggerated UNITA's strength, but there were genuine fears that South Africa intended to step up its military operations still further with the aim of putting an end to all SWAPO incursions into Namibia and of destroying the main defensive line drawn by Angolan troops across the country. With characteristic irony, the Angolan forces were now strengthened by the arrival of MiG helicopter gunships and Sam missiles from Russia, paid for from the profits of American oil installations in Cabinda and South African-owned diamond mines.

Once again the USA intervened when representatives from that country met with others from South Africa and Angola in Lusaka to discuss the possibility of a permanent cease-fire. The USA argued that

Angola must, surely, be only too relieved at being able to send home expensive Cuban troops if it were guaranteed protection against attack from South Africa. SWAPO, too, would be delighted to be given power in Namibia, while South Africa would not only save the expense of waging war to protect its frontiers but would be dealing with a SWAPO government which would have to rely on close economic integration with her powerful neighbour if it were to survive. Angola's future, it would seem, was to be determined as part of a general settlement in south-western Africa if America had its way. SWAPO, which had not been represented in Lusaka, was sceptical about the whole idea, and although Angola promised – in return for a South African withdrawal – to ensure that neither Cuban troops nor SWAPO guerrillas would be allowed to move into the areas vacated, it found it impossible to fulfil its promise completely.

External commitments jeopardized the proposed settlement. Dos Santos visited Cuba and signed an agreement with President Castro under the terms of which Cuban troops would be withdrawn from Angola, provided there was an end to aggression by South Africa, the USA, and their allies, together with a cessation of aid to Savimbi and independence for Namibia accompanied by the withdrawal of South African troops from that country. This seemed suspiciously like an attempt to reverse dos Santos's earlier claim that the withdrawal of Cuban troops was Angola's own internal affair and in no way related to Namibia. News of the agreement naturally disturbed South Africa. The USSR, for its part, had been none too pleased with the measure of agreement reached between Angola and South Africa in Lusaka but contented itself with a warning to Angola against any American attempt to set up separate puppet states in Cabinda and along the southern border.[19] Angola, however, seemed intent on carrying out the recommendations of the Lusaka agreement, not only by trying to intercept SWAPO guerrillas but also by announcing that its expressions of support for the African National Congress and SWAPO were no more than a confirmation of positions of principle and had no bearing upon its actions under the Lusaka Accord.[20]

UNITA showed no sign of reducing its military activities. In April 1984 Savimbi again said that he was anxious to form a government of national unity with the MPLA but threatened that if he did not get co-operation he would carry the war into the towns and cities. *The Times*, reporting this news, still referred to the MPLA as Marxist and described UNITA as pro-Western,[21] but six weeks later admitted that the title 'pragmatic nationalist' would be a more appropriate description of Savimbi.[22] Richard Dowden, reporting for *The Times* from Angola, said that Savimbi was vague when questioned about the differences between the policies of the MPLA and UNITA, and gave the impression that he was fighting because he thought he, rather than dos Santos, should rule Angola. He believed that South Africa supported him because it wanted a stable and friendly government in Angola, but insisted that if he were in power he would not be beholden to South Africa, though he would not tolerate guerrillas operating against South Africa from Angola.[23] In the meantime, he thought the USA should put more pressure on the Angolan government to take part in negotiations for an internal settlement.

In October 1984, dos Santos offered to give a commitment in advance that Cuban troops would be withdrawn from Angola in stages, in conjunction with the phased withdrawal of South African troops from Namibia. This was the first overt, official admission by the Angolan leader of any link between the two operations. Still confident of his position, Savimbi threatened that if UNITA were excluded from any peace negotiations his guerrilla forces would obstruct every effort to implement an agreement. It emerged, too, that when Angola spoke of the phased withdrawal of Cuban troops, it still envisaged the retention of 10,000 soldiers to protect the capital and Cabinda's oil refineries, while the rest would only begin to return to Cuba when UN peace keeping forces were in place in Namibia and South African troops in that country had been reduced to 1,500.[24]

The US government was beginning to tire of South Africa's insistence upon intervening in Angola's affairs. Cuba, too, threatened to reinforce its garrison in Angola because South Africa had failed to meet the terms of the Lusaka Accord, and ruled out any possibility of withdrawing its troops before Namibia became independent. Once again, Angola's future was thrown into doubt – deepening the human tragedy which the power struggle had created. A *New York Times* journalist, James Brooke, who visited the central-plateau region in January 1985, confirmed reports of the devastation created by the war – abandoned villages, untilled fields, the once prevalent herds of cattle long since stolen or eaten, the survivors suffering from malnourishment in a land which, little more than ten years ago, had produced so much grain that Angola had been able to export large quantities of it.[25]

At a conference of non-aligned ministers held in Luanda in September 1975, dos Santos called for mandatory sanctions against South Africa and urged the American people to stop their government from giving aid to UNITA. Nothing daunted, South Africa announced that it had carried out another hot-pursuit raid into Angola to deal with SWAPO fighters. But the tide was beginning to turn against Savimbi. Better training for the MPLA troops, provided by Portuguese counter-insurgency instructors, was beginning to take effect, and UNITA's advance was turned back. South Africa carried out a further raid across the border to assist Savimbi, but the action was unanimously condemned by the members of the UN Security Council. South Africa protested that there had been a dramatic change in the military supply situation in Angola in the past eighteen months because of the arrival of large numbers of Russian aircraft, and appealed to the USA to support a military operation to relieve the pressure on Savimbi's forces. Shortly afterwards, a government attack launched against UNITA in July met with a sudden and serious reverse, though whether this was due to South African intervention was not clear. What did become clear was that President Reagan was anxious to dissimulate over the aid he was ready to give to UNITA so that he was not inhibited from taking part in negotiations to settle the Namibian question.

Dos Santos himself was now strongly in favour of dialogue with the USA and South Africa in the hope of ending the war. The second party congress of the MPLA was faced with a formidable task if it were to make plans to settle the country's economy. Half a million people were in urgent need of food and 80 per cent of them were displaced from their homes and were without shelter, blankets, and cooking materials. Military spending absorbed between one-third and one-half of the revenue. Only the state oil company, which was responsible for 90 per cent of export earnings, was a clear economic success.

When Savimbi visited the USA in January 1986 he received a friendly welcome from the President and a clear indication of moral and political support. In spite of Congress opposition, Reagan shortly afterwards sent supplies of Stinger ground-to-air missiles to UNITA, an action which was widely condemned in Africa and caused even President Kaunda – who had throughout adopted a conciliatory attitude to the problems of Angola – to express doubts about America's sincerity as a peacemaker. Dos Santos also said he could no longer accept that the USA had a mediatory role in Angola, and he embarrassed the US State Department by revealing an agreement, signed in 1984 but kept secret, in which the USA allegedly promised to withhold aid from UNITA.[26]

In June 1986 the government launched a large-scale, dry-season attack against UNITA and once again South Africa responded by threatening the town of Cuito Cuanavale in southern Angola. In

September, Reagan won an important victory when the Democrat-controlled House of Representatives voted to continue covert aid to UNITA. Savimbi, meantime, in the course of a controversial visit to the European parliament, launched an appeal for peace talks in Angola without pre-conditions. These visits by Savimbi to America and Europe were distressing to the MPLA government which could not understand why a guerrilla leader should receive such official treatment. It was a reasonable complaint, because the action of the USA and the European countries involved suggested that they were convinced of their right to intervene in Angola's internal affairs. Even greater uncertainty was aroused by the announcement in March 1987 that US troops were to take part in joint manoeuvres in Zaire. These manoeuvres were said to be intended as protection for Mobutu's government, but the fact that they took place in an area containing the airstrip from which military supplies were being flow to UNITA did little to reassure the Angolan government.

In spite of these various disagreements, talks between Angola and the USA were re-opened in Brazzaville in April 1987, and in July the two countries pledged to continue negotiations towards achieving peace. Yet contradictions still continued to occur. Large quantities of arms arrived from Russia to help the government prepare for a new offensive against UNITA, while President Reagan promised further Stinger missiles and important anti-tank weapons to help UNITA in dealing with a recently arrived shipment of Russian tanks. The government was playing a risky game in gambling with such disparate partners because it was simultaneously begging the UN for international emergency assistance to meet the desperate shortage of food, particularly among the urban population where famine was threatening. Dos Santos was forced to admit that the enormity of the country's economic problems called for measures which might seem at odds with the socialist programme to which the MPLA was ostensibly committed. Foreign trade, he said in the course of a seminar on the country's economy, was vital to Angola's recovery, and it was dangerous to continue with measures that did nothing to resolve the country's economic problems. He did not propose a total change from a socialist to a private system, but he hoped to make the management of the economy more efficient by concentrating state effort upon the most urgent tasks and by keeping a watchful eye on those engaged in private activity.[27] Co-operation with Western countries was essential in this phase of national reconstruction, even to the extent of co-operating with the IMF.

The new government offensive met with heavy losses in spite of being led by Russian troops. South African forces played a vital role in the struggle and South Africa said that Russia's ultimate target was South Africa itself. This latter claim was made in an attempt to justify to the white electorate the heavy casualties suffered in the course of the fighting. Nevertheless, the South African government was determined to inflict such a damaging blow on the Angolan government that it would have to come to terms with UNITA. For a time it seemed that, in spite of lengthy discussions and President Reagan's anxiety to reach a solution before the end of his term of office, South African interests would be the factor which determined the outcome of events. However, suddenly, on 22 December 1988, the picture changed. An agreement was signed by Angola, Cuba, and South Africa under the terms of which Namibia was set on the road to independence and Cuban troops were to be withdrawn in stages from Angola. At the same time, South Africa formally waived its claim to intervene on behalf of UNITA.

The breakthrough, though resulting primarily from the persistent diplomacy of the USA, owed a great deal to an improvement in the relations between the USA and the USSR, both of which had played a significant role in the history of Angola since independence. The new understanding that was growing between the two countries made it possible for them effectively to impose their own terms upon the parties involved – the Angolan government being forced to accept the prospect of a Cuban troop withdrawal and South Africa having to contemplate Namibian independence on UN terms. Pretoria's former truculence and evasions suddenly seemed of little significance if the two great powers were prepared to guarantee Angola's independence and ensure that Namibia did indeed hold elections under UN supervision. South Africa, it should be said, was not wholly dissatisfied that the end of such costly military operations was in sight. But the problem of Angola's future was still unresolved. Generous external aid might provide the infrastructure upon which the revival of the economy might be attempted. There remained the task of determining how, and by whom, the country was to be governed. Savimbi firmly rejected the proposal, put forward by the leaders of a number of neighbouring African countries, that UNITA should be incorporated into the MPLA government. He wanted direct talks with the MPLA leading to the formation of a government of national unity which, in turn, would be followed within two years by multi-party elections. Again it seems as if the issue might well have to be determined by the fiat of external powers. Certainly, ambitious rivals for power will not be able to call upon either tribalism or ethnicity to influence this decision while 'great-power' strategy remains so deeply concerned with the outcome.

10 Zimbabwe: the latecomer

In the course of a lecture delivered in Zimbabwe in 1985, Professor Terence Ranger concluded that 'tribal identity is *not* inevitable, natural, unchanging, given, but a product of human creativity which can be re-invented and redefined'.[1] Much of what is deemed to be tribalism – even by many of Zimbabwe's inhabitants – is, he maintained, the invention of the colonial period, a categorization useful in promoting a number of settler or administrative objectives, though often adopted by the African population if they saw that to do so might be of help to them. The question is whether Professor Ranger's fears that such identities might become paramount, to the serious detriment of the black population, were in fact realized during the long struggle for independence and whether they still exert a malign influence today. Certainly, the English Press would appear to hold that view, and it is true that sharp and often corrosive divisions occurred among those fighting for majority rule. Journalists usually described those divisions as being between the Shona and Ndebele peoples, writing of them as if they were clear, tribal entities. Sometimes they also commented on the sub-tribal divisions which, they said, appeared among the Shona. Is this a true version of events?

Zimbabwe undoubtedly contains as rich a variety of ethnic and tribal groupings as other African countries and, as elsewhere in Africa, those groupings have adapted to new circumstances. Unlike the other countries dealt with in this book, it also has a sizeable white-settler population – many times more numerous than that of Kenya. Unlike Kenya, however, Zimbabwe – formerly Southern Rhodesia – was governed for more than half a century by white settlers who were intent upon remaining in charge. The determination with which they clung to that aim was demonstrated by their growing attachment to the idea of a unilateral declaration of independence if Great Britain persisted in demanding equality for Africans.

It was this attitude which gave rise to a feeling of intense dissatisfaction among many Africans, who saw their neighbours throughout the continent taking responsibility for their own government while they themselves seemed doomed to permanent subjugation. Hence the emergence of political movements like the African National Congress (ANC), which was banned in 1959 after all its leaders and some 500 supporters had been arrested on the declaration of a state of emergency by the government. Only Joshua Nkomo among the prominent members of the movement escaped because he was visiting Britain when action was taken against the Congress. Early in 1960, the National Democratic Party (NDP) was founded as the successor to the ANC. When its leaders were also arrested, Nkomo became president of the party.

These were genuinely nationalist movements, but it would be wrong to think of them as commanding the support of the majority of Africans in Southern Rhodesia. While many Africans deeply resented white domination, they did not see the emergent political parties as a viable alternative. Many of those who wanted political change would have been content at that stage for blacks to have a share in the government rather than demanding majority rule. If, therefore, the new constitution which came into force in 1961 – and which guaranteed Africans at least 15 seats in a parliament of 65 members – had been introduced before the arrest of the ANC and NDP leaders, it might well have proved widely acceptable. Indeed, a number of members of the NDP were still prepared to accept it, though it was overshadowed by the imminent breakdown of the Central African Federation and so did not go far enough to satisfy Nkomo and his followers.

When the NDP itself was banned in 1961, Nkomo founded the Zimbabwe African People's Union (ZAPU), and that in turn was banned in the following year. Thereafter, the victory of the hard-line white Rhodesian Front in the elections of December 1962 put paid to any hopes of the successful implementation of the 1961 constitution. In the circumstances, even Nkomo seemed to lack the aggressive edge looked for by some of his educated followers who broke away in 1963 under the leadership of the Reverend Ndabaninge Sithole and Robert Mugabe to form the Zimbabwe African National Union (ZANU). Violence took place between members of the two parties in a number of townships where the political movements could make a greater impact and where the African population was more easily terrorized by both groups intent upon forcing them to join their cause.[2] This was an inauspicious development in the campaign for majority rule. The divisive factor, however, was neither ethnic nor tribal, but one of personality, though no less deeply rooted on that account.[3] Later in the year, the first recruits of the Zimbabwe African National Liberation Army (ZANLA) – the military wing of ZANU – were sent to China for training. Nkomo, meanwhile, formed the People's Caretaker Council (PCC) and on 31 December 1963 the Central African Federation came to an end.

When Winston Field, the Rhodesian Front prime minister, failed to gain the British government's approval for an independent Rhodesia unless his party was prepared to grant equal status to Africans, he was replaced by Ian Smith. Though he did not immediately state that he intended to introduce UDI, Smith was clearly working towards that end. It was the knowledge of this that finally persuaded the leaders of ZANU that only armed struggle would achieve their objective of winning majority rule.[4] This was not, like the Mau Mau movement in Kenya, the frustrated gesture of incoherent peasants and labourers. It was a decision taken by educated men with a clear objective in mind, and it did not have mass support. Moreover, the arrest and detention of Nkomo, Sithole, and Mugabe in 1964 deprived the new parties of their most effective leaders and left them prey to still more disputatious lieutenants. From this time, both ZANU and the reactivated ZAPU were forced to carry on their work from Zambia.

The declaration of UDI on 11 November 1965 was, indirectly, a declaration of war by the white government against those who sought for African control of the country. Nkomo and his followers, though reluctantly forced to the conclusion that armed struggle might become essential, still hoped that Britain would intervene militarily to overthrow the RF government. The failure of the British government to assert its authority after discussions with Smith on board HMS *Tiger* in 1966 and *Fearless* in 1968 proved conclusively to both ZAPU and ZANU that they had nothing to hope for from British intervention.[5]

From this moment the two parties frequently claimed that a united front was needed to overthrow the white government, but no advance was made in that direction. Nkomo persisted in believing that ZANU was simply a small breakaway group which should rejoin the main body of his party. The ZANU leaders, however, would consider union only on equal terms and they believed that Nkomo lacked the dynamic qualities needed by a party leader. The fact that all the main leaders were in detention in Rhodesia while their supporters – now determined to wage a guerrilla war against the government – were dispersed in strictly separate camps in Zambia, made the exchange of ideas between the various elements within the two parties virtually impossible.

Within ZAPU itself there was dissension, mainly because of the difficulty experienced by sections of the party located in different camps in trying to maintain regular contact with each other. Even at this stage, however, the divisions which occurred sometimes did so along Shona/Ndebele-speaking lines.[6] The reason for this was simply that language differences added an almost intolerable complication to the difficulties already experienced by the guerrillas, and in so doing introduced a new element of suspicion between them. This was not tribalism in any political sense, and all parties were clearly united in their pre-eminent desire to rid the country of white domination. Nevertheless, disagreement over who should lead this enterprise made co-operation difficult, and the government's intelligence organization was able to widen the rifts by infiltrating the guerrilla organizations and encouraging distrust between potential rivals. The ZANLA guerrillas were not popular in their host country, Zambia, and this increased their sense of resentment against the Zimbabwe People's Revolutionary Army (ZIPRA), the ZAPU military group, which appeared to have the blessing of the Zambian government. So successful, too, were the Rhodesian security forces in gaining information about guerrilla movements that virtually every attempt to penetrate Rhodesia across the Zambezi River met with disaster. From 1969 to 1972 guerrilla incursions almost ceased.

A change in tactics by the African leaders was urgently necessary. James Chikerema, acting-chairman of ZAPU, opted for conventional warfare in addition to guerrilla activity. It was not an easy policy to put into effect, in view of the small number of guerrilla fighters and the inadequacy of their arms supplies and training. By contrast, the ZANLA leaders, influenced by their Chinese instructors who first arrived in 1969, and recognizing that they must somehow stir up more active support, decided upon a programme of politicizing the Rhodesian people before pursuing further military operations. It was to be of future importance that they also decided to direct their efforts towards north-eastern Rhodesia, an area which was more densely populated than the region immediately south of the Zambezi where the people were less hostile to the security forces than were the mainly Shona-speaking peoples who straddled the Rhodesia/Mozambique border in the north-east. The ZANLA guerrillas exploited the twofold advantage to be gained from operating in this area. First, over the Mozambican border, FREMLIMO opponents of Portuguese rule were taking a firm grip on Tete province and, unlike the Zambian government, were happy to provide a refuge for the guerrillas. Second, by invoking the spirit of Chaminuka (a prophet involved in the rising against British rule in 1896/97) and of Nehnda (a medium who had been executed during that struggle), they bound the people of the region to their cause.[7] By this latter action, however, ZANLA tended to become particularly associated with Shona-speaking elements in Rhodesia.

During the lull which preceded further military activity by the guerrillas, Abel Muzorewa, a bishop of the United Methodist Church, emerged as the most significant African leader out of detention. Muzorewa regarded himself as the spokesman for Joshua Nkomo, and although he was a political moderate, he was stout in his defence of African political claims. He was, as one of his colleagues who fell out with him freely admitted, a man of great courage and sincerity, but he was not schooled in the realities of nationalist politics.[8] Above all, he was totally lacking in the ruthlessness which was becoming essential for an effective leader. A Shona-speaker from Umtali, he nevertheless tried to address himself to the needs of all the African peoples of Rhodesia. In 1971 he mustered widespread support for the rejection of a settlement, which Smith had been tentatively negotiating with the British government, on the grounds that Africans would get better terms at a later stage. Smith persisted in his efforts to woo Muzorewa but without success.

It was not until December 1972 that ZANLA carried out its first guerrilla attacks in north-eastern Rhodesia. They marked the beginning of a new phase in the campaign which was ultimately to bring victory. Nevertheless, the guerrillas were anxious to avoid confrontation with security forces because, as Herbert Chitepo, the Lusaka-based chairman of ZANLA admitted, they were not yet in a position to achieve success by these means.[9] Instead, they increased their efforts at politicizing the African population and were prepared to use methods of terrorism to achieve their objective. In this way they were assisted by the ineptitude of the government in dealing with the inhabitants of the frontier zone in its efforts to prevent them from helping the guerrillas. Because the government had nothing positive to offer the people, the latter concluded that to support the guerrillas was the better option, and after the withdrawal of the Portuguese from Mozambique in September 1974 the ZANLA guerrillas had still further opportunities to continue their operations from bases in that country.

In the latter part of 1974 Smith agreed, under pressure from John Vorster, prime minister of South Africa, to release the detained African leaders with a view to initiating talks with them and of offering parity of representation in parliament. Sithole had already lost his hold on ZANU after denouncing the armed struggle some years earlier, and by 1975 he had been formally replaced as president of the party by Mugabe. Nkomo, on behalf of ZAPU, now claimed that he would accept nothing short of majority rule, but already Mugabe mistrusted the older leader's fixity of purpose and set little store by his words. An attempt by Muzorewa to establish an accord between the different parties resulted in the signing of a declaration of unity by Nkomo, Sithole, and Chikerema – who had acted as chairman of ZAPU during Nkomo's detention – but it proved ineffectual.

The Rhodesian intelligence forces exploited to the utmost the divisions between ZAPU and ZANU and also those within ZANU itself, where a violent power struggle was taking place. On the instigation of Rhodesian intelligence men, the ZANU leader, Chitepo, was killed by a car bomb in Zambia in March 1975. This aroused widespread mutual suspicion among ZANU members as well as encouraging President Kaunda, who was already angered by the disputes and the disturbances stirred up by ZANU in his country, to take action against the ZANLA guerrillas. Mugabe was convinced that the Zambian government had played some part in Chitepo's murder.[10] Meanwhile, the disarray in the ZANLA forces following these events, together with pressure from Vorster and the impact of economic sanctions imposed by foreign countries, encouraged Smith to open discussions with Nkomo.[11] The talks continued until 1976, but failed to reach any conclusion because Smith was determined not to accept majority rule. But the fact that Nkomo had agreed to take part in the deliberations confirmed Mugabe's doubts about his trustworthiness.

It was under further pressure from the American secretary of state, Henry Kissinger, and from South Africa that Smith agreed to hold talks with the African leaders in Geneva in October 1976, under British chairmanship, in return for an end to sanctions. Ostensibly, Smith had at last agreed to majority rule on the understanding that certain key ministries, including defence, should continue to be held by whites. The African representatives at the conference were selected by the African presidents of neighbouring states and included the by now virtually powerless Sithole, together with Bishop Muzorewa – who was the official leader of the United ANC but in fact commanded little support – and Nkomo and Mugabe. The two latter had supposedly formed an alliance under the name of the Patriotic Front (PF), but were united only in their common opposition to the proposals now put before them. In the course of discussions Nkomo again proved to be less of a hard-liner than Mugabe, but the conference broke up because no common ground could be reached among any of the parties involved and Smith had been saved the embarrassment of having to make known his real views on majority rule.

In January 1977, unity between the African parties suffered another setback when Jason Moyo, a particularly militant ZAPU leader who had been a staunch supporter of united action by ZIPRA and ZANLA forces against the government, was killed by a car bomb in Lusaka. Once again, suspicion was widespread and distrust increased between all parties. It is still not clear who was responsible for the murder. Smith, meantime, had accepted that he must make a pretence of accepting majority rule if he were to win outside support for his government, but he was reluctant to permit the African leaders to return to Rhodesia. He did, however, allow Sithole to return from Malawi in July 1977, and in order to reassure the government Sithole agreed to abjure terrorism. In so doing he lost the last vestige of support he had formerly commanded among those campaigning for majority rule.

It was to Nkomo that Smith again turned in an attempt to reach some sort of agreement. In September 1977 the prime minister flew to Lusaka to meet the African leader, but the result of the encounter was merely to anger Muzorewa, who believed that he alone could bring unity between blacks and whites, and Mugabe, who was not prepared to make any concessions to Smith but who could not be excluded from any discussions which held out any hope of success. Nkomo appeared to have ignored the strength of Mugabe's feelings and of the support which his rival could command, and in so doing he destroyed the very slender possibility of united PF action.

Having failed to make progress with Nkomo, Smith embarked upon an attempt to reach an internal settlement with Muzorewa, Sithole, and Chief Jeremiah Chirau, another Shona speaker, though he did so without real conviction. Muzorewa and Sithole insisted that the PF should be included in the talks, but while Nkomo might have been prepared to take part without Mugabe, the latter remained convinced that he would get a better deal if he were to continue the armed struggle. Eventually, in March 1978, Muzorewa, Sithole, and Chirau did reach an agreement with Smith, but Nkomo and Mugabe, for different reasons, refused to join in – the former from fear of the consequences, the latter because he was committed to continuing the fight. Andrew Young, the black American politician, was in no doubt after meeting Mugabe in 1978 that the latter was in fact 'fighting for personal power'.[12] The agreement accepted majority rule based upon universal adult suffrage and the immediate setting up of a transitional government which would include African ministers.

Muzorewa, honest and sincere though he was, lacked the political experience and personal qualities of leadership needed to hold together the African members of the transitional government, and he certainly lacked the power to compel or persuade Nkomo and Mugabe to bring the guerrilla war to an end. In fact, acts of terrorism were now intensified to demonstrate the power of ZANLA and ZIPRA and to frighten people away from the transitional government. In the latter endeavour the guerrillas were unsuccessful. There was still no active, widespread commitment to the leadership of either Mugabe or Nkomo.

Further secret negotiations opened by Smith with Nkomo, with the backing of President Kaunda who was anxious to disembarrass himself from the presence of ZIPRA forces in Zambia, were intended to get a stronger African leader into the transitional government. But the discussions foundered when ZIPRA forces shot down an Air Rhodesia passenger aircraft and murdered some of the survivors. In any case, the plan was unlikely to have been successful because Mugabe would never have accepted subordination to Nkomo and would simply have carried on the fight. The only result was that when news of the negotiations was leaked, the Patriotic Front became even more divided. The transitional government was too inept and the leaders, Muzorewa and Sithole, Chirau and Smith, were too much at variance to take advantage of this situation and it failed dismally to win popular support. By contrast, many European countries, and a number of Arab states, were becoming more friendly, though both Britain and the US urged Smith to call off the elections which had been planned under the internal agreement. Smith persisted however, and, in spite of widespread threats of disruption from both ZANLA and ZIPRA, the elections were successfully held in April 1979. Accusations that the security forces had intimidated the electorate had little foundation, a further indication that neither Mugabe nor Nkomo had convinced the majority of the people that they had much to gain from adopting their tactics. Muzorewa and his supporters in the UANC won 51 of the 72 African seats in parliament.

At midnight on 31 May 1979, Muzorewa succeeded Smith as prime minister of Zimbabwe–Rhodesia. His prospects of success in his new office were immediately vitiated, however, when seven of his party's MPs, under the leadership of Chikerema, resigned, and the prime minister lost his overall parliamentary majority. Sithole and his supporters also refused at first to take part in the proceedings of the new parliament, but by August they had relented. Further problems were presented by the reluctance of Britain and the USA to end sanctions and by Britain's refusal to recognize Muzorewa's government. The British government then undermined Muzorewa's position still further by demanding new elections under commonwealth supervision. The explanation for this move was that the new prime minister, Margaret Thatcher, had been pressed to intervene by Presidents Kaunda and Nyerere, speaking on behalf of Nkomo and Mugabe respectively, during the Commonwealth conference held in Lusaka in 1979. Significantly, Muzorewa had received no invitation to attend the conference.

The all-party discussions which opened in London in September 1979 to determine the constitutional future of Rhodesia demonstrated all too forcibly the complex nature of the divisions which existed in the country and the extent to which the desire for power motivated both Nkomo and Mugabe. Both these latter were anxious to introduce their own form of government into an independent Zimbabwe. Meanwhile, Muzorewa could muster the support of his delegates for the constitutional proposals put forward by Britain and Smith only with the greatest difficulty, and one member of the transitional government never did accept them. The PF at first rejected the proposals, but finally accepted them when the chairman of the conference, the British foreign secretary, Lord Carrington, threatened to go ahead and make a deal with Muzorewa without them. Nevertheless, only the firm intervention of President Samora Machel of Mozambique, who threatened to withdraw all support from ZANU, induced Mugabe to accept the proposed terms for a cease-fire.

Muzorewa had scarcely begun to feel the full weight of the opposition he faced. The British government, after getting the approval of the African leaders for an agreement, asked him to stand down from his office so that all parties could fight the elections on what the British optimistically described as equal terms. Muzorewa acquiesced in the proposals as a matter of conscience, but in so doing lost any hope he might have had of winning the elections. In the eyes of many of the Rhodesian people he had surrendered without a struggle an office he had won with their support, thus opening the way for more militant leadership. Mugabe, on the other hand, came out of the conference well, because of his intellectual superiority and his clear determination to get what he wanted.

The constitutional agreement was signed on 6 December, and Lord Soames was appointed as governor while Zimbabwe–Rhodesia temporarily reassumed its colonial status. The cease-fire agreement was then signed on 21 December, but there were fears it might not be observed by some of the ZANLA leaders who wanted to go on fighting until they controlled the whole of the country. Although the guerrillas were required to assemble at designated places and surrender their arms before voting took place, there was still concern lest fighting should continue unless ZANU won the elections. For this latter reason the support which Muzorewa initially attracted among the women of Mashonaland, and among the population of Manicaland generally, quickly ebbed away. Military force wielded by Africans, rather than by Europeans, now determined allegiances.

The overall advantage clearly lay with ZANU rather than with ZAPU because the former could deploy guerrillas throughout the greater part of the more populous eastern regions. ZAPU, for similar reasons, had almost the unanimous, but numerically more limited, backing of Ndebele speakers, of whom Nkomo was one. Only in Bulawayo, where there had been an influx of Shona-speaking workers, whose loyalty lay with their families in the east, was there any challenge to Nkomo's party in Matabeleland. Nkomo, Muzorewa, and Sithole all claimed support in south-eastern Rhodesia, but only Muzorewa's party was able to find effective political leaders in that region. It was the effectiveness of the intimidation carried out by ZANLA which won the day in the elections, however. Although some 20,000 ZANLA guerrillas reported to the collecting centres and handed in their arms, several thousand more mingled, still armed, with the electorate to ensure support for Mugabe's ZANU (PF).[13] Their presence had its effect and many who had been reluctant to commit themselves to any party clambered aboard the ZANU (PF) bandwagon. The steady flow back to the country of some 200,000 ZANU and ZAPU sympathizers from Mozambique and Zambia also weighted the scales against Muzorewa. Voting began in February 1980 and on 4 March the results were announced. Mugabe's party had won 57 seats, Nkomo's 20, Muzorewa's 3, and the rest none. Mugabe had thus achieved an outright majority in a 100-seat parliament in which 20 seats were reserved for whites.

Mugabe, as the future prime minister, immediately set out to reassure the white population by appointing two white ministers, and by promising that mines would not be nationalized and that there would be security of tenure for landowners if they made an adequate contribution to the country's prosperity. At the same time, and to satisfy Nkomo and his followers, most of whom were now described by foreign journalists – and probably thought of themselves as being – Ndebele, he agreed to a coalition with ZAPU and offered Nkomo the presidency of the country. Nkomo rejected the latter offer, seeking instead to become minister of defence, and when that post was not forthcoming, accepting the ministry of home affairs. His party gained three other seats in the cabinet and three posts of deputy minister. Admitting that there were not enough Africans with ministerial experience to create an effective government, Mugabe then asked that Soames or another British minister should remain in a guiding role for up two years.[14] The British government rejected the proposal because it was anxious to get out of a situation that had been a cause of embarrassment for some time. Consequently, at one minute after midnight on 18 April 1980, Zimbabwe came into being as an independent country with the uncontroversial Reverend Canaan Banana as its president.

Though Mugabe professed to be a Marxist, his government was not particularly friendly towards the USSR which had previously rejected ZANU (PF) in favour of ZAPU. His initial policy was to treat Zimbabwe as unaligned in its dealings with foreign powers until they showed whether or not they were friendly. Though he demonstrated great restraint in his dealings with ZIPRA and ZAPU, neither of which was particularly co-operative, he was surprisingly harsh in his treatment of Muzorewa, who was imprisoned on unspecified charges.

The problems facing the new government were not simply political in character. Economically, there was much lost ground to recover. Formerly an exporter of maize – the basic food of the African population – Zimbabwe had become a large-scale importer because of the insecurity engendered by the guerrilla war. The hope of financial recovery based upon the export of the country's chief foreign exchange earner, tobacco, was undermined by the decline in world prices due to widespread over-production. In spite of these problems, it was internal political divisions that created the most fundamental difficulties for the government. The absorption of the former ZANLA and ZIPRA guerrillas into a new national army, incorporating the soldiers of the former Rhodesian army, presented considerable problems. In November, fighting broke out in Bulawayo between former ZANLA and ZIPRA troops, and order was restored only with the greatest difficulty. The white population, too, remained ill at ease, in spite of frequent reassurances from the government. The fear of Mugabe's Marxist opinions was only partly assuaged by his signing of the Lomé Convention in November 1980 which established links between Zimbabwe and the EEC.

In January 1981, Nkomo was removed from the ministry of home affairs and offered the public service ministry after he had condemned the government's decision to transfer control of five South African-owned newspapers to the Zimbabwe Mass Media Trust. The move, he protested, would enable ZANU to use the Press as its private mouthpiece. Early in February, there were clashes between rival factions within the army in Bulawayo and Gwelo. The fighting soon attracted a number of guerrillas who had not yet been disarmed, and it was some time before Nkomo was able to persuade his ZIPRA supporters to surrender their weapons. Even after that, a few hundred held on to their arms and took to the bush in Matabeleland Province, prepared to resist a government led by men they did not believe they could trust. It was with reluctance that most of these were finally disarmed in May 1981.

Timely rains, and the reassurances given by Mugabe to white farmers, resulted in a bumper maize crop in 1981. But the profit which might have accrued from exporting surplus maize was lost because the shortage of rolling stock and a lack of co-operation from a hostile South Africa made the transport of both maize and tobacco extremely difficult. This resulted in Zimbabwe's first visible balance-of-trade deficit since 1968. The country's dependence upon communications passing through South Africa made reprisals impossible. As Mugabe freely admitted, it also prevented the government from putting into effect a policy of economic sanctions against its neighbour, although the prime minister remained one of the most outspoken advocates of such measures being taken by other countries. In fact, in March 1982 it was necessary to renew Zimbabwe's preferential trade agreement with South Africa. Not to have done so would have cost the country 50 million dollars in exports and would have put 6,500 jobs at risk. These were losses which Mugabe could not contemplate in view of the feelings of insecurity which already existed in Zimbabwe. At the same time, his relations with the white population at home and with potential foreign investors were not helped by his announcement in a New Year message in 1982 that, in pursuance of a socialist programme, the state would play an increasingly important role in every aspect of the economy, including agriculture and mining. The further proposal, made known in March 1982, that the constitution was to be changed, gave further cause for anxiety among potential investors – in spite of assurances that any property they acquired would be secure.

Nkomo, too, was angered by Mugabe's insistence that only policies approved by ZANU (PF) would be implemented. This, Nkomo pointed out, was at variance with the agreement which Mugabe had signed in Lancaster House and which affirmed the sovereignty of parliament. He was consequently in no mood to accept a plan for the merger of ZANU (PF) and ZAPU which was put forward in February 1982. Mugabe, in turn, was incensed by the discovery of arms caches on farmland belonging to Nkomo's supporters. They had almost certainly been hidden there for defensive purposes in the event of an emergency, but Nkomo and three other members of his party were dismissed from the government – charged with having been plotting to overthrow the ruling party.

Distrust between the leaders had communicated itself to their followers. Fears of a violent clash between the two parties proved to be unjustified, but a plot was said to have been uncovered involving members of the Rhodesian Front and some of Nkomo's supporters and aiming at the secession of Matabeleland Province. Shortly afterwards, the remnant of the ZIPRA guerrillas who had not previously laid down their arms began a series of raids in Matabeleland which were to continue intermittently for more than five years. Nkomo condemned these dissidents while criticizing the government for pursuing the policy of a one-party state – which, he said, could only cause fear and opposition among the members of ZAPU. He denounced in equally strong terms an attack on the homes of the prime minister and of another minister, Enos Nkala, in Harare, the name given in 1982 to Salisbury. Mugabe, however, was not propitiated, and accused Nkomo of being linked with the attacks.

The guerrilla operations in Matabeleland Province led to fierce reprisals by the army – consisting mainly of Shona speakers – and these acts aroused sympathy for the guerrillas among people who were forced into regarding themselves as Ndebele by the hostility of Mugabe's supporters, although they might otherwise have condemned the guerrilla movement. Hundreds of people were arrested in Bulawayo in an attempt to track down the dissidents. The government was still further roused in July when twelve fighter planes were destroyed in a night attack on an air-base at Gweru. A number of white and black members of the airforce were arrested. Yet Nkomo still took it upon himself to approach Mugabe in August, proposing that discussions should be held between their two parties. He was genuinely anxious to put an end to the violence in Matabeleland, but he felt strongly that the brutality employed against civilians by 5 Army Brigade, trained by North Koreans, was excessive and was only likely to stiffen opposition to the government. Nor was he reassured by the announcement that a sixth brigade was to be raised from Shona-speaking areas and trained by North Koreans. Mugabe, it seems, thought that Ndebele speakers were not wholly to be trusted and he wanted to make up for the defection of a number of former ZIPRA members from the national army. Inevitably the violence continued, and there were several casualties when guerrillas – believed to be supporters of ZAPU – attacked cars, buses, and a train in western Matabeleland in December 1982. To be able to identify oneself as Shona was now to belong to the ruling group. The Ndebele, on the other hand, regarded themselves as an unjustly oppressed minority. To that degree had ethnic identities hardened.

All these problems were exacerbated by drought which caused great distress to the farming community, as well as ensuring a continuing deficit in the balance of payments. The devaluation of the currency by 20 per cent in December 1982 was a blow to the whole population but was deemed to be necessary in order to meet the requirements of the IMF, which was contemplating a loan to help the government to stabilize the economy.

Though the economy continued to be a serious problem, the division within the Patriotic Front was an even greater source of distress. What, before independence, had been essentially a split between two small, rival, guerrilla groups based outside Rhodesia, had become since independence a struggle between two large language groups inside Zimbabwe, each of which was increasingly assuming an ethnic, even tribal identity. Their geographical location now identified ZANU (PF) and ZAPU, both in their own eyes and in the eyes of the outside world, with the Shona and Ndebele speakers respectively.

In March 1983 the government ordered the army to seek out dissidents in Bulawayo. Nkomo fled to Botswana and thence to Britain. A liberal white politician and former prime minister, Garfield Todd, said that a conflict of terror was taking place in Matabeleland. The Roman Catholic bishops of Zimbabwe also condemned army brutality in the province. Mugabe insisted that the army's action was the nation's response to the excesses of a guerrilla force which was striving to wreck the country's plans for regeneration. Though he rejected the bishops' charges, he did, however, offer to investigate every criticism of the army which was backed by evidence. But the government's reputation for justice was tarnished when six former members of ZIPRA were found not guilty of plotting to overthrow the government and of illegally possessing arms, but were then served with detention orders without any further charges being brought against them. They were later ordered to be held indefinitely without trial, though one of them, Dumiso Dabengwa, was released in November on the order of the High Court.

In August, Nkomo returned to Zimbabwe, but met with an unfriendly reception when he reclaimed his seat in the assembly from which his opponents had tried, unsuccessfully, to exclude him on the ground that he had unconstitutionally absented himself for more than twenty-one consecutive days. Another attack was then made on Bishop Muzorewa, who was arrested when about to fly to the USA. He denied that he had planned to have talks en route with the South African government, and he protested vigorously against an order for his indefinite detention. But the government's uneasiness was further reflected when a warning was issued to the Reverend Ndabanyingi Sithole not to conspire against the government.

The replacement of the minister of home affairs, Herbert Ushewokunze, early in 1984 – because of his misuse of emergency powers – produced no noticeable change in government policy. His successor, Simbi Mubako, almost immediately imposed a dusk-to-dawn curfew over a considerable part of southern Matabeleland, claiming that his having sent a large number of troops to the area had had a salutary impact upon guerrilla activities. Nkomo, however, denounced the atrocities – which, he said, were being carried out by the troops. Once again, Roman Catholic bishops intervened, accusing the army of preventing food supplies from reaching the area, in the hope that by so doing they would put an end to rebel activities. The ban on food supplies was lifted in response to the complaints but, after visiting southern Matabeleland, Mugabe accused the bishops of becoming agents of Nkomo. He himself, he said, was satisfied with the army's behaviour. The curfew was lifted in August 1984, but the antipathy existing between the two leaders encouraged their supporters to commit acts of violence under the impression that they were defending their very existence.

That Mugabe should be intolerant of opposition, particularly when he believed it to be aimed at promoting sectional interests, was understandable. The rehabilitation of the country was an enormous task. Inflation was rising steadily. The foreign debt had doubled and redoubled. Cuts in departmental expenditure had become inevitable at a time when the need for further expenditure on a variety of projects called for the availability of greater financial resources. New taxes had had to be imposed upon people who could ill afford to pay them. In such circumstances, the need to divert effort and finance into dealing with armed dissidents was a distraction the country could well do without. The spread of insurgency beyond the borders of Matabeleland in the middle of 1984 was particularly disquieting; and it explained, if it did not wholly justify, the ban on opposition party meetings in the centre of the country and in western Mashonaland.

Mugabe had always insisted that it was his intention to introduce one-party government when the time was opportune. His reiteration of that aim, and the suggestion that it would be implemented after the elections in February 1985 if a majority of the people wanted it, was regarded by Nkomo as a direct attack on himself and his supporters. Mugabe, however, was confident of his majority, and in September 1984 he ordered the release of Bishop Muzorewa – detained since November 1983 – leaving him free to lead his United African National Council in the elections. He also lifted the ban on opposition party meetings but threatened to reimpose it if the parties encouraged violence.

His generosity was short-lived. Moven Ndlovu, a ZANU (PF) senator, was murdered in the southern border town of Beitbridge. Instigated by ZANU (PF) supporters, riots broke out and the nine rural council members, consisting of six ZAPU supporters and three whites, fled. Mugabe at once dismissed the two remaining ZAPU cabinet ministers, and three senior ZAPU officials were detained under emergency laws. The time had come, he said, for ZAPU to be declared an enemy of the people. Shortly afterwards, Gini Ntuta, a ZAPU member of parliament, was shot dead on his farm in Matabeleland. Early in 1985, Nkomo himself found it increasingly difficult to address public meetings because of the violent disruption created by supporters of ZANU (PF). At the end of February, five members of Muzorewa's UANC were shot dead at Hwange railway station after a party meeting, and on the same day supporters of ZANU and ZAPU fought a pitched battle in the streets of Bulawayo. A few days later, government troops cordoned off the town, ostensibly in order to carry out a search for rebels and to prevent a recurrence of violence. Nkomo protested that their real aim was to demoralize his supporters, and again the Roman Catholic church denounced the violent methods used by the army in Matabeleland.

In the midst of these disturbances it had been impossible to prepare electoral registers and to delimit constituency boundaries. As a result, the elections planned for March were postponed until June 1985. The High Court rejected ZAPU's plea that this still did not allow them adequate time to choose candidates and allocate them to constituencies. When the elections did take place at the end of June and in early July, Ian Smith's Conservative Alliance of Zimbabwe, which had been steadily losing support, won a surprisingly convincing victory in the voting for white seats. The result angered Mugabe, who insisted that Smith's followers had not displayed the loyalty which the government might reasonably have expected. He therefore threatened to abolish white representation at an early date, irrespective of the terms of the Lancaster House agreement. In the elections for black seats, ZANU (PF) increased its representation from 57 to 63, even scoring some victories in Matabeleland. The implications of this are unclear unless it meant that the military superiority of the government had convinced some former opponents that resistance was futile. ZAPU won 14 seats, 6 less than in the previous election. Sithole's party won 1 seat in his home Manica Province, but Muzorewa's UNAC failed to win a single seat.

ZAPU was particularly angered by the appointment of Enos Nkala as minister of home affairs. Though he was a Ndebele speaker, Nkale had been a harsh critic of all opponents of the government and he now responded to his own critics by threatening to ban, and later to destroy, ZAPU. The pressure on ZAPU was growing steadily. Sidney Malunga, a senior party official and member of parliament, was arrested. So, too, was Nick Mabodoko, mayor of Bulawayo. ZAPU was evicted from its headquarters in Harare, and Nkomo's passport was seized. Amid this turmoil, Bishop Muzorewa announced his retirement from politics.

Hopes of a more stable future were roused by talks of a merger between ZANU (PF) and ZAPU and by the promise of record maize and tobacco crops. Hopes of union, however, were alternatively fanned and quenched throughout 1986. Towards the end of January, three senior officials of ZAPU were charged with treason. Yet, only a week later, three other ZAPU officials, including Nkomo's brother, were released after six months' detention. In March, Nkomo stated in Bulawayo that the move towards unity was making no progress, but shortly afterwards he joined with his arch-enemy, Nkala, in an appeal for peace in Matabeleland. In the same month, two other ZAPU Leaders, Vote Moyo and Lookout Masuku, were released from detention. Masuku, former commander of ZIPRA, had been detained under emergency regulations in 1983 after having been acquitted of a charge of stockpiling arms to be used to overthrow the government. His release was approved on grounds of ill-health and within a month he died of a rare brain disease. Speaking at his funeral, Nkomo compared the rule of Mugabe to that of Hitler, but the prime minister refused to be provoked and insisted that talks about unity still held out hope of success. Nor did he hesitate to dismiss the transport minister – formerly the troublesome home affairs minister, Hubert Ushewokunze – who, when accused by the public-accounts committee of nepotism and of the mismanagement of the national railway system and Air Zimbabwe, claimed that the charges were a plot manufactured by an ethnic group seeking to dominate the country.

Another to suffer for failing to support the party unquestioningly was Edgar Tekere, a former chairman of ZANU (PF), who in May

1987 was dismissed from his post as provincial party leader after criticizing some of his cabinet colleagues.[15] Mugabe had no more time for members of his party who appeared to be stirring up internal animosity than he had for those who encouraged any form of separatism under the guise of ZAPU political manoeuvring. Yet his own supporters were frequently guilty of acts of provocation based upon ethnic hatred. When the results of the parliamentary elections were declared, women members of ZANU (PF) drove supporters of opposition parties from their homes in Harare, Bindura, and Gweru, and a purge of the army had resulted in the dismissal of some forty officers, most of them former ZIPRA leaders.[16] In August 1986, some 150 homes and their maize stocks were burnt by members of the ZANU (PF) youth brigade assisted by special constables. Ostensibly their aim was to kill ZAPU officials but the zeal of the attackers was sharpened by their own assumption of a Shona identity and by the knowledge that their victims were almost all Ndebele.

The see-sawing relations between ZANU (PF) and ZAPU continued throughout 1986. In July, senior ZAPU officials were among more than 100 people arrested in Beitbridge, but in August, ten other leading supporters were released from detention. The government's feeling of insecurity was reflected in the renewal of the state of emergency in July, although new laws passed in April had given the authorities increased emergency powers and had encouraged the belief that a further extension of the state of emergency would be unnecessary. There were, it is true, guerrilla activities in Matabeleland, and they may have accounted for the government's impatience and its anxiety to clamp down on all attempts to subvert law and order. But its measures failed to put an end to the troubles in Matabeleland, and there were also raids along the eastern border with Mozambique in reprisal for the role played by Zimbabwe's troops in assisting her neighbour's government to counter guerrilla activities.

The first important change in the constitution since independence was announced in July 1987 when a bill was published which abolished the 20 parliamentary seats reserved for whites. Now the white voters' roll was to be merged with the common roll and, pending the next general election, the 80 African members of parliament would sit as an electoral college to choose 20 new members who would be obliged to support the ruling party. This would mean that ZANU (PF) controlled 85 out of 100 votes in the house. Surprisingly the move reawakened hopes of an amalgamation between the two leading parties, but once again they drew back after the constitution amendment bill was approved in September 1987. The very day after

President Banana appended his signature, Enos Nkala launched another attack on ZAPU, announcing that he had ordered all the party's offices to be closed. He was supported by Mugabe who, though stating that the closure was a temporary measure to allow police to carry out searches, insisted that there was adequate evidence to support the view that ZAPU was closely linked with guerrilla activities in Matabeleland. The measure of the government's fundamental hostility to ZAPU was further demonstrated in October when ZANU (PF) refused to nominate any ZAPU supporters to the 20 vacant seats in parliament, preferring to support a number of white candidates, men who had been openly hostile to ZANU (PF) in the past.[17]

Mugabe's frustration was compounded by the problems arising from the country's economy. After the promise of excellent harvests for all the country's main crops, a sudden severe drought destroyed the quality of the tobacco crop, the main hope of providing foreign earnings, while any prospect that maize would become available for export was blighted and the country's ample reserves were urgently required for home consumption. Simultaneously, considerable sums of money had to be spent on providing arms for the troops fighting in Mozambique and on importing oil to meet the shortfall from normal sources caused by sabotage to the oil pipeline which passed through Mozambique. The high rate of company tax also discouraged independent Zimbabwean businessmen from playing the active role in reviving the country's economy which Mugabe expected of them. He was particulary anxious to minimize Zimbabwe's dependence upon foreign capital because it only increased the country's debts, but his anti-capitalist policies did little to endear him to the business community. His wish to demonstrate his involvement in the sanctions campaign against South Africa aroused even more opposition, and he had to abandon his plans because he was forced to acknowledge the potentially disastrous repercussions which his policy would have on the country's economy.

It was not only the more prosperous citizens of Zimbabwe who were worried by the government's policies. The murder of sixteen white missionaries in the south of the country on 25 November, though probably planned by anti-government guerrillas, was a protest by landless people after it had been decided that some 40,000 black squatters should be evicted from land owned by white settlers, powers having been given to local authorities to use police if necessary to achieve the objective.[18] Most of the squatters were concentrated in the east of the country and were not all evicted forcibly. But some 12,000 were removed in the volatile region of Matabeleland and guerrillas encouraged the people, who were already resentful of the army's excesses, to resist government policy. Those same guerrillas, posing as liberators, had been responsible for considerable damage to essential services in Matabeleland which had seriously delayed progress there.[19]

A breakthrough occurred on 22 December 1987 when Mugabe and Nkomo signed an agreement to unite their parties. It came as a surprise, because throughout 1987 relationships between the two parties had blown hot and cold – as they had in previous years. In April, Mugabe had broken off discussions with Nkomo because he said they were serving no purpose. On that occasion it had been Nkomo's turn to insist that his party was committed to unity. In August, talks had begun again after ZAPU had agreed to drop some of its claims – including its demand for a new name to be given to the united party. Under the terms of the December agreement, the title ZANU (PF) was to be retained, and Mugabe was to be the new party's president. Mugabe's insistence upon the name ZANU (PF) – the only non-negotiable element in the discussions as far as he was concerned – was a clear indication of his pride in the role his supporters had played in establishing Zimbabwe as an independent nation. In holding on to it he himself was in no sense motivated by feelings of ethnic exclusiveness, but that might not have been equally true of some of his supporters. Nkomo's acceptance of the title, albeit reluctant, demonstrated that he, too, was willing to forgo any element which suggested a division between the two groups. Equally significant was the joint approval by the two leaders of vigorous measures to put an end to guerrilla action in Matabeleland.

An editorial in *The Times* on 24 December 1987 viewed the agreement with something less than confidence, reiterating the refrain that the two parties brought to the marriage memories of bitterness and bloodshed based on tribalism rather than on ideological differences. It was an opinion that had gained respectability largely because of the way in which ZAPU had continuously refused to cooperate with ZANU (PF), with the result that the government had put increasing pressure upon ZAPU's leaders. But the real impetus for ethnic distrust had come from the actions of a handful of dissidents whose guerrilla campaign in Matabeleland had led to vicious and indiscriminate reprisals by the army against the Ndebele. This, in its turn, had stirred up what had come to be accepted as ethnic resentment among the army's victims. It was a situation not unlike that in Uganda under Obote's second presidency when the army took reprisals against the Ganda as part of its campaign against guerrillas.

On 31 December 1987, Mugabe was sworn in as executive president. Banana retired and the office of prime minister – formerly occupied by Mugabe – was abolished. Nkomo became vice-president, an appointment which he shared with the existing vice-president, Simon Muzanda, but it was the latter, not Nkomo, who was accorded the title of state deputy president. Nkomo did, however, become second secretary of ZANU (PF). Shortly afterwards, when Mugabe shuffled his cabinet, Nkomo became one of three senior ministers in the president's office and a member of a five-man inner cabinet, along with Mugabe himself, Muzenda, Bernard Chidzero, and Maurice Nyagumbo. Two other ZAPU ministers were given cabinet posts. Efforts were also made through the good offices of Didymus Mutasa – the speaker of the house of assembly, who himself came from Manicaland – to induce Phineas Sithole, the member of parliament for Southern Manicaland, to join in the formation of a one-party state.

In April 1988, ZAPU held its last party congress and accepted the merger with (or more accurately its absorption into) ZANU (PF). A week later, ZANU (PF)'s own congress also endorsed the merger, but within a fortnight an armed gang had killed a Roman Catholic missionary and injured another in an attack in Matabeleland. This act coincided with the offer by Mugabe of an amnesty to dissidents in Matabeleland – provided they would come forward and hand in their arms. Surprisingly, in view of the hatred for the government so long encouraged by the guerrillas, the response to the offer was good. Virtually the whole dissident force – a dwindling group of former members of ZIPRA who had deserted from the national army to oppose Mugabe's government – came forward. They proved to have been both well-armed and well-organized, but their surrender was an important turning-point in communal relations throughout the country. It was their actions which had led to confrontation between the two main groups into which the country had become divided, and their withdrawal from the battlefield augured well for unity.

The onus now rested on the leaders, because it was their ambitions which, initially and throughout the long struggle for independence, had divided the peoples of Zimbabwe into rival camps. To Mugabe fell the responsibility for ruling firmly yet with magnanimity in partnership with a man whom he had always regarded as being too ready to compromise his principles. But it was upon Nkomo that the greater burden fell. He had, for so long, been a leading figure in Zimbabwe's campaign for independence, and it would require a great effort on his part to accept second place to a man who had been his greatest opponent. It would take time, too, for the concept of rival ethnic identities, to which the power struggle had given birth, to be subsumed by the spirit of Zimbabwean nationalism. Professor Ranger's fear that ethnic identities might become paramount may now be in process of decline, and the emphasis – as he believed it should be – may now be placed upon promoting the well-being of those who most need help. Certainly, if the country is to develop anything more than a subsistence economy, such unity of purpose is essential. But the road ahead will be an uneven one. The revelation of corruption among senior members of the government has done nothing to reinforce public confidence in the leadership, and even President Mugabe's prompt and praiseworthy measures agains the offenders could so easily be interpreted by his opponents as an act of discrimination against certain tribal groups. Such is the delicacy of the path the leaders must tread if they are to prevent local feelings of insecurity from developing into open hostility to the government.

11 Conclusion

In most of the countries dealt with in this book, a generation of Africans has grown up which has never known European rule. Yet the negative sense of identity with which their fathers greeted the end of imperialism has rarely been replaced, for either generation, by a positive attachment to the new nation states. It is not suggested that those states are in any sense sacrosanct. What can be argued is that there is no obvious political alternative. Nevertheless, there has been a marked tendency for people to seek security in more familiar, more localized communities.

This has not necessarily been an atavistic movement. Many of the societies in which Africans have sought refuge from the problems of the modern world are themselves relatively new, though the majority draw their strength from common ethnic roots. Significantly, in only a few instances have these groups shown any desire to sever their links with the nations of which they form a part. Perhaps Buganda provides the most notable, if not the only, manifestation of this tendency. There, unquestionably, although much of what passes for tradition is of a recent vintage, the strength of the movement lies in the conviction, shared by most Ganda, that they are a people deeply and uniquely rooted in the past. Yet, under the stress of events, even the Ganda seem less wedded to the concept of exclusiveness than they were. The Somali of Kenya, and the inhabitants of the Casamance in Senegal, have both indicated their desire to cut themselves off from their new governments. But neither has rejected the idea of participating in a larger political unit. They simply want to choose the society to which they belong. In Nigeria, recently invoked ethnicity has joined hands with religious fervour and traditional pride to challenge the unity of the new state. But federation, not dissolution, is now the accepted remedy. In Katanga, too, what began as a separatist movement has been translated into the hope that a new central government might be found to replace that of President Mobutu.

If, then, there is little evidence of any desire to dismember the countries which came into being at independence, why have local loyalties exerted so powerful an influence upon so many people and have they, in practice, undermined the workings of the new states? The answer to the first part of the question lies largely in the non-fulfilment of the expectations raised by independence. The material condition of most Africans is no better, and is in many instances worse, than it was under imperial rule. This is due in part to the genuine lack of resources in many parts of the continent, to the population explosion which has affected every country, to prolonged periods of drought in certain areas, to corruption and ineptitude among some of those responsible for managing the economy, but perhaps most fundamentally to the fact that the countries were not created to stand alone. In the age of imperialism, each had formed a part of a larger economic circle of which the metropolitan country had been the hub. Even before independence this had disadvantages as well as advantages for the countries on the periphery, but at least the imperial authorities, in their own interests, were concerned to see their dependencies survive. Probably, too, they expected the economic relationships they had established in the imperial era to continue after independence, the principal difference being that they would no longer have even the nominal responsibility for the well-being of their former subject peoples. Most of the new governments, however, wanted to exercise a measure of flexibility in their external relations. As a result, although foreign aid has usually been forthcoming, it has not always been distributed in such a manner as to enable the lopsided economies of most African countries to survive in the hurly-burly of world markets. Only recently has the IMF imposed directives aimed at stabilizing economic systems which were already in a state of decomposition. These measures have had dire consequences for the people called upon to tighten still further their already constricting belts. President Mobutu, however, has had the confidence and temerity to challenge the IMF, as, too, did President Babangida of Nigeria, though he took the precaution of proposing a reasonable alternative to the IMF's proposals. That Zaire has survived in spite of the behaviour of its president has owed a great deal to American views about its strategic role in Africa. With the possible settlement of the military conflict in neighbouring Angola, Mobutu may no longer be able to act with such insouciance.

Whether or not the attempts now being made to improve the

economic balance of the countries of Africa through the use of intermediate technology will meet with success is difficult to predict. Clearly it is out of the question for the continent to return to the practices of the pre-imperial era, to be preserved as a sort of anthropological museum. But it is far from certain, even if it were known to be possible, that recapturing a mythical golden age of self-sufficiency in food production by using intermediate technology will satisfy the aspirations of the countries' leaders, however much it might appeal to the mass of the people. Many of the latter, having suffered from years of drought or of shortages brought about by civil war or inadequate planning, might settle for anything which would bring peace and plenty. But the taste which the leaders have acquired for the products of the outside world – and not merely those of a material character – would be difficult to surrender, yet it can only be satisfied by external charity or by developing an exchange economy. Few leaders would wish to be wholly at the mercy of outside aid with its attendant pressures. It takes a Senghor or a Diouf to accept such dependency without loss of integrity, and such acceptance does not go unchallenged by their fellow countrymen, who may well be as sincere in their criticisms as is Diouf in pursuing his policies. In defence of the critics, it could certainly be argued that the industrialized world seems in no hurry to encourage rival developments in Africa. It is still content to look to that continent to produce only such raw materials as are currently in demand. The exploitation of those materials remains largely in the hands of outsiders – who have the capital as well as the expertise to use them to advantage. To those interested primarily in a balanced economy, that may, of course, seem an eminently sensible way of ordering things.

With such obvious limits upon both wealth and the opportunities wealth provides, it is not surprising that many Africans have lost confidence in the power of their central government to fulfil their early hopes. Even in those countries where a great leader at first inspired confidence, disillusionment has followed. Consequently, men have turned to those institutions they believed they could trust: the family or the clan; those who spoke their own language; to traditional, or more often to neo-traditional, authorities – who are easy of access, sympathetic, not remote and uncomprehending. The dreams inspired by independence were replaced by the pragmatism of survival and security.

But the more educated sections of the community were not ready to settle for acquiescence. If the spoils of independence were limited, they concluded that they must fight to acquire them. It was these educated people who were largely responsible for enlisting local support – usually again from those who spoke their own language or with whom they could claim some cultural or clan affinity – in their struggle for power. It is to the movements they created, rather than to any recrudescence of pre-imperial polities, that British journalists have mainly – if not exclusively – given the title of tribalism. Building upon the outward forms of administrative unity introduced by the imperial powers, and fortified by myths and memories of an earlier sense of community, these educated leaders have made their bid for power and hence for the patronage which would sustain their followers. Inspired by them, the resignation of many of the rest of the population has been converted into active ethnicity. 'Tribal' groups have emerged, their strength buttressed by suspicion of the aims of other, similar groups, each striving to control the same limited resources.

Not all those leaders were as intentionally divisive as, say, Chief Awolowo was in Nigeria. Most of them would have preferred to head a united country. Individual ambition, blended to a greater or lesser degree with unselfish idealism, has been their main motivation, not factionalism. However, for the reasons given, they found it difficult – save in the brief euphoria of the independence movement – to command the adherence of the whole people. Forced to rely upon localized support, some – like Oginga Odinga in Kenya – have deplored the limited vision of their supporters. Many more have accepted the situation, and, either from expediency or from genuine concern, have shared the anxiety of their followers that they should not be permanently excluded from whatever benefits independence might offer by the triumph of similar, rival factions.

If ethnicity has been less prominent in Angola, this is mainly because the power struggle had taken on a military form some time before independence. The one essentially ethnic movement, that led by Holden Roberto, was squeezed out by more competent military leadership. The surviving leaders were then supported by armies of freebooters who had been led to believe that defeat would mean perpetual deprivation and who contrived to command the fearful, often reluctant, backing of those over whose territory they could exercise military domination. The majority of these latter have little sense of loyalty to any of the leaders, but crave for peace under whatever government can ensure stability. The military struggle in Zimbabwe, which also pre-dated independence, has produced a different result. There, exaggerated neo-ethnicity has indeed played an important role in determining the outcome. Yet the recent response to an agreement between the leaders suggests that the lines drawn between the contestants were, in some measure, artificial. They were, it is true, the product of geographical circumstances as well as of loyalty to men who could be seen as representing the interests of differing language groups. That the Ndebele had been led to believe they would suffer if Mugabe and his Shona supporters were to triumph there can be little doubt. It was, however, a belief which was initially fostered by rival leaders and by the consensus of foreign journalists rather than by innate ethnic antagonism.

Not all the countries of Africa have conformed to this divisive pattern. Guinea, for example, has achieved a considerable measure of cohesion, but only through the flight of thousands of dissenters. The challenge to Senegal's unity comes mainly from a group of vocal intellectuals who have certainly not stimulated ethnic rivalry and probably have no wish to do so, or from geographically peripheral culture groups who feel neglected by the central government. This is mainly due to the special position enjoyed – at least by the inhabitants of the communes – in France's scheme of West African administration, and the advantage taken of this by western powers interested in maintaining a presence in West Africa after independence. The proportionately large number of people who possess a high level of European-style education, and the wide dissemination of the Wolof language, have ensured that politics have remained a national rather than a regional concern, and the co-operation between the politicians and the traditional Muslim leaders has guaranteed the support of the mass of the people. A greatly modified version of this situation is to be found in Zaire, though the façade of unity which exists there is largely due to the success of President Mobutu, with US aid, in crushing local expressions of dissatisfaction which otherwise would almost certainly have led to the same 'tribal' movements as have occurred in other countries.

Can it be said, then, that 'tribalism', in the distorted and varied versions in which we have seen it, does pose a threat to the states of Africa. The answer must certainly be in the affirmative. Opposition to governments which have inherited the authoritarianism of the imperial era may be valuable. But so long as there is competition among those who would like to govern the countries of Africa, and so long as central governments seem unable, and can be accused of being unwilling, to meet the basic needs of all the people, so long, too, as they are unable to maintain their authority by military force, will it be possible to enlist local support in the struggle for power. The support will be given for essentially defensive purposes, but it can still constitute a challenge to stable government. The challenge may not take a violent form, but the possibility of violence will always be present as long as even basic provision cannot be made for the whole of the people. This explains why military governments have played such an important role in many countries, even where the military have been initially reluctant to intervene. But 'tribalism' is in only limited instances the root cause of Africa's problems. It is its availability to reinforce the discontent created by inadequate or inadequately administered economies that constitutes its main threat to stability.

Notes and references

1 THE IMPERIAL LEGACY

1. *The Times*, reporting events in Zimbabwe, 12 April 1986.
2. *ibid.*, 12 March 1981.
3. *Sunday Times*, reporting events in Uganda, 28 July 1985.
4. cf. Eugen Weber (1979) *Peasants into Frenchmen: the Modernization of France 1870–1914*, p. 492, London: Chatto & Windus.

2 UGANDA: THE KINGDOM AND THE POWER

1. *Observer*, 24 June 1979.
2. *Daily Telegraph*, 15 November 1979.
3. *ibid.*, 19 July 1979.
4. *Guardian*, 27 January 1986.
5. *The Times*, 18 and 19 July 1983.
6. Oliver Furley (1987) *Uganda's Retreat from Turmoil?* Conflict Studies 196, London: The Centre for Security and Conflict Studies, provides a shrewd interpretation of Museveni's career in Uganda.
7. *Le Soleil*, 25 February 1987.
8. Michael Twaddle (1974) 'Ganda receptivity to change', *Journal of African History*, XV (2), pp. 303–15.

3 GHANA: A CONFEDERATION OF REGIONS?

1. Flt. Lt. J.J. Rawlings, interviewed by Davina Doughan, in *West Africa*, 9 February 1987, p. 259.
2. Mije Barnor (1987) 'The role of the NCD', *West Africa*, 12 January 1987, pp. 67–8.
3. *Ghanaian Times*, 20 February 1987.
4. Kwesi Aning (1986) 'Government and Press in Ghana, 1957–1985', BA (Hons) dissertation, University of Ghana, unpublished, p. 82.
5. *West Africa*, 28 March 1988, p. 541.
6. Eugene Adjei Sekyi (1986) 'Freedom and justice in Ghana, 1957–1972', BA (Hons) dissertation, University of Ghana, unpublished, p. 12.

7. K. Nkrumah (1968) *Dark Days in Ghana*, pp. 42–3, London: Lawrence & Wishart.
8. F.K. Drah (1974) 'Ghana since independence', in *History of Ghana*, p. 47, Accra: Cultural Programme of the American Women's Association.
9. Alfred Kofi Korankye (1985) 'Parliamentary Democracy in Ghana, 1959–1972', p. 34, BA (Hons) dissertation, University of Ghana, unpublished.
10. Rosamond Hammonf (1986) 'From "liberation" to "redemption": causes of military intervention in the government of Ghana after independence', p. 32, BA (Hons) dissertation, University of Ghana, unpublished.
11. *The Times*, 14 January 1972.
12. *ibid.*, 6 July 1976.
13. Mije Barnor (1987) 'The role of the NCD', *West Africa*, 12 January 1987, pp. 67–8.
14. *West Africa*, 9 February 1987, p. 259.
15. Yao Graham (1987) 'The fourth republic', *West Africa*, 16 March 1987, pp. 504–7.
16. *Financial Times*, 6 March 1987.
17. Nana Kwarteng Amaniampong, quoted in the *People's Daily Graphic*, 20 February 1987.

4   NIGERIA: FEDERATION BY CONSENSUS

1. S. Egite Oyovbaire (1985) *Federalism in Nigeria*, p. 12, London and Basingstoke: Macmillan.
2. Obafemi Awolowo (1960) *Awo*, pp. 167–77, Cambridge: Cambridge University Press.
3. Billy Dudley (1982) *An Introduction to Nigerian Government and Politics*, p. 55, London and Basingstoke: Macmillan.
4. Rotimi Timothy Subero (1988) 'Federalism and Nigeria's political future: a comment', *African Affairs*, 348, July, pp. 431–2.
5. *West Africa*, 20 July 1987, pp. 1389–90.
6. *ibid.*, 6 July 1987, pp. 1282–4.
7. *African Concord*, 13 August 1987, p. 19.
8. Larry Diamond (1987) 'Issues in the constitutional design of a third Nigerian republic', *African Affairs*, 343, April 1987, p. 210.
9. *West Africa*, 16 February 1987, p. 340.

5   KENYA: THE PRESIDENT'S COUNTRY

1. M. Tamarkin, 'The roots of political stability in Kenya', *African Affairs*, 308, July 1978, pp. 297–9.
2. Mordechai Tamarkin (1983–4) 'Recent developments in Kenyan politics: the fall of Charles Njonjo', *Journal of Contemporary African Studies*, 3 (1/2) pp. 60–1.
3. Odinga set out his views clearly and unequivocably in his 1967 autobiography, *Not Yet Uhuru*, London: Heinemann Educational Books.

4. Norman N. Miller (1984) *Kenya: the Quest for Prosperity*, p. 50, Boulder, Colorado: Westview Press, and London: Gower.
5. The Belgian Congo, later Zaire, became independent in 1960 and was immediately torn by civil war, with some of the peoples of Kasai and Katanga Provinces setting up secessionist states.
6. Tom Mboya (1970) *The Challenge of Nationhood*, p. 47, London: Heinemann Educational Books.
7. Joseph Karimi and Philip Ochieng (1980) *The Kenyatta Succession*, pp. 12–13, Nairobi: Transafrica.
8. David Goldsworthy (1982) *Tom Mboya: the Man Kenya Wanted to Forget*, pp. 264–86, London: Heinemann.
9. Tamarkin, 'Recent developments in Kenyan politics', pp. 63–4.
10. Karimi and Ochieng, *op. cit.*, *passim*.
11. *Daily Telegraph*, 10 November 1979.
12. Tamarkin, 'Recent developments in Kenyan politics', p. 74.
13. *Guardian*, 1 June 1982.
14. *The Times*, 21 October 1982.
15. *ibid.*, 13 December 1984.

6 SENEGAL: UNITY IN DIVERSITY

1. Ouma Kane (1986) 'Le Fuuta-Toora des Satigi aux Almaani', 1512–1807 (in three volumes), thesis presented for the degree of Docteur d'Etat, Dakar, vol. 2, pp. 575–756.
2. El Hadji Rowane M'Baye (1973) 'Contribution à l'étude de l'Isalm au 'Sénégal', pp. 122–3, Mémoire présenté pour un maîtresse d'Arabe, University of Dakar, unpublished.
3. Mamadou Dia (1986) *Mémoires d'un Militant du Tiers-Monde*, pp. 14–27 and 50–8, Paris: Publisud.
4. Mansour Bouna Ndiaye (1986) *Panarama politique du Sénégal*, pp. 79–81, Dakar: Les Nouvelles Editions Africaines; and Dia, *op. cit.*, 49–51.
5. Ndiaye, *op. cit.*, 89–90.
6. Magatte Lô (1985) *Sénégal, l'heure du Choix*, see *passim*, Paris: Editions L'Harmattan; and Dia, *op. cit.*, pp. 143–66.
7. cf. Donal B. Cruise O'Brien (1978) 'Senegal', in John Dunn (ed.) *West African States*, pp. 179–80, Cambridge: Cambridge University Press.
8. Sheldon Gellar (1982) *Senegal, an African Nation between Islam and the West*, pp. 115–18, Boulder, Colorado: Westview Press; and Hampshire: Gower.
9. Mar Fall (1986) *Sénégal, L'Etat Abdou Diouf, ou le temps des incertitudes*, pp. 34–7, Paris: Editions L'Harmatton.
10. *West Africa*, 28 September 1987, pp. 1884–5.
11. *ibid.*, 21 December 1987, p. 2484.
12. *Le Soleil*, 2 March 1987.
13. Moriba Magassouba (1985) *L'Islam au Sénégal: Demain les mollahs?* pp. 193–207, Paris: Editions Karthala.

7   GUINEA: UNITED AGAINST THE WORLD

1. A. Sékou-Touré (1962) *L'Action politique du Parti démocratique de Guinée pour l'émancipation de la jeunesse guinéenne*, p. 26, Conakry, quoted in Lapido Adamolekun (1976) *Sékou-Touré's Guinea*, p. 128, London: Methuen & Co.
2. cf. Saa Marcel Tinkiano (1974–5) 'La résistance à l'intrusion Française en pays Kisi', Mémoire de diplome de fin des études, Conakry: Institut Polytechnique Gamal Abdel Nassar (IPGAN), unpublished; Abdourahame Diallo (1973–4) 'La lutte de libération nationale en Guinée à travers la presse de combat', Mémoire de diplome, Conakry: IPGAN, unpublished; Sékar Mohamed Camera, (1974–5) 'Le non du 28 Septembre 1958, son impact politico-idéalogique sur le processus de désintégration de l'empire colonial Français', Mémoire de diplome, Conakry: IPGAN, unpublished; Amara Djoubar Souna (1971–2) 'Les methods de la contre-révolution, Mémoire de diplome, Conakry: IPGAN, unpublished.
3. Quoted in Adamolekun, *op. cit.*, 147–8.
4. *The Times*, 10 April 1984.
5. R.W. Johnson (1978) 'Guinea', in John Dunn (ed.), *West African States*, pp. 43–4, Cambridge: Cambridge University Press.
6. *Daily Telegraph*, 22 June 1979.
7. *ibid.*
8. Lapido Adamolekun (1984) 'Reflections on Guinea: the economic prospects', *West Africa*, 12 November 1984, pp. 2264–5.
9. *West Africa*, 12 May 1987, pp. 956–7.
10. *ibid.*, 17–23 October 1988, p. 1974.

8   ZAIRE: THE AUTHENTIC AFRICA?

1. *The Times*, 25 January 1972.
2. *ibid.*, 1 May 1972.
3. *ibid.*, 24 November 1972.
4. *ibid.*, 11 December 1973.
5. *ibid.*, 20 June 1975.
6. *ibid.*, 15 August 1977.
7. *ibid.*, 16 September 1977.
8. *ibid.*, 8 August 1978.
9. *Sunday Times*, 28 May 1978.
10. *Barclays Country Reports, Zaire*, 27 March 1980.
11. *The Times*, 15 July 1987.
12. *West Africa*, 18 April 1988, pp. 676–7.
13. *ibid.*, 22 February 1988.

9   ANGOLA: NO MAN'S LAND

1. John Stockwell (1979) *In Search of Enemies: a CIA History*, pp. 38–9 and *passim*, London: Futura Publications.

2. Henry Brandon (1975) 'Ford despairs over Angola', *Sunday Times*, 31 December 1975, and *The Times*, editorial, 22 December 1975.
3. *The Times*, 25 and 31 January 1976.
4. *ibid.*, 14 February 1976.
5. *ibid.*, 17 March 1976.
6. *Sunday Times*, 1 August 1976.
7. *Barclays Country Reports, Angola*, 28 October 1976.
8. Basil Davidson, writing in the *Sunday Times*, 3 July 1977.
9. Bruce Loudon, writing in the *Sunday Times*, 29 May 1977.
10. *Daily Telegraph*, 11 December 1978.
11. *ABERCOR Country Reports, Angola*, December 1979.
12. *ibid.*, April 1982.
13. Michael Hornsby, writing in *The Times*, 2 June 1984.
14. *Sunday Times*, 30 August 1981.
15. *Guardian*, 28 July 1982.
16. *The Times*, 20 November 1982.
17. *West Africa*, 28 February 1983.
18. *Cristian Science Monitor*, 18 July 1983.
19. *Observer*, 25 March 1984.
20. *The Times*, 28 March 1984.
21. *ibid.*, 2 April 1984.
22. *ibid.*, 17 May 1984.
23. *ibid.*, 3 July 1984.
24. For a detailed statement of the Angolan government's position at this stage, see the letter from President dos Santos to the Secretary-General of the UN, dated 20 November 1984, published as an advertisement in *The Times*, 24 November 1984.
25. *The Times*, 7 January 1985.
26. *Observer*, 6 April 1986.
27. *West Africa*, 7 September 1987.

10   ZIMBABWE: THE LATECOMER

1. Terence Ranger (1985) *The Invention of Tribalism in Zimbabwe*, p. 19, Gweru: Mambo Press.
2. Ken Flower (1987) *Serving Secretly: An Intelligence Chief on Record, Rhodesia into Zimbabwe, 1964 to 1981*, London: John Murray.
3. Kenneth Young (1967) *Rhodesia and Independence*, p. 85, London: Eyre & Spottiswoode.
4. *ibid.*, p. 261.
5. Kees Maxey (1975) *The Fight for Zimbabwe: the Armed Conflict in Southern Rhodesia since UDI*, p. 6, London: Rex Collings.
6. *ibid.*, p. 15.
7. Flower, *op. cit.*, pp. 105–6.
8. *Guardian*, 27 September 1973.
9. Flower, *op. cit.*, p. 136.
10. *ibid.*, pp. 147–50.
11. William Minter and Elizabeth Schmidt (1988) 'When sanctions worked:

the case of Rhodesia re-examined', *African Affairs*, 247, April 1988, p. 233.

12. Flower, *op. cit.*, 197.
13. *ibid.*, 255.
14. *ibid.*, 266.
15. *The Times*, 5 May 1987.
16. *ibid.*, 6 May 1987.
17. *Sunday Times*, 25 October 1987.
18. Karl Maier, reporting in the *Independent*, 30 November 1987.
19. Jan Raath, reporting in *The Times*, 28 November 1987.

Select bibliography

NEWSPAPERS, PERIODICALS, ETC.
(Published in London unless otherwise stated.)

Africa
African Concord
Africa Now
Daily Telegraph
Financial Times
Ghanaian Times (Accra)
Guardian
Independent
Jeune Afrique (Paris)
Le Soleil (Dakar)
Observer
People's Daily Graphic (Accra)
Sunday Telegraph
Sunday Times
The Times
Weekly Review (Nairobi)
West Africa

BOOKS, ARTICLES, ETC.

General

Crowder, Michael (ed.) (1984) *Cambridge History of Africa*, vol. 8, London: Cambridge University Press.
Duignan, Peter and Jackson, Robert H. (eds) (1986) *Politics and Government in African States, 1960–1985*, London: Croom Helm.
Hobsbawn, Eric and Ranger, Terence (eds) (1983) *The Invention of Tradition*, Cambridge: Cambridge University Press.
Hodder-Williams, Richard (1984) *An Introduction to the Politics of Tropical Africa*, London: George Allen & Unwin.
Ibingira, Grace Stuart (1980) *African Upheavals since Independence*, Boulder: Colorado: Westview Press.

Suret-Canale, Jean (1972) *Afrique Noire occidentale et centrale: de la colonisation aux indépendances, 1945–1960*, Paris: Editions Sociales.

Uganda

Avirgan, T. and Honey, M. (1982) *War in Uganda: the legacy of Idi Amin*, London: Zed Press.
Furley, Oliver (1987) *Uganda's Retreat from Turmoil?* Conflict Studies 196, London: Centre for Security and Conflict Studies.
Gertzel, Cherry (1974) *Party and Locality in Northern Uganda, 1945–1962*, London: Athlone Press.
Hansen, Holger Bernt and Twaddle, Michael (eds) (1988) *Uganda Now: Between Decay and Development*, London: James Currey; Athens: Ohio University Press, and Nairobi: Heinemann.
Jorgensen, Jan Jelmert (1981) *Uganda: a Modern History*, London: Croom Helm.
Karugire, S.R. (1980) *A Political History of Uganda*, Nairobi and London: Heinemann.
Kasfir, Nelson (1976) *The Shrinking Political Arena: Participation and Ethnicity in African Politics, With a Case Study of Uganda*, Berkeley, Los Angeles, and London: University of California Press.
Low, D.A. (1962) *Political Parties in Uganda, 1949–1962* London: Athlone Press.
Mamdani, Mahmood (1983) *Imperialism and Fascism in Uganda*, London: and Nairobi: Heinemann Educational Books.
—— (1976) *The Politics of Class Formation in Uganda*, Nairobi: Heinemann.
Mazrui, Ali A. (1970) 'Privilege and protest as integrative factors: Buganda's status in Uganda', in Robert L. Rotberg and Ali A. Mazrui (eds) *Protest in Black Africa*, New York: Oxford University Press.
Mujaju, Akiiki B. (1987) 'The gold allegations motion and political development in Uganda', *African Affairs*, 345, October 1987, pp. 479–504.
Sathyamurthy, T.V. (1986) *The Political Development of Uganda 1900–1960*, London: Gower.
Twaddle, Michael (1974) 'Ganda receptivity to change', *Journal of African History*, XV (2), pp. 303–15.

Ghana

Afrifa, A.A. (1967) *The Ghana Coup*, London: Frank Cass.
Amanoo, Joseph G. (1988) *The Ghanaian Revolution*, London: Jafint Co.
Armah, Kwesi (1974) *Ghana: Nkrumah's Legacy*, London: Rex Collins.
Crook, Richard (1986) 'Decolonization, the colonial state and chieftaincy in in the Gold Coast', *African Affairs*, 338, January 1986, pp. 75–105.
Jones, Trevor (1976) *Ghana's First Republic, 1960–1968*, London: Methuen.
Le Vine, Victor T. (1975) *Political Corruption: the Ghana Case*, Hoover Institute Publications 138, Stanford University.

Limann, H. (1983) *Democracy and Ghana: Select Speeches of President Hilla Limann*, London: Rex Collings.

Nkrumah, Kwame (1961) *I Speak of Freedom*, London: Panaf.

Pinkney, Robert (1972) *Ghana under Military Rule, 1966–1969*, London: Methuen.

Rado, Emil (1986) 'Notes towards a political economy of Ghana today', *African Affairs*, 341, October 1986, pp. 563–72.

Rathbone, Richard (1978) 'Ghana', in John Dunn (ed.) *West African States*, pp. 22–35, London: Cambridge University Press.

Nigeria

Akinola, Anthony A. (1988) 'Nigeria: the quest for a stable political future', *African Affairs*, 348, July 1988, pp. 441–5.

Clarke, J.D. (1987) *Yakubu Gowon: Faith in a United Nigeria*, London: Frank Cass.

Diamond, Larry (1987) 'Issues in the constitutional design of a third Nigerian republic', *African Affairs*, 343, April 1987, pp. 209–26.

Dudley, Billy (1982) *An Introduction to Nigerian Government and Politics*, London and Basingstoke: Macmillan.

Horowitz, Donald (1985) *Ethnic Groups in Conflict*, Berkeley and Los Angeles: University of California Press.

Kirk-Greene, Anthony and Rimmer, Douglas (1981) *Nigeria Since 1970: a Political and Economic Outline*, London, Sydney, Auckland, and Toronto: Hodder & Stoughton.

Laitin, David D. (1986) *Hegemony and Culture: Politics and Religious Change Among the Yoruba*, Chicago: University of Chicago Press.

Opia, Eric Agume (1972) *Why Biafra?* San Rafael, California: Leswing Press.

Orabator, S.E. (1987) 'The Biafran crisis and the midwest', *African Affairs*, 344, July 1987, pp. 367–83.

Oyediran, Oyeleye (ed.) (1981) *The Nigerian 1979 General Elections*, Nigeria and London: Macmillan.

Oyovbaire, S. Egite (1985) *Federalism in Nigeria*, Basingstoke and London: Macmillan.

Subero, Rotimi Timothy (1988) 'Federalism and Nigeria's political future', *African Affairs*, 348, July 1988, pp. 431–39.

Teal, Francis (1988) 'Domestic policies, external constraints and economic development in Nigeria since 1950', *African Affairs*, 346, January 1988, pp. 69–81.

Williams, Gavin and Turner, Terisa (1978) 'Nigeria', in John Dunn (ed.), *West African States*, pp. 132–72, London, 132–72.

Azikiwe, Nnamdi (Zik) (1961) *Selections from the Speeches of Nnamdi Azikiwe*, Cambridge: Cambridge University Press.

Kenya

Gertzel, Cherry (1970) *The Politics of Independent Kenya, 1963–1968*, London and Ibadan: Heinemann.

Goldsworthy, David (1982) *Tom Mboya: the Man Kenya Wanted to Forget*, Nairobi and London: Heinemann.

Gordon, D.F. (1986) *Decolonization and the State in Kenya*, Boulder, Colorado: Westview Press.

Karimi, Joseph and Ocheng, Philip (1980) *The Kenyatta Succession*, Nairobi: Transafrica.

Kenyatta, Jomo (1968) *Suffering Without Bitterness: the Founding of the Kenya Nation*, Nairobi: East Africa Publishing House.

Mboya, Tom (1970) *The Challenge of Nationhood*, London, Ibadan, and Nairobi: Heinemann.

Miller, Norman N. (1984) *Kenya: the Quest for Prosperity*, Boulder, Colorado, and Gower, London: Westview Press.

Odinga, Oginga (1967) *Not Yet Uhuru*, London, Ibadan, Nairobi, and Lusaka: Heinemann.

Tamarkin, Mordechai (1978) 'The roots of political stability in Kenya', *African Affairs*, 308, July 1978, pp. 297–320.

—— (1983/4) 'Recent developments in Kenyan politics: the fall of Charles Njonjo', *Journal of Contemporary African Studies*, 1/2, 59–77.

Senegal

Cruise O'Brien, Donal B. (1975) *Saints and Politicians: Essays in the Organisation of a Peasant Society*, London: Cambridge University Press.

—— (1978) 'Senegal', in John Dunn (ed.) *West African States*, London: Cambridge University Press.

Dia, Mamadou (1986) *Mémoires d'un militant du tiers monde*, Paris: Publisud.

Fall, Mar (1986) *Sénégal: l'état Abdou Diouf ou le temps d'incertitudes*, Paris: Editions L'Harmattan.

Fatton, Robert Jr. (1987) *The Meaning of a Liberal Democracy: Senegal's Passive Revolution, 1975–1985*, Boulder, Colorado, and London: Lynne Reinner Publishers.

Foltz, William J. (1966) 'Senegal', in James S. Coleman and Carl G. Rosenberg Jr. (eds) *Political Parties and National Integration in Tropical Africa*, Berkeley and Los Angeles: University of California Press.

Gellar, Sheldon (1982) *Senegal: An African Nation between Islam and the West*, Boulder, Colorado: Westview Press, and Hampshire: Gower.

Lô, Mangat (1985) *Sénégal: l'heure du choix*, Paris: Editions L'Harmattan.

Magassouba, Moriba (1985) *L'Islam au Sénégal: Demain les mollahs?* Paris: Editions Karthala.

Milcent, Ernest (1962) 'Senegal', in Gwendolin Carter (ed.) *African One-Party States*, pp. 87–148, Ithaca, New York: Cornell University Press.

Mouna Ndiaye, Mansour (1986) *Panorama politique du Sénégal ou les mémoires d'un enfant du siècle*, Dakar, Abidjan, and Lomé: Les Nouvelles Editions Africaines.

Guinea

Adamolekun, Lapido (1976) *Sékou Touré's Guinea*, London: Methuen.
Cowan, L. Gray (1962) 'Guinea', in Gwendolen M. Carter (ed.) *African One-Party States*, pp. 149–236, Ithaca, New York: Cornell University Press.
du Bois, Victor D. (1986) 'Guinea', in James S. Coleman and Carl G. Rosenberg Jr. (eds) *Political Parties and National Integration in Tropical Africa*, Berkeley and Los Angeles: University of California Press.
Johnson, R.W. (1978) 'Guinea', in John Dunn (ed.) *West African States*, pp. 36–55, London: Cambridge University Press.

Zaire

Panaf Great Lives (1978) *Sékou Touré*, London: Panaf.
Callaghy, Thomas M. (1984) *The State–Society Struggle: Zaire in Comparative Perspective*, New York: Columbia University Press.
Colvin, Ian (1968) *The Rise and Fall of Moise Tshombe*, London: Leslie Frewin.
O'Brien, Conor Cruise (1962) *To Katanga and Back*, London: Hutchinson.
Gérard-Libois, Jules (1966) *Katanga Secession*, Madison, Milwaukee, and London: University of Wisconsin Press.
Hoskyns, Catherine (1965) *The Congo Since Independence: January 1960–December 1961*, London, New York, and Toronto: Oxford University Press.
Kanza, Thomas (1972) *Conflict in the Congo*, Harmondsworth, Middlesex: Penguin.
Lumumba, Patrice (1962) *Congo, My Country*, London: Pall Mall Press.
MacGaffey, Janet (1983) 'How to survive and become rich amidst devastation: the second economy in Zaire', *African Affairs*, 328, July 1983, pp. 351–66.
Young, Crawford (1965) *Politics in the Congo: Decolonization and Independence*, New Jersey: Princeton University Press, and London: Oxford University Press.
Young, C. and Turner, T. (1985) *The Rise and Decline of the Zairean State*, Madison: University of Wisconsin Press.

Angola

Chilcote, Ronald H. (ed.) (1972) *Protest and Resistance in Angola and Brazil*, Berkeley, Los Angeles, and London: University of California Press.
Davidson, Basil (1972) *In the Eye of the Storm: Angola's People*, Harmondsworth, Middlesex: Penguin.
Hallett, Robin (1978) 'The South African intervention in Angola, 1975–76', *African Affairs*, 308, July 1978, pp. 347–86.
Harsch, Ernest and Thomas, Tony (1976) *Angola: the Hidden History of Washington's War*, Washington: Pathfinder Press.
Henderson, Lawrence W. (1979) *Angola: Five Centuries of Conflict*, Ithaca and London: Cornell University Press.

Klinghoffer, A.J. (1980) *The Angolan War: A Study in Soviet Policy in the Third World*, Boulder, Colorado: Westview Press.

Marcum, John A. (1978) *The Angolan Revolution, vol. 2: Exile Politics and Guerrilla Warfare, 1962–1976*, Cambridge, Mass. and London: MIT Press.

Somerville, Keith (1986) *Angola: Politics, Economics and Society*, London: Frances Pinter, and Boulder, Colorado: Lynne Rienner.

Stockwell, John (1979) *In Search of Enemies: a CIA History*, London: Futura Publications.

Wolfers, Michael and Bergerol, Jane (1983) *Angola in the Front Line*, London: Zed Press.

Zimbabwe

Davidow, Jeffrey (1984) *A Peace in South Africa: The Lancaster House Conference on Rhodesia, 1979*, Boulder, Colorado, and London: Westview Press.

Flower, Ken (1987) *Serving Secretly: Rhodesia into Zimbabwe, 1964–1981*, London: John Murray.

Martin, David and Johnson, Phyllis (1981) *The Struggle for Zimbabwe*, London and Boston: Faber & Faber.

Maxey, Kees (1975) *The Fight for Zimbabwe: The Armed Conflict in Rhodesia Since UDI*, London: Rex Collings.

Meredith, Martin (1979) *The Past is Another Country: Rhodesia, UDI to Zimbabwe*, London: André Deutsch.

Minter, William and Schmidt, Elizabeth (1988) 'When sanctions worked: the case of Rhodesia re-examined', *African Affairs*, 347, April 1988, pp. 207–37.

Muzorewa, Abel Jendekai (1979) *Rise Up and Walk*, London: Evans Brothers.

Nkomo, Joshua (1984) *Nkomo, the Story of my Life*, London: Methuen.

Peel, J.D.Y. and Ranger, T.O. (eds) (1983) *Past and Present in Zimbabwe* Manchester: Manchester University Press.

Ranger, Terence (1985) *The Invention of Tribalism in Zimbabwe*, Gweru Zimbabwe: Mambo Press.

Smith, David and Simpson, Colin, with Ian Davis (1981) *Mugabe*, London Sphere Books.

Stoneman, Colin (ed.) (1981) *Zimbabwe's Inheritance*, London and Basingstoke: Macmillan.

Verrier, A. (1984) *The Road to Zimbabwe, 1890–1980*, London: Jonathan Cape.

Index

Note: Political parties and organizations have been entered under their acronyms.